BIRNBAUM GUIDES

2009

Disneyland

RESORT ®

Expert Advice from the Inside Source

Wendy Lefkon EDITORIAL DIRECTOR

Jill Safro EDITOR

Frieda Christofides DESIGNER

Jessica Ward ASSISTANT EDITOR

Alexandra Mayes Birnbaum CONSULTING EDITOR

Jody Revenson CONSULTING EDITOR

THE OFFICIAL GUIDE

Stephen Birnbaum FOUNDING EDITOR

DISNEY EDITIONS

NEW YORK
AN IMPRINT OF DISNEY BOOK GROUP

For Steve, who merely made this all possible

For information address Disney Editions, 114 Fifth Avenue, New York, New York 10011-5690.

ISBN 978-1-4231-1050-7

Printed in the United States of America

Other 2009 Birnbaum's Official Disney Guides

Disney Cruise Line
Walt Disney World
Walt Disney World Dining
Walt Disney World For Kids
Walt Disney World Pocket Parks Guide
Walt Disney World Without Kids

Contents

95 Disney's California Adventure

From the glittering lights of Hollywood to the swells of the Pacific to the thrill rides of an amusement pier, Disney pays tribute to the glories of the Golden State in this, Disneyland's sister theme park. Our exclusive coverage reveals all there is to see and do—follow our advice and Hot Tips on how to tour the area like a pro and be sure to catch all of the park's greatest hits.

111 Good Meals, Great Times

Whether it's a simple snack or a multicourse meal, the Disneyland Resort offers something for every palate and pocketbook. For a change of scenery, venture a bit further afield into Orange County, other inland communities, or nearby beach towns. Our entertainment section reflects the area's wide range of possibilities, from the nightclubs in the Downtown Disney District to the dinner shows, concert halls, and lounges of Orange County.

131 Sports

Perhaps you dream of catching the perfect wave, hiking along cliffs above the Pacific coast, polishing your serve, or simply taking in a spectator sport. It's a cinch to fulfill your fondest athletic fantasies in the land of sun and surf.

137 Orange County & Beyond

Besides the Disneyland Resort and other family-oriented attractions, Orange County is home to impressive art museums, a presidential library, two seaside resort towns, a famous mission, a mammoth glass cathedral, and state-of-the-art performance venues. After you have thoroughly explored Disney's environs, why not plan a trip to see other parts of Southern California? The options are as diverse as the landscape itself.

A Word from the Editor

Walt Disney, the man who pioneered the realm of family entertainment, was at once an artist, entrepreneur, and creative visionary. He was also a dad. And, like many of the folks who visit Disneyland each year, Walt treasured the time he spent with his children. In fact, while his two daughters were growing up, Walt accompanied them to carnivals, zoos, and local amusement parks. It was something of a Saturday tradition for the Disney family. During these outings he would often make the same observation: The youngsters were happily entertained, but the adults didn't have much to do. It didn't seem right that he'd be stuck sitting on a bench while the kids had all the fun. To his way of thinking, a park should appeal to the sense of wonder and exploration in guests of *all* ages. His vision became a reality on July 17, 1955, when Disneyland opened in Anaheim, California.

Now, more than fifty years later, Walt's original theme park is as beloved as ever. While Disneyland Park is wonderfully familiar to us—practically a second home— Disney's California Adventure is a newer playing ground, and finding the best ways to take it in is an adventure in itself. Even now, it remains a work in progress, with stand-out attractions such as Toy Story Mania! and Turtle Talk with Crush being added to further guest satisfaction.

When Steve Birnbaum launched this guide, he made it clear what was expected of anyone who worked on it. The book would be meticulously revised each year, leaving no attraction untested, no meal untasted, no hotel untried. First-hand experiences like these, accumulated over the years, make this book the most authoritative guide to the Disneyland Resort. Our expertise, however, was not achieved by being escorted through back doors of attractions. Instead, we've waited in lines with everyone else, always hoping to have a Disney experience like any other guest.

Of course, there's more to the Disneyland Resort than the theme parks. There's also a dining, shopping, and entertainment district known as Downtown Disney, and three Disney hotels. It all adds up to a total that is truly greater than the sum of its parts. And, though it has a half century of history under its belt, this is just the beginning—as per its founder's wishes: "Disneyland will never be completed. It will continue to grow as long as there is imagination left in the world."

Take Our Advice

In creating this book, we have considered every possible aspect of your trip, from planning it to plotting day-to-day activities. We realize that even the most meticulous vacation planner needs detailed, accurate, and objective information to prepare a successful itinerary. To achieve that goal, we encourage the submission of factual information and insight from Disneyland staffers—but the decision to use or lose such information is entirely at the discretion of the editor.

We have also packaged handy bits of advice in the form of "hot tips" throughout the book. These helpful hints come directly from the copious notes we've taken during our countless trips to the Disneyland Resort and the surrounding Anaheim area. We've also used our "Birnbaum's Best" stamp of approval wherever we deemed it appropriate, highlighting our favorite attractions and restaurants—the crowd-pleasers we feel stand head, shoulders, and ears above the rest.

You, the reader, benefit from the combination of years of experience—coupled with access to up-to-date inside information from the Disneyland staff—that makes this guide unique. We like to think it's indispensable, but you be the judge of that 150 pages from now.

Credit Where Credit Is Due

We hope we are not omitting any names in thanking Annika Chase, Drew Cohen, Bob Deuel, Matt Gray, Michelle Harker, Pat Harris, Mike Hyland, Susan Leonetti, John McClintock, Doug McIntyre, Christian Petersen, Bill Rowland, Andrea Rivas, Frankie Lobono, and George Savvas. Special thanks to Pam Dahl, who has done so much to ensure the factual accuracy of *Birnbaum's Official Guide to Disneyland*.

Kudos to Michelle Olveira for her outstanding fact-checking, and to copy editors extraordinaire Warren Meislin and Jill Rapaport. We would also like to tip our hats to Nisha Panchal, Sara Liebling, Mike Carroll, Brendan Carroll, and Gabrielle Bill, for their editorial support and production panache.

Of course, no list of acknowledgments would be complete without mentioning our founding editor, Steve Birnbaum, whose spirit, wisdom, and humor still infuse these pages, as well as Alexandra Mayes Birnbaum, who continues to be a guiding light—to say nothing of a careful reader of every word.

The Last Word

Finally, it's important to remember that every worthwhile travel guide is a living enterprise; the book you hold in your hands is our best effort at explaining how to enjoy the Disneyland Resort at the moment, but its text is no way etched in stone. Disneyland is always changing and growing, and in each annual edition we refine and expand our material to serve your needs better. Just before the grand opening of Disneyland, Walt Disney remarked that the main attraction was still missing—people. That's where you come in.

Have a wonderful time!

Don't Forget to Write!

No contribution is of greater value to us in preparing the next edition of this book than your comments on its usefulness and your own experiences at the Disneyland Resort. Drop us a postcard or send a letter to the address on the right.

Official Disney Guides
Birnbaum's Disneyland 2009
Disney Editions
114 Fifth Avenue, 14th Floor
New York, NY 10011

Getting Ready to Go

Anyone who visited the Anaheim area over the last few years was sure to see evidence of the Disney Imagineers at work. Behind closed gates, construction went on day and night, and finally, the results were unveiled— a 500-acre Disneyland Resort, with Walt Disney's original theme park, Disneyland (although many Disney-philes may still refer to it fondly as the "Magic Kingdom"), at its heart. Besides this "Happiest Place on Earth," guests will find Disney's California Adventure theme park, the Downtown Disney District, and Disney's Grand Californian Hotel & Spa—which completes the trio of Disney's on-property hotels. Of course, you'll want to do and see it all, but where should you start? When should you go? And then there are the all-important questions of how to get there and where to stay. Maybe you want to extend your vacation—perhaps you'll include a visit to (or a stay at) the beach or one of the other nearby attractions. . . .

That's a lot to think about. But don't worry. By the time you've read through this chapter, you'll have all the information you need to make smart decisions. So read on, and remember: A little advance planning goes a long way.

When to Go

When you weigh the best times to visit the Disneyland Resort, the most obvious possibilities seem to be Christmas, Easter, and summer vacation—particularly if there are children in the family. But there are a few good reasons to avoid these periods—the major one being that almost everybody else wants to go then, too. Keep in mind, however, that the pedestrian traffic at Disney's California Adventure is always lighter than it is at Disneyland Park.

If you can only visit during one of these busy times and worry that the crowds might spoil your fun, there are some tactics for making optimum use of every minute and avoiding the lines—notably, go to the park early to get a jump on the day (and on the crowds), take advantage of the time-saving Fastpass system whenever possible, and remember that Disney keeps the parks open later during busy seasons. Note that "early entry" is offered on select days to guests staying at Disneyland hotels, Walt Disney Travel Company guests, and day guests with a 3-day (or more) park hopper ticket.

On the other hand, choosing to visit when the parks are least crowded may mean that you miss some of the most entertaining parades and special events. For instance, Disneyland park's Fantasmic! show and the fireworks might not be on the entertainment schedule, and certain attractions may be closed for annual refurbishment.

A wonderful time to visit Disneyland—when it's not too crowded but everything is still open—is the period between Thanksgiving and Christmas, when the Christmas parade takes place and carolers add festive music to the mix. Other good times to visit are the period after summer—September through early October—and after New Year's Day.

When Not to Go: If crowds make you queasy, keep in mind that Saturday is usually the busiest day year-round. In summer, Monday and Friday are the next busiest. If you decide to visit Disneyland Park during a weekend, opt for Sunday. And remember that the weeks before Christmas through New Year's Day, Easter week, and the period from early July through Labor Day are packed.

Crowd Patterns

Least Crowded

- Second week in January to Presidents' week

- Two weeks after Easter Sunday to Memorial Day week

- End of Labor Day week to Columbus Day

- End of Thanksgiving weekend to mid-December

Average Attendance

- End of Presidents' week to week before Easter

- Sundays in spring, autumn, and winter, except holiday weekends

- Memorial Day week to beginning of summer vacation

- Labor Day week

- Columbus Day to day before Thanksgiving

Most Crowded

- Any Saturday

- Sundays during summer and holiday weekends

- Presidents' week

- Weeks before and weeks after Easter Sunday

- Beginning of summer through Labor Day weekend

- Thanksgiving weekend (Thursday through Sunday)

- Week before Christmas through first week of January

Keeping Disney Hours

Operating hours tend to fluctuate according to the season, so call 714-781-4565 or 714-781-7290, or visit *www.disneyland.com* for updates.

DISNEYLAND PARK: This park is typically open from about 9 A.M. to 8 P.M. Monday–Thursday, 10 A.M. to 10 P.M. on Friday and Sunday, and 8 A.M. to 11 P.M. on Saturday. Hours are often extended in the summer and during holiday seasons.

DISNEY'S CALIFORNIA ADVENTURE: The park generally opens at 10 A.M. and closes at about 6 P.M. on weekdays, and later on weekends. Call 714-781-4565 for specifics.

DOWNTOWN DISNEY: Some shops and restaurants in this shopping and entertainment district open as early as the theme parks do, but most stick to the following hours: 10 A.M. to 11 P.M. Sunday–Thursday, 10 A.M. to midnight on Friday and Saturday.

TRANSPORTATION: The monorail generally begins making its 2½-mile loop about the time

Disneyland opens (for early entry "Magic Mornings"), and continues running until about 15 minutes before the park closes. Trams transporting guests between the Mickey and Friends parking structure or the Timon parking lot and the theme parks begin picking up guests about 60 minutes before the first park opens, and continue transporting guests back to parking areas until about an hour or so after the last park closes. If for some reason you miss the last tram, know that there is always some sort of transportation available to Mickey and Friends (usually in the form of a van).

Disneyland Weather

If dry, sunny weather is your ideal, Anaheim may seem like a dream come true. Rainy days are few and far between and generally occur between the months of November and April, which is also the coolest time of year. During this season, Santa Ana winds sometimes produce short periods of dry, crisp, warm desert weather and sparkling-clear skies that unveil distant mountains usually hidden by smog. In summer, thin, low morning clouds make it prudent to plan expeditions to the beach for the afternoon, when the haze burns off and the mercury rises. Mornings and nights are generally cool. The average daytime year-round temperature is 73 degrees.

	TEMPERATURE AVERAGE		RAINFALL AVERAGE (INCHES)
	HIGH	LOW	
January	69	45	2.47
February	69	47	2.86
March	70	48	2.55
April	73	51	0.66
May	75	56	0.13
June	79	60	0.09
July	84	62	0.03
August	86	63	0.01
September	85	62	0.06
October	80	56	0.26
November	74	51	0.82
December	70	46	1.29

Holidays & Special Events

The Disneyland Resort sponsors special events during the year. Here are a few highlights. Find out about specific events by calling 714-956-6413 or visiting *www.disneyland.com*.

JANUARY–FEBRUARY

Valentine's Day: Sweethearts will swoon over the romantic backdrop that Disneyland Park provides on this love-struck holiday.

Mardi Gras: With its Creole and Cajun cuisine and boutiques, Disneyland's New Orleans Square offers the most traditional Mardi Gras setting. Expect Ralph Brennan's Jazz Kitchen, in Downtown Disney, to be hopping, too.

MARCH–MAY

Easter: The parks remain open late the week before and the week after Easter, making this a popular time to visit. At the Disneyland Hotel, guests may feast at an Easter Sunday buffet presented in the grand ballroom. The event is hosted by Disney characters. Reserve at least two months in advance (714-781-3463). Seating is limited.

Mother's Day: Disney characters honor Mom during a special buffet in the Disneyland Hotel's Grand Ballroom. Reserve at least two months in advance (714-781-3463). Seating is limited for this very popular event.

JUNE–AUGUST

Summer Flag Retreat: Disney's All-American College Band performs for nine weeks during the summer (usually beginning in mid-June), Tuesday through Saturday, at about sundown.

The performance takes place in front of the flagpole in Town Square; it includes patriotic Sousa marches and concludes with "The Star-Spangled Banner," which brings any guests not already standing to their feet.

Fourth of July: This is one of the busiest days of the year—and one to avoid if you're easily overwhelmed by crowds. The more-patriotic-than-usual day features exceptionally festive fireworks at Disneyland Park.

LATE SEPTEMBER–OCTOBER

Halloween Festivities: At Disneyland, "HalloweenTime" lets guests celebrate in not-so-scary ways, including the Main Street Pumpkin Festival and Woody's Halloween Roundup. Both offer sing-alongs and activities for guests. The Haunted Mansion Holiday transformation gives this spooky spot a *Nightmare Before Christmas* motif—inside and out. At Disney's California Adventure, HalloweenTime celebrates Disney villains and encourages trick-or-treating on special ticket nights known as "Mickey's Halloween Treat."

NOVEMBER–DECEMBER

Thanksgiving Weekend: The four days of this holiday weekend are filled with musical entertainment and the first installments of Disneyland's Christmas Fantasy Parade and It's a Small World Holiday, both of which kick off on Thanksgiving Day. The parks observe extended hours. At the Disneyland Hotel, the characters host "A Disney Family Thanksgiving" buffet in the Grand Ballroom. Reserve at least two months in advance (714-781-3463)—seating is limited and in high demand for this perennial favorite.

Christmas Festivities: By early November, Main Street in Disneyland Park is festooned with greenery and hundreds of poinsettias, while a 60-foot Christmas tree decorated with about 5,000 colorful lights and ornaments further embellishes the scene. Carolers stroll up and down Main Street, and on one of the first two weekends of December, a massive choir walks down Main Street in a Candlelight Ceremony and Procession. It features a live orchestra and special guest narrator who reads the biblical Christmas story. There is also a special, holiday-themed fireworks show, "Believe In Holiday Magic." It is not to be missed.

In Fantasyland, It's a Small World is transformed into a world of holiday magic and music. A Christmas Fantasy Parade also takes place. Haunted Mansion Holiday (see Late September–October, above) extends through the Christmas festivities.

The weeks before the holiday rank among the best times of year to visit the Disneyland Resort. The week afterward, however, is one of the busiest, so plan accordingly.

MAGICAL MILESTONES

Walt Disney once said, "Disneyland will never be completed. It will continue to grow as long as there is imagination left in the world." Truer words were never spoken. Here's a sampling of major milestones and important dates in Disney history.

1901

Walter Elias Disney is born on December 5 in Chicago, Illinois. He spends his boyhood in Marceline, Missouri.

1922

Walt and collaborator Ub Iwerks start Laugh-O-Gram Films, an animation studio located in Kansas City, Missouri. (The business lasts one year.)

1923

Walt and his brother Roy open the Disney Bros. Studio in Hollywood, California.

1928

Disney's studio introduces the world to the immortal Mickey Mouse with *Steamboat Willie,* the world's first cartoon with a synchronized sound track. (Walt Disney himself provides the voice for Mickey.)

1932

Flowers and Trees wins the Disney Studios its first Academy Award.

1937

Disney releases *Snow White and the Seven Dwarfs,* the world's first feature-length animated film.

1940

Great works of classical music meet Disney animation with the release of *Fantasia.*

1955

Disneyland opens its doors in Anaheim, while television's original *Mickey Mouse Club* begins a four-year run.

1967

Disneyland debuts Pirates of the Caribbean—one of the most popular and beloved attractions of all time.

1971

Walt Disney World opens near Orlando, Florida.

1989

Disney animation experiences a renaissance of sorts with the release of the Studio's 28th animated film, *The Little Mermaid.*

1992

A bit of Disney magic travels overseas with the opening of Disneyland Paris.

2001

For the first time since its opening, the Disneyland Resort gets a new theme park: Disney's California Adventure.

2003

The Many Adventures of Winnie the Pooh makes its debut in Disneyland Park's Critter Country.

2004

The Twilight Zone™ Tower of Terror starts shaking up guests at Disney's California Adventure.

2006

Captain Jack Sparrow joins the merry marauders in the Pirates of the Caribbean.

2007

Pirates invade Tom Sawyer Island, and the Finding Nemo Submarine Voyage opens at Disneyland Park.

2008

Toy Story Mania! opens at Disney's California Adventure.

Weddings & Honeymoons

The Disneyland Resort's customized Fairy Tale Weddings program lets brides and grooms create an affair to remember at one of the three Disney hotels—either indoors or out. Couples may go the traditional route or plan a themed event with invitations, decorations, souvenirs, napkins, and thank-you notes emblazoned with their favorite Disney character couples, including Cinderella and her Prince, and Mickey and Minnie Mouse.

One spot for tying the knot is the rose garden gazebo at the Disneyland Hotel, in a picturesque garden setting where the bride or couple may arrive in Cinderella's crystal coach. Another choice is the courtyard area at Disney's Grand Californian. A fantasy reception may follow (at any of these hotels), at which the couple is greeted by a fanfare of trumpets. Mickey and Minnie Mouse may arrive to help the newlyweds with the cake-cutting moment.

A Disney wedding coordinator assists with the arrangements for the wedding and reception—everything, that is, except providing a guest's very own Prince or Princess Charming.

The bridal salon (at the Disneyland Resort Center, between the Disneyland Hotel and Paradise Pier Hotel) helps guests through the planning and preparation stages, and even through those pre-ceremony jitters.

For more information about creating a happy occasion in a happy location, contact the Disneyland Fairy Tale Weddings department, which coordinates events at all three hotels and in Disneyland: 714-956-6527. To learn more about Disneyland honeymoons, contact Disneyland Resort Travel Sales at 800-854-3104.

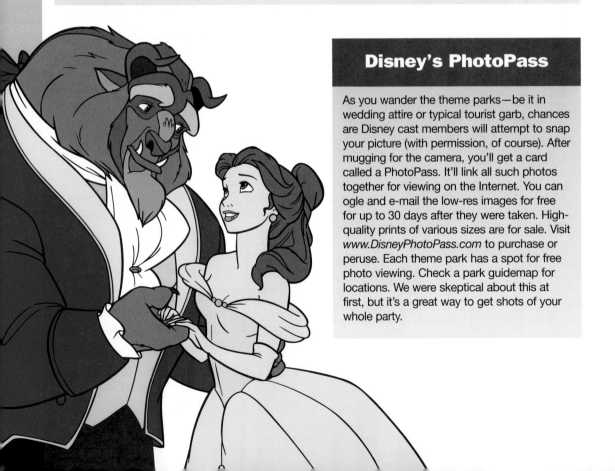

Disney's PhotoPass

As you wander the theme parks—be it in wedding attire or typical tourist garb, chances are Disney cast members will attempt to snap your picture (with permission, of course). After mugging for the camera, you'll get a card called a PhotoPass. It'll link all such photos together for viewing on the Internet. You can ogle and e-mail the low-res images for free for up to 30 days after they were taken. High-quality prints of various sizes are for sale. Visit *www.DisneyPhotoPass.com* to purchase or peruse. Each theme park has a spot for free photo viewing. Check a park guidemap for locations. We were skeptical about this at first, but it's a great way to get shots of your whole party.

Planning Ahead

Collect as much information as you can about the attractions you're interested in from the sources listed below. Then consider all the possibilities before making any definite travel plans.

Information

For current information about special events and performance times, the latest ticket prices, operating hours, rides under refurbishment, and other Disneyland Resort specifics, contact:

Disneyland Resort Guest Relations;
Box 3232; Anaheim, CA 92803; 714-781-4565 (for recorded information), or 714-781-7290 (to speak directly with a Disney employee); *www.disneyland.com.*

If you are staying at one of the Disneyland Resort hotels (see the *Accommodations* chapter), contact Guest Services at the hotel for help in planning your visit to both the parks and the surrounding area.

www.disneyland.com

For up-to-date online information, head to *www.disneyland.com*, the official Disneyland Resort Web site. Using the handy Trip Wizard, you can actually plan your vacation, find out about the three Disneyland Resort hotels, book travel packages, and order park tickets, plus check park hours and show schedules. You can also book your Disneyland vacation online through *www.disneytravel.com.*

Inside the Disneyland Resort: Cast members (the folks who work at Disneyland) can answer many questions. Information stations in Disneyland Park include City Hall, in Town Square; and the Information Board on the west side of Central Plaza, at the far end of Main Street. In Disney's California Adventure, the Guest Relations Lobby is located on the east side of the Entry Plaza, before the Golden Gate Bridge, and Information Boards can be found by the sun icon at the far end of the Gateway Plaza. At any Disneyland Resort hotel, visit the lobby for assistance.

For other area information, contact these bureaus of tourism:

Anaheim/Orange County Visitor & Convention Bureau; Visit them at *www.anaheimoc.org* or call 714-765-8888 during business hours to reach a representative. You can visit them at 800 W. Katella Ave.; Anaheim, CA 92802.

California Tourism; *www.visitcalifornia.com*

Huntington Beach Visitors & Conference Bureau; 301 Main St., Suite 208; Huntington Beach, CA 92648; 714-969-3492 or 800-729-6232; *www.surfcityusa.com.*

Laguna Beach Conference & Visitors Bureau; 252 Broadway; Box 221; Laguna Beach, CA 92651; 949-497-9229 or 800-877-1115; *www.lagunabeachinfo.com.*

Long Beach Area Convention & Visitors Bureau; One World Trade Center, Third Floor; Long Beach, CA 90831; 562-436-3645 or 800-452-7829, ext. 100; *www.visitlongbeach.com.*

Los Angeles Convention & Visitors Bureau; 685 S. Figueroa St.; Los Angeles, CA 90017; 213-689-8822 or 800-228-2452; *www.lacvb.com.* An additional location is 6801 Hollywood Blvd.; Hollywood, CA 90028; 323-467-6412.

Newport Beach Conference & Visitors Bureau; 110 Newport Center Dr., Suite 120; Newport Beach, CA 92660; 949-719-6100 or 800-942-6278; *www.visitnewportbeach.com.*

Orange Chamber of Commerce & Visitor Bureau; 439 E. Chapman Ave.; Orange, CA 92866; *www.orangechamber.com;* 714-538-3581.

San Diego Convention & Visitors Bureau; 2215 India St., San Diego, CA 92101; 619-232-3101; *www.sandiego.org.*

Reservations

With the Disneyland Resort's recent expansion, advance planning has become essential. To get your choice of accommodations, especially for visits during the busy spring and summer seasons, make lodging reservations as far in advance as possible—at least six months ahead, if you can, since area hotels fill up rather quickly during these months. For visits at other times of the year, check with the Anaheim/Orange County Visitor & Convention Bureau (714-765-8888) to see if any conventions are scheduled when you want to travel. Some of these events can crowd facilities enough to warrant altering your plans.

Travel Packages

The biggest advantage to purchasing a travel package is that it almost always saves you money over what you'd pay separately for the individual elements of your vacation, or it offers special options not available if you simply buy a ticket at the ticket booth. This is especially true the longer you stay. And there is the convenience of having all the details arranged in advance by someone else.

Finding the best package for yourself means deciding what sort of vacation you want and studying what's available. Don't choose a package that includes elements that don't interest you—remember, you're paying for them. And if it's Disney theming and "extras" you want, consider a Walt Disney Travel Company package.

The Walt Disney Travel Company offers packages that include a stay at a Disney hotel and a Park Hopper Ticket. It's possible to add extras, such as a character breakfast in the park or a guided tour of Disneyland, as well as admission to another Southern California attraction, such as Sea World or Universal Studios Hollywood. Purchase extras separately.

Besides booking guests into an official Disneyland Resort hotel, the Walt Disney Travel Company also works closely with more than 40 Good Neighbor hotels and motels (see pages 42–47 for details), and they are included in its packages as well. To book a vacation package at the Disneyland Resort, contact a travel agent, or call the Walt Disney Travel Company at 714-520-5060.

The Disneyland Resort is also featured in a wide variety of non-Disney-run package tours, including those sponsored by individual hotels, airlines (United Vacations and Alaska Airlines Vacations both offer fly-drive packages, for instance), and organizations. AAA Vacations packages are available to members and non-members alike, while AAA Disney Magic Moments packages represent savings and benefits for members only.

This book's selective guide to Anaheim-area hotels and motels can help you decide initially which property best suits your travel style, needs, and budget (refer to the *Accommodations* chapter). Pick one, then contact a travel agent or the desired hotel directly to make a reservation or book a Disneyland Resort package. Happy hunting!

What to Pack

Southern California isn't so laid-back that you only need to pack a few pairs of shorts and a T-shirt. Nor is it a place that demands formal attire. Casual wear will suffice in all but the fanciest restaurants, and even there, men can usually wear sports jackets without ties. Bathing suits are an obvious must if you plan to take advantage of your hotel's swimming pool or go for a walk on a long, surf-pounded Pacific beach. It's also a good idea to bring along a bathing suit cover-up and sunglasses (and don't forget the sunscreen). Tennis togs or golf gear may be necessary if you plan to hit the courts or the course. The weather in summer can be hot, but because Southern California air-conditioning can be over efficient, take a lightweight sweater or jacket to wear indoors.

In winter, warm clothing is a must for evening; during nighttime visits to the parks, a heavy jacket may be a godsend. Whatever the time of year, come prepared for the unexpected: Pack an umbrella, a T-shirt, and a jacket—just in case the weather suddenly turns wet or unseasonably warm or cool.

Making a Budget

Vacation expenses tend to fall into five major categories: (1) transportation (which may include costs for airfare, airport transfers, train tickets, car rental, gas, parking, and taxi service); (2) lodging; (3) theme park tickets; (4) meals; and (5) miscellaneous (recreational activities, souvenirs, postcards, film, toiletries, and expenses such as pet boarding, etc.).

When budgeting, first consider what level of service suits your needs. Some prefer to spend fewer days at the Disneyland Resort, but stay at a deluxe hotel like the Grand Californian or dine at pricier restaurants. Others want a longer vacation with a value-priced Good Neighbor hotel and less expensive meals. The choice is up to you. (Having said that, we do feel that a great deal of the Disney experience comes from staying on-property and recommend at least making room in your budget for accommodations at the more moderately priced Disneyland or Paradise Pier hotel.)

Once you've established your spending priorities, determine your price limit. Then make sure you don't exceed it when approximating your expenses—without a ballpark figure to work around, it's easy to get carried away.

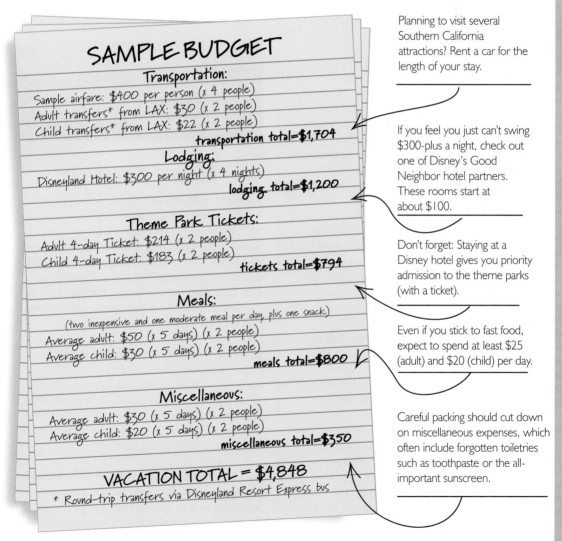

SAMPLE BUDGET

Transportation:
Sample airfare: $400 per person (x 4 people)
Adult transfers* from LAX: $30 (x 2 people)
Child transfers* from LAX: $22 (x 2 people)
transportation total=**$1,704**

Lodging:
Disneyland Hotel: $300 per night (x 4 nights)
lodging total=**$1,200**

Theme Park Tickets:
Adult 4-day Ticket: $214 (x 2 people)
Child 4-day Ticket: $183 (x 2 people)
tickets total=**$794**

Meals:
(two inexpensive and one moderate meal per day, plus one snack)
Average adult: $50 (x 5 days) (x 2 people)
Average child: $30 (x 5 days) (x 2 people)
meals total=**$800**

Miscellaneous:
Average adult: $30 (x 5 days) (x 2 people)
Average child: $20 (x 5 days) (x 2 people)
miscellaneous total=**$350**

VACATION TOTAL = $4,848
* Round-trip transfers via Disneyland Resort Express bus

Planning to visit several Southern California attractions? Rent a car for the length of your stay.

If you feel you just can't swing $300-plus a night, check out one of Disney's Good Neighbor hotel partners. These rooms start at about $100.

Don't forget: Staying at a Disney hotel gives you priority admission to the theme parks (with a ticket).

Even if you stick to fast food, expect to spend at least $25 (adult) and $20 (child) per day.

Careful packing should cut down on miscellaneous expenses, which often include forgotten toiletries such as toothpaste or the all-important sunscreen.

This is an example of a moderately priced budget for a family of four (two adults and two kids staying at the Disneyland Resort for four nights and five days during "off-peak" times). Totals include tax; theme park admission prices are likely to increase in 2009.

Money-Saving Strategies

Cost-Cutting Tips

LODGING: The most important rule is not to pay for more than you need. Budget chains don't offer many frills, but they are usually clean and provide the essentials; many even have a swimming pool, albeit a small one.

You can also save by checking the cutoff age at which children can no longer share their parents' room for free. Many of the hotels and motels in the Anaheim area allow children under 18 to stay free. A few places have a cut-off age of 15 or 17, so it's good to find out before making a reservation. And ask about special rates or discounts, especially if you are a California resident, a member of AAA or AARP, or are in the military.

Bed-and-breakfasts sometimes represent an excellent buy. While B&Bs are scarce in Anaheim proper, there are some on the coast, within an hour of the Disneyland Resort.

Hostels and campgrounds also offer lower-priced lodging alternatives. Contact the Anaheim/Orange County Visitor & Convention Bureau at 714-765-8888 for a listing of those areas closest to the Disneyland Resort.

FOOD: The budget-minded (and who isn't?) should plan to have meals in coffee shops or fast-food restaurants, or save your splurges for the buffets, to get your fill and your money's worth. If you want to try an upscale place, go for lunch; the entrées are often the same as those at dinnertime, but usually cost less.

Pack a picnic and enjoy meals outside. There's a small picnic area just to the left of Disneyland's entrance. (It's surrounded by trees—so it's easy to miss—but last we checked it was still there.) Vending machines dispense soft drinks. Snacks may be brought into the parks, but not glass bottles.

You can also save significantly on meals by choosing lodging with kitchen facilities and opting to eat in some of the time. The savings on food may more than cover the additional cost of accommodations. Don't forget to pack snack items, too—especially if you are traveling with small children.

In the Anaheim area, a number of places offer refrigerators or full kitchen facilities (look for suite hotels); some also provide complimentary breakfast.

TRANSPORTATION: When calculating the cost of driving to the Disneyland Resort, consider your car's gas mileage, the price of gasoline, and the expense of the accommodations and food en route. If you are thinking of traveling by plane, don't forget about the cost of getting from your home to the airport and later to your hotel. Also factor in the cost of renting a car at your destination, if that's part of your plan. Remember to ask if your hotel charges for parking (the rates tend to vary quite a bit) or shuttle transportation to the Disneyland Resort—these daily charges can tack a substantial amount on to a family's room bill.

> ### HOT TIP!
> For information on special offers for many of Anaheim's hotels, restaurants, and attractions, visit *www.anaheimoc.org* or call 714-765-8888.

Disney Discounts

ANNUAL PASSPORT: Bearers are granted special savings on Disneyland hotel accommodations (pending availability); Disneyland restaurants; select merchandise throughout the parks and Downtown Disney and select guided tours. For an extra $59, Annual Passholders may have parking priveleges. Premium Annual Passholders may park for free in the Mickey and Friends parking structure.

DISNEY VISA: Members who pay for purchases with the Disney Rewards Visa card earn points that can be redeemed for various discounts and Disney items throughout the year. Note that purchases do not have to be made at Disneyland, and all purchases count. Details are subject to change.

AUTOMOBILE ASSOCIATION OF AMERICA (AAA): Auto Club members can order park tickets as well as special vacation packages through local AAA offices. Contact your local AAA office for details.

DISCOUNT FOR SENIORS: Senior citizens get a $2 discount on Single Day park tickets.

Theme Park Tickets

Most admission media (with the exception of annual passes) are now called "tickets" rather than "passports." Single Day One Park tickets let you visit just one park. Park Hopper tickets allow you unlimited park-hopping between Disneyland Park and Disney's California Adventure. Admission tickets to the parks include unlimited use of all attractions (except arcades) once inside.

Ticket Options

One-Day Tickets feature admission to one Disneyland Resort theme park, while One- and Two-Day Park Hopper tickets allow admission to both parks. Three- to Six-Day Tickets (which expire 14 days after first use) allow you to "hop" between Disneyland and Disney's California Adventure.

The two main types of annual passports are known as the Deluxe and Premium versions. Each affords the bearer shopping and dining discounts, as well as "park-hopping"—that is, visiting both theme parks on the same day.

The Premium Annual Passport is valid year-round and includes parking (it has no block-out periods). The Deluxe Annual Passport is valid many days of the year but has block-out periods, such as each Saturday from March through June (passholders may enter the park on a blocked-out day by paying $40). An optional one-time parking fee, currently $59, is available to Deluxe Annual Passholders. Premium passholders can park for free.

Annual passes are sold at the ticket booth near the turnstiles and processed at the Plaza Pavilion on Main Street.

There are usually special passes available for purchase by Southern California residents. Offers change from time to time, so be sure to inquire before you visit. Call 714-781-4565 or visit *www.disneyland.com* for details.

Purchasing Tickets

Long lines have been known to form at the Disney ticket booths—especially in the morning, as the parks open for business. Avoid the wait by buying your tickets ahead of time. If that's not incentive enough, consider the possibility of saving a little money by purchasing tickets prior to your arrival.

Where to Buy Tickets: All tickets are sold at park ticket booths. Some Disney Stores sell tickets, too (they do not offer one-day tickets). Call or visit your local store for specifics.

Tickets by Mail: Send check or money order and ticket request (plus a $10 fee for orders over $200) to Disneyland Ticket Mail Order Services; Box 61061; Anaheim, CA 92803. It's also possible to order by calling Ticketing & Reservations at 714-781-4400 (up to 30 days ahead). Allow 10 business days for processing.

Tickets Online: Select tickets are available at *www.disneyland.com*. (You'll need to print them and present your "eTicket" when you arrive at the turnstile.) There are often special offers, such as five days for the price of three.

Tickets by Phone: Call 714-781-4043 and have a credit card handy. Allow five days for delivery, ten during busy times of the year.

How to Pay for Tickets: Cash, traveler's checks, personal checks, American Express, Visa, MasterCard, JCB Card, and the Discover Card are accepted. Personal checks must be imprinted with name and address, and accompanied by a government-issued photo ID.

Note that ticket structures and pricing are apt to change. For the latest information, visit *www.disneyland.com*.

Ticket Prices

Although prices are always subject to change, the following will give you an idea of what you can expect to pay. Prices and ticketing structure are likely to change in 2009. For current prices, call 714-781-4565, or visit *www.disneyland.com*.*

	Adults	Children**
One-Day Ticket (one park)	$66	$56
One-Day Ticket (hopper)	$91	$81
Two-Day Ticket (hopper)	$132	$112
Three-Day Ticket	$189	$159
Four-Day Ticket	$214	$184
Five-Day Ticket	$234	$204
Six-Day Ticket	$239	$209
Two-Park Deluxe Annual Passport	$259	
Two-Park Premium Annual Passport	$379	

*Discounts may be available through the Web site.

**3 through 9 years of age; children under 3 free

Customized Travel Tips

Traveling with Children

When you tell your kids that a Disney vacation is in the works, the challenge is keeping them relatively calm until you actually arrive at the Disneyland Resort.

PLANNING: Get youngsters involved in plotting the trip from the outset, putting each child in charge of a small part of the vacation preparation—such as writing for travel brochures, choosing which attractions to see and in what order to see them, and deciding which other activities to include in your Southern California visit.

EN ROUTE: Certain resources can stave off the "Are we there yet?" chorus, such as travel games, books and magazines, and snacks to quiet rumbling stomachs. If you drive, take plenty of breaks along the way. If you fly, try to time your departure and return flights for off-peak hours and during the off-season, when chances are better that an empty seat or two will be available. During takeoffs and landings, encourage toddlers to suck on bottles and pacifiers to keep ears clear, and supply older kids with gum or water.

IN THE HOTELS: During the summer, several hotels offer special kids' programs at no (or low) charge. Some offer babysitting services or babysitting referrals year-round. Pinocchio's Workshop at the Grand Californian is available to take requests for "day of" child activity services for hotel guests. There is a charge for all of the above services.

IN THE THEME PARKS: The smiles that light up your kids' faces as they enter a Disney theme park will repay you a thousandfold for any fuss en route. No place in the world is more aware of the needs of children—or their parents—than this one.

Favorite Attractions: Fantasyland and Mickey's Toontown in Disneyland Park are great places to start with small kids, who delight in the bright colors and familiar characters. In Disney's California Adventure, A Bug's Land, Playhouse Disney—Live on Stage!, and Monsters, Inc.—Mike and Sulley to the Rescue! have big kid appeal. If you have children of different ages in your party, you may have to do some juggling or split the group up for a few hours, so that older kids won't have to spend their whole vacation waiting in line for Dumbo. Some rides, like Snow White's Scary Adventures, may be too scary for some youngsters. If they're afraid of the witch, skip the attraction.

Strollers: They can be rented for $10 ($18 for two) at the Stroller Shop, located to the right as you enter the main gate in Disneyland park and on the right side as you enter Disney's California Adventure. If you plan to park-hop, know that you can take the stroller with you. If you leave the park but plan to return, keep the receipt and get another stroller at no additional charge (provided that it's the same day).

Baby Care: Baby Care Centers feature toddler-size flush toilets that are quite cute—and completely functional. In addition, there are changing tables, a limited selection of formulas, strained baby foods, and diapers for sale, plus facilities for warming baby bottles (you can wash out your bottles here, too). A special room with comfortable chairs is available for nursing mothers.

The decor is soothing, and a stop here for diaper changing or feeding is a tranquil break for parent and child alike. The Baby Care Centers are located on the east side of the Central Plaza, at the Castle end of Main Street in Disneyland, and near Cocina Cucamonga in the Golden State area inside Disney's California Adventure.

Changing tables and diaper machines are also available in many restrooms.

Note: We recommend that parents of toddlers pack waterproof diapers. They'll come in handy for children who want to spend time splashing in the parks' interactive fountains.

Where to Buy Baby Care Items: Besides being at the Baby Care Centers, disposable diapers and baby bottles are sold at select shops throughout the parks.

Lost Children: When a child disappears or fails to show up on time, it's reassuring to know that Disney's security force and cast members are carefully trained to follow specific procedures when they encounter a lost child.

Up to age 10, a youngster may be taken to Child Services, adjacent to First Aid, where Disney movies and books provide temporary amusement. The child's name is registered in the lost children's logbook there. Kids 11 and older may leave messages and check in often at City Hall in Disneyland Park, or Guest Communications in the entrance area of Disney's California Adventure.

Traveling Without Children

Disneyland is as enjoyable for solo travelers and couples as it is for families for several reasons: Its ambience encourages interaction, and the attractions are naturally shared events.

PLANNING: Read Disney literature carefully before you arrive to familiarize yourself with the resort's layout and activities. Also, request tourist information from other places in Southern California that you intend to visit.

Food for Thought: Sightseeing takes energy, and only healthy meals can provide it at a consistent level. Don't try to save money by skipping meals. Prices at the parks (particularly at Disneyland) and nearby "off-property" eateries are relatively reasonable, and there are healthful options, even in the fast-food restaurants. And don't forget to stay well-hydrated—running around theme parks all day is a lot of work!

Health Matters: If you visit in summer, avoid getting overheated; August in particular can be sweltering. Protect yourself from the sun with a hat and plenty of sunscreen, rest in the shade often, and beat the mid-afternoon heat with a cold drink or a snack in an air-conditioned spot.

If you feel ill, speak to a Disney cast member or go to First Aid and lie down for a while. Above all, don't take unnecessary risks. If you have a back problem, heart condition, or other physical ailment, suffer from motion sickness, or are pregnant, you should steer clear of

rough rides. Any restrictions are noted at the entrance to each ride in the park, as well as at the end of the individual listings in theme park chapters of this book.

Lost Companions: Traveling companions do occasionally get separated. If someone in your party wanders off or fails to show up at an appointed meeting spot, head for City Hall in Disneyland or Guest Relations in California Adventure. Here you will find a book in which guests can leave and receive messages for one another during the day.

MEETING OTHER ADULTS: Downtown Disney, with its mix of restaurants and nightclubs, is the best spot to mingle. While each of Disney's three hotels has lounges worth visiting, those at the Grand Californian are among the most sophisticated on property. As far as the parks go, Disney's California Adventure tends to attract more grown-ups than Disneyland Park does.

Travelers with Disabilities

The Disneyland Resort is rather accessible to guests with disabilities, and as a result, it makes a good choice as a vacation destination. But advance planning is still essential.

Getting to Anaheim

Probably the most effective means of ensuring a smooth trip is to make as many advance contacts as possible for every phase of your journey. It's important to make phone calls regarding transportation well before your departure date to arrange for any special facilities or services you may need en route.

The Society for Accessible Travel & Hospitality (347 Fifth Ave., Suite 605; New York, NY 10016; 212-447-7284; *www.sath.org*) has member travel agents who book trips for

Height Ho!

At attractions with age and/or height restrictions, a parent who waits with a child too young or too small to ride while the other parent goes on the attraction may stay at the front of the line and take a turn as soon as the first parent comes off. This is called the "rider switch" policy, and if lines are long, it can save a lot of time. Be sure to ask the attendant, and he or she will explain what to do.

travelers with disabilities, keeping special needs in mind. Membership costs $49, or $29 for seniors 63 and older and for students.

The following travel agencies specialize in booking trips for travelers with physical disabilities: Accessible Journeys (35 W. Sellers Ave.; Ridley Park, PA 19078; *www.accessiblejourneys.com*, 610-521-0339 or 800-846-4537) and Flying Wheels Travel (143 W. Bridge St.; Owatonna, MN 55060; 507-451-5005; *www.flyingwheelstravel.com*).

Hertz (800-654-3131) and National (888-273-5262) have a few hand-control cars available for rent at the airports in Southern California. Be sure to order your car at least 48 hours in advance.

Though less convenient, it is also possible to access the area by public transportation. All buses operated by Anaheim Resort Transit (888-364-2787 or visit *www.rideart.org*), and the Orange County Transportation Authority (714-560-6282 or *www.octa.net)*, the public bus company that serves Orange County, are outfitted with lifts so that travelers using wheelchairs can board them easily. Many routes pass Disneyland.

Sightseeing tour buses are another option. Though only a few of them are wheelchair accessible, all have storage facilities for collapsible chairs, making this a possibility for travelers who have a companion to help them on and off the bus. Coach America is wheelchair accessible. It offers tours to many Disneyland Resort–area attractions. Make reservations (at least 48 hours in advance if a wheelchair lift will be needed) by calling 714-978-8855 or 800-828-6699.

Scootaround rents standard and electric wheelchairs, as well as scooters. Pick-up and delivery is available to all hotels in the Disneyland Resort area. Call 888-441-7575 or visit *www.scootaround.com*. Wheelchair Getaways of California rents wheelchair accessible vans and has pick-up and delivery options for most hotels in the area. Call 800-659-1972 or visit *www.wheelchairgetaways.com*.

Lodging

Most hotels and motels in Orange County have rooms equipped for guests with disabilities, with extra-wide doorways, grab bars in the bathroom for shower or bath and toilet, and sinks at wheelchair height, along with ramps at curbs and steps to allow wheelchair access. Unless otherwise indicated, all the lodging described in the *Accommodations* chapter provide rooms for travelers with disabilities.

Inside the Disneyland Resort

Cars displaying a "disability" placard will be directed to a section of each Disney parking lot, next to the tram pickup and drop-off area.

Wheelchairs and Electric Convenience Vehicles (ECVs) can be rented at the Stroller Shop just inside the main gate in Disneyland and across from Guest Relations in the Entry Plaza of California Adventure. The rental price ($10 per park per day for wheelchairs, $35 for ECVs) includes a refundable deposit of $20. A small number of wheelchairs may be available to rent from Disney's three hotels; inquire at the front desk. We recommend you bring your own stroller or wheelchair whenever possible.

Most waiting areas are accessible, though some attractions have auxiliary entrances for guests using wheelchairs or other mobility devices, who may be accompanied by up to five other party members using the special entry point. The Main Street train station is not wheelchair accessible. However, guests using wheelchairs may access the train in New Orleans Square, Mickey's Toontown, or Tomorrowland.

Accessibility information is provided in a special brochure (see "Park Resources" below). In all cases, guests with mobility disabilities should be escorted by someone in their party who can assist as needed.

In some attractions, guests may remain in their wheelchair or ECV; in others, they must be able to transfer in and out of their wheelchair or ECV. In a few attractions, they must be able to leave their wheelchair or ECV and remain ambulatory during the majority of the attraction experience.

Park Resources

Contact Guest Relations at 714-781-7290 for information on *Services for Guests with Visual Disabilities, Services for Guests with Hearing Disabilities, Services for Guests with Service Animals,* and *Attraction Access for Guests Using Wheelchairs and Electric Convenience Vehicles (ECVs).* Information is also available at *www.disneyland.com* and at City Hall inside Disneyland and at Guest Relations in Disney's California Adventure.

All the shops and food locations in the theme parks are designed to be completely accessible to guests in wheelchairs.

For Guests with Visual Disabilities: A tape recorder and cassette describing the park, along with the *Braille Guidebook*, are available upon request at City Hall in Disneyland and at Guest Relations in California Adventure.

Service animals are permitted almost everywhere, except on attractions that involve a great deal of motion. In such instances, the service animal waits with a Disney cast member while the guest goes on the ride.

For Guests with Hearing Disabilities: Several dozen attractions provide a written story line for guests to follow while they experience the attraction. Check at City Hall in Disneyland and Guest Relations in California Adventure for more information.

Closed captioning is available in the pre-show areas of select attractions—inquire at the attraction entrance; contact Guest Relations for the use of a handheld closed-captioning unit (available for free with a $100 deposit). Reflective captioning is available at several shows as well; inquire at each attraction. Quantities are limited—be sure to reserve ahead of time and confirm before you leave home.

Text typewriters (TTYs) are located in between the main entrance to Disneyland and the kennels, and at the pay phones near the exit from Space Mountain. In Disney's California Adventure, TTYs can be found in the Bay Area by Golden Dreams, beside King Triton's Carousel, and inside the Guest Relations lobby.

Sign language interpretation is available for select shows and attractions. Reservations must be made at least seven days in advance. To make this arrangement, contact Resort Tour Services at 714-817-2229.

Volume-control telephones are located throughout the theme parks. Audio tours and closed captioning devices are available to borrow at City Hall and the Guest Relations Lobby for a $20 refundable deposit.

DISNEYLAND RESORT TOURS

The following "behind-the-scenes" tours provide guests with an opportunity to explore Disneyland and Disney's California Adventure in entertaining and informative ways. Annual Passholders, AAA members, and Disney's Visa cardholders receive a 20 percent discount. For details, visit *www.disneyland.com*.

• **Cruzin' Disney's California Adventure** (Daily; 7:30 A.M.): This 3-hour guided, behind-the-scenes tour allows guests a chance to view the park from a special perspective—from a Segway personal transporter. Guests must be at least 16 years old (those under 18 must be accompanied by an adult), be between 100 and 250 pounds, and able to safely step on and off the Segway. (It is not as easy as it looks! Guests should be in good physical condition to participate.) Ample instuction is provided. Cost is $99 per person. Park admission is not required.

• **Welcome to Disneyland** (Daily): A 2½-hour journey that takes you through Disneyland Park and Disney's California Adventure, with stops at several attractions, shows, and interactive experiences. It includes VIP viewing for select shows, and priority seating for some restaurants. It costs $25 per person. Valid Disneyland Park admission is required.

• **A Walk in Walt's Footsteps** (Daily): Led by a knowledgeable guide, the tour covers the whole park. If you already have a park ticket, you pay an extra $59 (per person, all ages) for the 3½-hour tour. It includes lunch, a pin, a peek at the exclusive Club 33, and a special visit to a classic Disneyland attraction, focusing on Audio-Animatronics.

• **Discover the Magic** (Saturday and Sunday): This family tour promises a unique experience for the whole family—while promoting the idea that Disneyland is a community where Disney characters live and play. The tour lasts about 3 hours and is recommended for families with kids ages 5 to 9. Strollers are discouraged, and kids under 18 must be accompanied by an adult. Cost is $59 for the first two tickets, $49 for each additional ticket. Park admission is required.

• **Holiday Time at Disneyland** (Daily during the run of the Christmas parade): This tour is designed for families or groups looking for a unique way to celebrate the holidays together, or guests looking for a personalized experience. The tour, which makes everyone feel like a VIP, shares the history of Disneyland's holiday traditions, includes visits to attractions that have had special holiday makeovers, and special seating for A Christmas Fantasy, Disneyland's holiday parade. Tours may be booked up to 30 days in advance. Availability is limited for all tours. Cost is $59 per person. For more information or to book a tour, call 714-781-4400. Park admission is required.

How to Get There

Most visitors to the Disneyland Resort arrive by car. Many of those who live nearby own an annual pass and drive down frequently to spend a day or weekend at the resort. But for those traveling any significant distance, it tends to cost less to fly than to drive, and certainly saves time. During your days at the Disneyland Resort, you can rely on Disney transportation (in the form of trams, double-decker buses, and monorails) to take you anywhere you want to go on-property. Plan to rent a car for the days you'll venture off-property, or rely on local tours to see the area sights. If you prefer to leave the driving to someone else altogether, traveling by bus or train are alternatives.

By Car

SOUTHERN CALIFORNIA FREEWAYS:
Driving almost anywhere in Orange County, or farther afield, requires negotiating a combination of freeways and surface streets. But once you familiarize yourself with a few names and numbers, navigating becomes much more manageable.

The freeways are well marked and fast, barring (common) traffic snags. That said, they can be rather frenetic. Major thoroughfares may merge with little or no notice. Monstrous traffic jams are the rule, not the exception. And proper names of most roads change, depending on where you are. I-5, for instance, is called the Santa Ana Freeway in Orange County, but in the Los Angeles area it becomes the Golden State Freeway; to the south it's the San Diego Freeway. It's a good idea to learn both the name and the route number of any freeway on which you plan to travel. The exit signs will most likely indicate one or the other but not both.

It's also useful to have an idea of the overall layout of the freeways. Several run parallel to the Pacific coast and are intersected by others running east and west. While this scheme is fairly straightforward, it is complicated by a couple of freeways that squiggle diagonally across the map.

CALIFORNIA DRIVING LAWS: Under California law, seat belts are required for all front- and backseat passengers; right turns at red lights are legal unless otherwise posted, as are U-turns at intersections; and pedestrians have the right-of-way at crosswalks.

AUTOMOBILE CLUBS: Any one of the nation's leading automobile clubs will come to your aid in the event of a breakdown en route (be sure to bring your membership card with you), as well as provide insurance covering accidents, arrest, bail bond, lawyers' fees for defense of contested traffic cases, and personal injury. They also offer useful trip-planning services—not merely advice, but also free maps and route-mapping assistance.

MAPS: Many car rental agencies provide helpful maps, but it's still wise to buy one before your trip. Or drop by a visitor information office; it can usually provide a map showing tourist attractions, major roads, and some minor streets. Local gas stations and bookstores often sell maps, as do some hotel gift shops. Routes can also be plotted ahead of time through *http://maps.google.com*; *www.mapquest.com*; or *http://maps.yahoo.com*.

By Air

Anaheim lies about 45 minutes southeast of Los Angeles by car. Most Disneyland Resort guests who arrive by plane disembark at Los Angeles International Airport (LAX), one of the busiest in the world. It handles approximately 1,580 departures and arrivals daily of more than 70 commercial airlines. Major carriers serving Los Angeles include American, Continental, Delta, and United.

Much closer to Anaheim, Orange County's John Wayne Airport, in Santa Ana, is less than a half hour away from Disney and is served by 11 commercial airlines and more than 200

HOT TIP!
Freeway traffic updates can help you avoid a jam. Tune in to 980 AM or 1070 AM (in Anaheim and Los Angeles).

flights a day. It is sometimes possible to find the same fare to John Wayne/Orange County Airport (SNA) as to LAX, and if it's a nonstop flight, so much the better. There aren't as many direct flights available, but given the airport's proximity to Disneyland, it's worth considering. Another airport vying for attention is the Long Beach Airport (LGB). It is also near Anaheim, but few airlines serve it on a nonstop basis. At press time, JetBlue offered service from several major U.S. cities. Visit *www. jetblue.com* for information.

HOW TO GET THE BEST AIRFARE: These days, airfares are constantly in flux, changing from day to day, seemingly hour to hour. That makes it important to shop around—or have your travel agent do so. It pays (literally) to keep these suggestions in mind:

• Find out the names of all the airlines serving your destination, and then call them all. Tell the airline's reservationist how many people are in your party, and emphasize that you're interested in economy. Ask if you can get a lower fare by slightly altering the dates of your trip, the hour of departure, or the duration of your stay—or, if you live halfway between two airports, by leaving from one rather than the other or by flying into a different area airport.

• Fly weekends on routes heavily used by business travelers, and midweek on routes more commonly patronized by vacationers.

• Purchase your tickets online. Airlines often offer lower fares or bonus frequent flier miles for tickets purchased through their Web site.

• Keep an eye on your local newspapers for advertisements announcing new or special promotional fares.

AIRPORT TRANSPORTATION: Frequent scheduled bus service is offered by Disneyland Resort Express (call 714-978-8855 or 800-828-6699; or *www.anaheimsightseeing.com*). It not only goes to the Disneyland Resort hotels and the properties in Anaheim, but also several hotels in Buena Park (seven miles away and the home of Knott's Berry Farm). The bus stops at each LAX airline terminal, outside the baggage claim area; look for the green bus stop signs on the center island and for DISNEYLAND RESORT EXPRESS in the windshield (of course, the elaborate Disney theming makes the buses pretty easy to spot!).

Those who fly into John Wayne Airport (named after one of Orange County's most famous residents), 16 miles from the Disneyland Resort, have an easier time of it. The ride into town takes half the time. From the baggage claim area, proceed to the Ground Transportation Center. Then cross the street and get to the ticket booth. Look for the motor coach that has the words DISNEYLAND RESORT EXPRESS displayed in the windshield.

SuperShuttle (call 800-258-3826 or visit *www.supershuttle.com*) also serves area airports. At Los Angeles International Airport, claim your luggage, then step out to the orange Shared Ride Van sign on the outer island and contact a blue-uniformed guest service rep for information. A van should arrive within 15 to 30 minutes.

To Anaheim from the Airports

	Disneyland Resort Express bus	SuperShuttle
Los Angeles Int'l Airport	$20 ($30 round-trip) per adult $17 ($22 round-trip) per child 3–11	$16 per person
John Wayne Airport	$15 ($25 round-trip) per adult $13 ($17 round-trip) per child 3–11	$10 per person
Long Beach Airport	Resort Express service is not available, but it's possible to take a Yellow Cab for about $60 each way.	$35 for the first guest in the party, $9 for each additional guest.

Children under 3 ride free. Prices were accurate at press time, but are subject to change.

Reservations are required when arriving at John Wayne or Long Beach airports. At John Wayne, proceed to the transportation center across the street and look for the island marked "Van Shuttle Service." At Long Beach Airport, look for your van across from the main terminal in the car rental return lot. Vans should arrive at either location within 15 to 30 minutes. To return to any airport, check with your hotel front desk the day before the departure for bus schedules and reservation information.

HOT TIP!

The SuperShuttle often carries a smaller group than the Disneyland Resort Express. Expect fewer stops before reaching your destination.

CAR RENTALS: Several major car rental agencies have locations at LAX, John Wayne, and Long Beach airports, in Union Station, at many hotels, and elsewhere in Anaheim. Expect to pay between $189 and $370 a week for a midsize car, and $68 to $114 for a three-day weekend, with unlimited mileage included. Some rental companies to choose from are Avis (800-230-4898), Budget (800-527-0700), Dollar (800-800-3665), Hertz (800-654-3131), and National (800-227-7368).

It pays to call all the agencies to get the best available deal. Be sure to ask about any special promotions or discounts. Loss Damage Waiver (LDW) coverage is essential for your protection in case of an accident, but it can add a lot to your bill (usually at least $9 a day). Most packages that include a rental car do not include the LDW. If you have your own car insurance, check with your carrier to see what they cover.

An increasing number of credit-card companies offer free collision damage coverage for charging the rental to their card, and some may provide primary coverage. That means your credit card company may deal with the rental company directly in the event of an accident, rather than compensate you after your insurance has kicked in. It's worth a phone call to find out.

If you're renting a car at Los Angeles International Airport, the drive to the Disneyland Resort is only 31 miles, but it will take about 45 minutes with no traffic, or up to two hours if the roads are congested. From John Wayne Airport, the drive takes about 25

minutes (without traffic). Expect a drive of about a half hour from Long Beach Airport (again, that's without heavy traffic).

PHOTO BY JILL SAFRO

By Train

Amtrak (800-872-7245; *www.amtrak.com*) and Metrolink commuter service (800-371-5465; *www.metrolinktrains.com*) go to and from L.A.; trains stop at Anaheim's Angel Stadium, about two miles from Disneyland. Yellow Cabs can be called from the station: 714-535-2211. The fare to Disneyland is about $10 each way.

Union Station in Los Angeles is served by a number of trains from the rest of the state, as well as the Northwest, the South, and the Midwest. To get to Anaheim from L.A., you can take Amtrak's Pacific Surfliner or rent a car. Hertz and Budget rental agencies have counters at Union Station by which to arrange rental. Call the companies directly for hours.

By Bus

Buses make sense if you're traveling a fairly short distance, if you have plenty of time to spend in transit, if there are only two or three people in your party, or if cost-control is key.

Buses make the trip from Los Angeles and San Diego, though they usually make a few stops along the way. Travel from most other destinations usually requires a change of vehicle in L.A. Transfers are usually made at 1716 E. 7th St. at Alameda in downtown L.A. The Anaheim Greyhound bus terminal is located at 100 W. Winston Rd., about one mile east of the Disneyland Resort; *www.greyhound.com*; 800-231-2222; Yellow Cabs can get you to Disneyland for about $7; 714-535-2211.

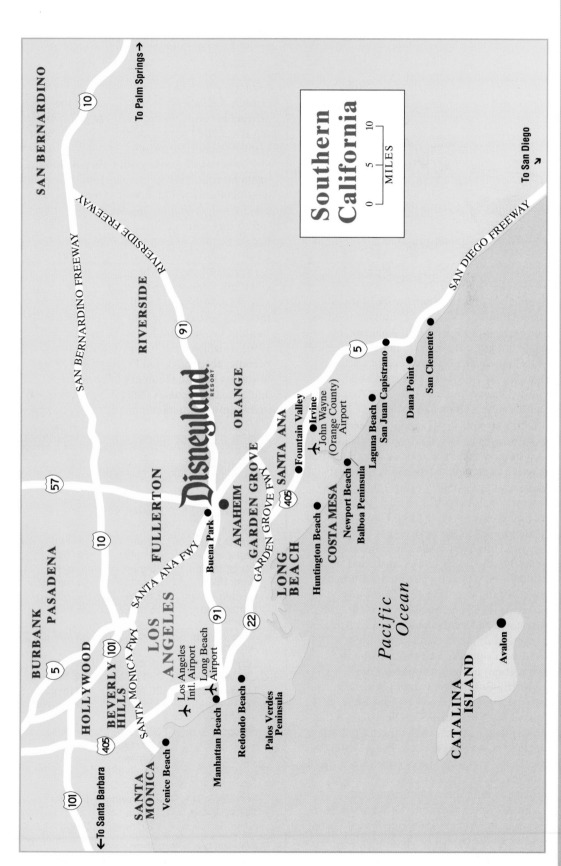

Southern California

MILES

0　　5　　10

To Palm Springs →

SAN BERNARDINO

RIVERSIDE FREEWAY

SAN BERNARDINO FREEWAY

RIVERSIDE

91

Disneyland
RESORT

ORANGE

ANAHEIM

GARDEN GROVE

GARDEN GROVE FWY

SANTA ANA

405

FULLERTON

Buena Park

57

SANTA ANA FWY

LOS
ANGELES

BURBANK

PASADENA

HOLLYWOOD

BEVERLY
HILLS

5

10

101

101

SANTA
MONICA

←To Santa Barbara

405

SANTA MONICA FWY

Los Angeles
Intl. Airport

Long Beach
Airport

Manhattan Beach

Redondo Beach

Palos Verdes
Peninsula

Venice Beach

91

22

LONG
BEACH

Huntington Beach

COSTA MESA

Newport Beach

Balboa Peninsula

Fountain Valley

Irvine

John Wayne
(Orange County)
Airport

5

Laguna Beach

San Juan Capistrano

Dana Point

San Clemente

SAN DIEGO FREEWAY

To San Diego ↗

Pacific
Ocean

CATALINA
ISLAND

Avalon

25

Getting Oriented

Southern California's patchwork of small communities has undeniably blurred borders. The Disneyland Resort is in Anaheim, but you might not know if you were in that city or one of its immediate neighbors except for the signs. Buena Park lies to the northwest, Garden Grove to the south, Santa Ana to the southeast, and Orange to the east.

Farther south—in Huntington Beach, Newport Beach, Laguna Beach, and San Juan Capistrano—there's a bit more breathing room between communities. Heading northwest from Anaheim, you'll come to Los Angeles International Airport.

Continuing northwest into L.A., you'll find Santa Monica to the west, and, to the east, Beverly Hills, West Hollywood, and Hollywood. On the beach farther north and west is Malibu, and inland to the east are Burbank (home of the Walt Disney Studios) and Glendale. The San Fernando Valley lies further north and a bit inland from Los Angeles proper, while Santa Barbara, Southern California's northern boundary, is on the coast, about two hours to the north.

North–South Freeways: There are two. I-5 (the Santa Ana Freeway) runs from Vancouver, Canada, to San Diego, and is the principal inland route in Southern California, linking Los Angeles and San Diego. I-405 (the San Diego Freeway) sprouts from I-5 north of Hollywood, veers toward the coast, then rejoins I-5 at Irvine, south of Anaheim.

East–West Freeways: Of the roads that intersect the two principal north–south arteries, one of the closest to the Disneyland Resort is Route 22, also known as the Garden Grove Freeway; it begins near the ocean in Long Beach and runs beyond the southern border of Anaheim. Route 91, called the Artesia Freeway on the west side of I-5 and the Riverside Freeway on the east, lies about eight miles north of Route 22.

Further north you'll reach I-10, called the Santa Monica Freeway from its beginning point near the Pacific shore in Santa Monica to just east of downtown Los Angeles. At this juncture, it jogs north and then turns east again, becoming the San Bernardino Freeway. I-10 is located about 12 miles north of Route 91.

North of I-10 (anywhere from two to eight miles, depending on your location) is U.S. 101, which heads south from Ventura and then due east, crossing I-405. It is known as the Ventura Freeway until a few miles east of I–405, at which point it angles south and becomes the Hollywood Freeway; at a point a few miles beyond the intersection with I-405, it angles south, becomes the Hollywood Freeway, and eventually merges into I-5.

Travel Times

To/from the Resort	Approx. Distance	Drive Time
Balboa	30 miles	40 min.
Buena Park	7 miles	12 min.
Carlsbad	50 miles	60 min.
Costa Mesa	20 miles	30 min.
Dana Point	30 miles	40 min.
Garden Grove	5 miles	10 min.
Huntington Beach	15 miles	25 min.
John Wayne Airport	16 miles	25 min.
Laguna Beach	30 miles	45 min.
Las Vegas	280 miles	5-6 hrs.
Long Beach	20 miles	30 min.
Los Angeles (downtown and airport)	31 miles	45–90 min.
Newport Beach	20 miles	30 min.
Palm Springs	180 miles	3–4 hrs.
San Diego	87 miles	90 min.
San Juan Capistrano	32 miles	45 min.
San Simeon	270 miles	5–6 hrs.
Santa Ana	5 miles	10 min.
Santa Barbara	110 miles	2 hrs.

Drive times are under optimal conditions; rain or rush-hour traffic could increase or even double the time.

HOW TO GET THERE: The Disneyland Resort is on Harbor Blvd. between Katella Ave., Disneyland Dr., and Ball Rd., 31 miles south of downtown Los Angeles and 87 miles north of San Diego. Many visitors drive to Disneyland from elsewhere in Southern California, while those who come from farther away fly into one of the area airports, rent a car, and drive from there. Once at their hotel, guests may prefer to use the hotel's shuttle or Anaheim Resort Transit (ART) to and from Disneyland.

Southbound I-5 Exit: To get to Disneyland, southbound I-5 (the Santa Ana Freeway) travelers should exit at Disneyland Dr., turn left, cross Ball Rd., and follow signs to the most convenient parking area.

Northbound I-5 Exit: Northbound travelers should exit I-5 at Katella Ave., proceed straight to Disney Way, and then follow signs to the most convenient parking area.

From John Wayne/Orange County Airport: Take I-405 north to CA-55 north to I-5 north. Watch carefully for highway signs once out of the airport. Exit at Katella Ave. exit, head straight to Disney Way, then follow signs to the most convenient parking area.

From Los Angeles International Airport: Take I-105 east to I-605 north to I-5 south. Take Disneyland Dr. exit toward Ball Rd. Merge onto Disneyland Dr. and proceed to the most convenient parking area.

Exit off Orange Freeway: Travelers on the 57 freeway should exit on Katella Ave. and proceed west to Harbor Blvd. Turn right on Harbor and follow signs to the most convenient parking area.

ANAHEIM SURFACE STREETS: The Disneyland Resort is in the center of the Anaheim Resort, a 1,100-acre garden district which also includes the Anaheim Convention Center. Disneyland is bounded by Harbor Blvd. on the east, Disneyland Dr. (a segment of West Street) on the west, Ball Rd. on the north, and Katella Ave. on the south.

Harbor Blvd., near Ball Rd., is the most convenient place to pick up I-5 (Santa Ana Freeway) going north to Los Angeles. Katella Ave. past Anaheim Blvd. is the most convenient entrance to southbound I-5 going to Newport Beach and points south.

Note: Be sure to park in a designated lot or feed the parking meter often. Parking fines can run between $25 and $280 in Anaheim.

LOCAL TRANSPORTATION: The Orange County Transportation Authority (OCTA; 714-560-6282; *www.octa.net*) provides daily bus service throughout the area, with limited weekend service. Several lines stop at Disneyland, but know that public transportation can involve considerable waiting and transferring. Fares are $1.25 for a one-way fare or $3 for a one-day unlimited pass. Seniors 65 and older and people with disabilities pay 50 cents one-way or $1 for a one-day pass. Exact change is required.

If you have wanderlust but lack wheels, your best bet is to sign up for a bus tour, such as one of those offered by Gray Line of Anaheim (800-828-6699). Hotel and motel desks can provide information on tour schedules and prices, and even arrange to have you picked up at the hotel.

Anaheim Resort Transit (*www.rideart.org*; 888-364-2787) is a multi-route guest transit system serving the Anaheim Resort area. Passes may be purchased from many area hotels, public sales outlets, and various kiosk locations. Drivers do not sell passes. Adult fares (kids age nine and under ride for free) are $3 for one day, $6 for two days, and $12 for five days.

The Metropolitan Transportation Authority (MTA) serves Los Angeles County and the major attractions of Orange County (213-626-4455 or 800-266-6883; *www.mta.net*). Exact change is required.

TAXIS: The only licensed taxi company officially authorized to serve the Disneyland Resort is Anaheim Yellow Cab Company (714-535-2211). Cab fare to John Wayne Airport from the Disneyland Hotel runs about $40; if you're going to LAX, figure about $90 (or more, depending on traffic); Long Beach Airport runs about $60 plus gratuity. Prices for town cars are slightly higher. Taxis can be called to pick you up at train and bus stations.

Planning Your Itinerary

For those lucky enough to live in the Los Angeles/Orange County area, the Disneyland Resort offers the opportunity to return frequently. And over the past few years, Disney has given locals more incentive to do just that. With a second theme park and a shopping, dining, and dancing district, the "things to do" list at Disney has tripled in length since the turn of the millennium. Seasoned visitors and first-timers alike will do well to plan each step of their visit far in advance—make the travel arrangements as soon as vacation dates are set (refer to the "Trip Planning Timeline" below to make sure you don't miss any crucial steps), and then study the following chapters of this book to decide how you'd like to spend each day of the trip.

How many days should you spend with the Mouse? Well, that's up to you, but to experience the Disneyland Resort at its best, we recommend a stay of about four full days—you'll have enough time to see every attraction, parade, and show (plus revisit all of your favorites), lounge by your hotel's pool, enjoy a character meal, shop for souvenirs, and dance the night away. If you'd like to visit other area attractions, like Sea World, Universal Studios, or Hollywood, add on one day for each excursion. But don't try to cram too much into one visit; this is a vacation, after all.

Once you've decided how many days you're going to dedicate to Disney, it's time to decide how you'll split up your time on-property. We suggest that you begin with a day at Disneyland Park (for the original and quintessential Disney experience), followed by a visit to Disney's California Adventure (to sample the attractions and shows). On the third day return to Disneyland and hit the park's highlights, plus any attractions you missed on the first day, and save time for souvenir shopping. Day four should be dedicated to your preferred park and some downtime by the pool or in Downtown Disney's shopping plaza. Evenings can be spent in the park, if it's open late, or in Downtown Disney's clubs, lounges, and movie theaters. The options are plentiful.

On the next four pages, we've provided full-day schedules to guide you through four days in the theme parks (with special tips for families with young children and priorities for days when the lines are at their longest). The schedules are meant to be flexible and fun (not Disney boot camp), so take them at your own pace and plan breaks to relax: Have a Mickey Mouse Ice Cream Bar, browse through the shops, feed the ducks, or just pick a bench and watch the crowds rush by.

Trip Planning Timeline

First Things First

- Make hotel and transportation reservations as far ahead as possible. Call 714-520-5050 to purchase theme park tickets and to book Disney hotel accommodations (see page 38 for details); remember that a deposit must be paid within 21 days of the reservation. Log all confirmation numbers in a notebook and call to confirm before you leave home.

- Decide where you will be on each day of your vacation, and create a simple schedule.

6 Months

- Unless you opted for a vacation package that includes theme park admission, it's time to purchase Disney park tickets (see page 17 for ticket options and ordering methods). Your tickets should arrive in about a week.

3 Months

- Find out park hours, the attraction refurbishment schedule, and details on any special events by calling 714-781-4565 or by visiting www.disneyland.com; add this information to your day-by-day schedule.

Up to 2 Months

- Make priority seating arrangements (they're necessary at certain Disney restaurants; call 714-781-3463), and add the information to your day-by-day schedule. Refer to the *Good Meals, Great Times* chapter for details on Disneyland Resort.

2 Weeks

- Airline confirmation and travel vouchers should have arrived by now. Contact your travel agent or the travel company if they haven't shown up yet.

1 Week

- Reconfirm all reservations and finalize your day-by-day schedule.

- Add all your important telephone numbers (doctor, family members, house sitter) to your trip planning notebook, and be sure to bring it and your day-by-day schedule with you.

1 Day

- Be sure to pack any park tickets you may have purchased, as well as photo ID.

Disneyland Park One-Day Schedule

- Disneyland's breakfast options have expanded of late. If you don't nosh at the hotel, consider eating at Café Orleans, Riverbell Terrace, Plaza Inn, or Carnation Café.
- Take in the sights as you walk down Main Street, but don't stop to shop or snack now (you'll have time for that later). Instead, head straight to Adventureland's Indiana Jones† and Jungle Cruise before making your way to Splash Mountain† and The Many Adventures of Winnie the Pooh, in Critter Country. (If you plan to dine at the Blue Bayou, be sure to make a reservation in advance by calling 714-781-3463.)
- Backtrack to New Orleans Square and visit the Haunted Mansion and Pirates of the Caribbean before breaking for an early lunch.
- Next, see the show at the Golden Horseshoe Saloon, take a relaxing river cruise on the Mark Twain, or raft over to Pirate's Lair on Tom Sawyer Island before tackling Big Thunder Mountain† in Frontierland.
- Walk through the Castle into Fantasyland and visit Snow White, Pinocchio, Peter Pan, and Mr. Toad. Then see Alice, the Mad Tea Party, the Matterhorn, and It's a Small World.

IF YOU HAVE YOUNG CHILDREN

First, head to Fantasyland and visit each area attraction (note that some are scary for small children) before heading to Mickey's Toontown. Then visit Critter Country to enjoy The Many Adventures of Winnie the Pooh.

Scope out a spot on a Main Street curb at least an hour before the parade. For smaller crowds, watch the parade from the viewing area near It's a Small World.

Take tykes for a ride on the Disneyland Railroad and It's a Small World. If you need cooling off, backtrack to Toontown and splash around at Donald's Boat.

Ride the Jungle Cruise, then see the Tiki Birds in Adventureland and Tarzan's Treehouse before returning to your favorite rides.

LINE BUSTERS

When the park is packed, head to the Disneyland Railroad, Enchanted Tiki Room, Pirates of the Caribbean, Haunted Mansion, and Disneyland: The First 50 Magical Years.

†Fastpass is available for this ride. Retrieve your time-saving Fastpass before visiting the land's remaining attractions. To learn how the system works, see page 60.

Continued on page 30

HOT TIP!

If you enter the park via monorail, you'll begin your tour in Tomorrowland. Hit the land's major attractions if you wish, and then ride the railroad to Main Street and follow this schedule from there.

Disneyland Delights

These attractions form the quintessential Disneyland experience:

Indiana Jones Adventure • Pirates of the Caribbean
Haunted Mansion • Big Thunder Mountain Railroad
Splash Mountain • Peter Pan's Flight • Matterhorn Bobsleds
It's a Small World • Mr. Toad's Wild Ride
Jungle Cruise • The Many Adventures of Winnie the Pooh
Buzz Lightyear Astro Blasters • Space Mountain
Finding Nemo Submarine Voyage

Continued from page 29

Disneyland Park One-Day Schedule

- Keep an eye on the time and try to fit the afternoon parade into your schedule.
- Make your way to Mickey's Toontown and see as many of this land's attractions as you can, making Roger Rabbit's Car Toon Spin† a priority.
- Hop on the Disneyland Railroad and disembark in Tomorrowland. Hit the Finding Nemo Submarine Voyage, Buzz Lightyear Astro Blasters, and Space Mountain before heading for dinner.

Note: If the park is open late, board the monorail in Tomorrowland and dine in Downtown Disney before returning to the park.

- After dinner, catch a screening of Honey, I Shrunk the Audience before riding Autopia†, Star Tours†, or Astro Orbitor.
- Take little ones to Mickey's Toontown before it closes for the day—it closes earlier than the rest of the park when there is a fireworks presentation (generally one hour before the show starts).
- On nights when Fantasmic! is presented, make a point of getting to Frontierland in plenty of time to see it. (Check park guidemap for the schedule, or inquire at City Hall.) If there is more than one performance scheduled, the later one is usually less crowded.
- Stroll back to Main Street. Shop, stop for dessert, see the Walt Disney Story, and watch the fireworks burst over the castle.
- If there's time, take a second spin on your favorite attractions.

MEET THE CHARACTERS!

There are lots of places to mix and mingle with Disney characters in this park. Some of the best spots include Toontown (Mickey, Minnie, Donald, Goofy, and more), Critter Country (Pooh and pals), and Fantasyland's Princess Fantasy Faire (princesses). Check a park map for specific times and locations. And don't forget the camera!

†Fastpass is available for this ride. Retrieve your Fastpass before visiting the land's remaining attractions.

Top Shops

Whether you're browsing or buying, Disneyland is a shopper's paradise. Here are a few of the spots where wallets get a workout:

Candy Palace • Emporium • **Main Street Magic Shop**
Market House • The Disney Gallery
Jewel of Orleans • **Pieces of Eight**
Pioneer Mercantile • The Star Trader
South Seas Traders • **Villains Lair**

HOT TIP!

If you'd like to meet Mickey Mouse, make a beeline for his Toontown house—the big cheese greets guests in the movie barn out back. For the shortest wait, get there as soon as Toontown opens. And don't forget your camera!

Disney's California Adventure One-Day Schedule

- Begin your California adventure by snagging a Fastpass for a high-flying ride on Soarin' Over California†. (It tends to run out of Fastpass assignments early, as does Tower of Terror.)

- Depart from Condor Flats and head into the Hollywood Pictures Backlot, via the Sunshine Plaza. Enjoy a thrilling trip at the Twilight Zone™ Tower of Terror†. Refer to a park guidemap for the Hyperion Theater's next showtime, and plan to arrive at the theater at least 30 minutes before the show. In the meantime, enjoy Monsters, Inc.—Mike & Sulley to the Rescue!, Muppet*Vision 3D† and Disney Animation (don't miss Turtle Talk with Crush). Take toddlers to the show at Playhouse Disney.

- Head to A Bug's Land and don your insect eyes for a creepy-crawly screening of It's Tough to be a Bug! (though it may scare little ones).

- Now it's time for a little mountain climbing: Make your way over to Grizzly Peak, and get set to get wet on the drenching Grizzly River Run† white-water raft ride. If you're up for it (and properly shoed), then visit the Redwood Creek Challenge Trail.

- Keep an eye on the time, and find a curbside spot in the San Francisco district about 20 minutes before the parade starts.

- Pick up some wine-pairing tips or sample California's finest at the Golden Vine Winery.

- Tour the micro-factories of the Pacific Wharf before proceeding on to Paradise Pier's daredevil rides.

- Work your way around Paradise Bay, stopping for each attraction, but making sure California Screamin'† and Toy Story Mania! are top priorities.

- Stroll along the boardwalk and try some midway games, or enjoy a sweet treat. If there's a parade scheduled, be sure and catch it.

IF YOU HAVE YOUNG CHILDREN

Head straight to the Hollywood Pictures Backlot part of the park. Stop in to see the Muppets before experiencing Monsters, Inc.— Mike & Sulley to the Rescue! Head over to Animation for Turtle Talk with Crush. Next, pay a visit to Playhouse Disney. Then maneuver young water lovers through the sprinkler maze and gardens of A Bug's Land. Note that It's Tough to be a Bug! often frightens young children.

Try the kid-friendly obstacle course on the Redwood Creek Challenge Trail (save time for some campside storytelling).

Take a spin on the carousel and visit the SS Rustworthy, a water-spouting boat and play area, before spending some time at Paradise Pier's Midway.

LINE BUSTERS

When lines abound at Disney's California Adventure, we suggest the following: the Golden State's micro-factories, Bountiful Valley Farm, Redwood Creek Challenge Trail, King Triton's Carousel, the SS Rustworthy, and Paradise Pier's Midway.

†Fastpass is available for this ride. Retrieve your Fastpass before visiting the area's remaining attractions.

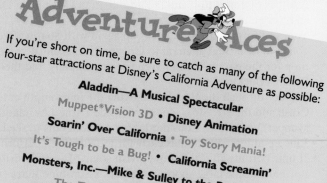

Adventure Aces

If you're short on time, be sure to catch as many of the following four-star attractions at Disney's California Adventure as possible:

Aladdin—A Musical Spectacular

Muppet*Vision 3D • Disney Animation

Soarin' Over California • Toy Story Mania!

It's Tough to be a Bug! • California Screamin'

Monsters, Inc.—Mike & Sulley to the Rescue!

The Twilight Zone™ Tower of Terror

A Second Day in Disneyland Park

Returning for a second or third day in each of the theme parks means more time to savor the atmosphere, try any attractions you missed the first day, and revisit all the old and new favorites. Knowing that there will be a second day also makes for a much less harried pace on day one. Longer stays also allow time for full-day excursions to attractions like Universal Studios Hollywood or Knott's Berry Farm (see *Orange County & Beyond* chapter for day-trip options).

- Start the morning with a character breakfast at the Plaza Inn (you can also share a morning meal with the characters outside the park at Goofy's Kitchen in the Disneyland Hotel, the Grand Californian's Storytellers Cafe, or PCH Grill in Disney's Paradise Pier Hotel).
- Head to Tomorrowland and ride Space Mountain, Star Tours, Buzz Lightyear Astro Blasters, and other favorite attractions.
- Hop on the train to Mickey's Toontown. See the sights and spend some time mingling with resident Disney characters.
- Visit It's a Small World and the nearby character greeting area, and then tour Fantasyland.
- Stroll, shop, and stop for lunch on Main Street, U.S.A.
- Watch the afternoon parade from the Main Street Railroad depot, or secure a curbside spot.
- Ride a Main Street Vehicle up to Town Square and then continue on foot toward Adventureland.
- Stop at the Enchanted Tiki Room and Tarzan's Treehouse before heading on to New Orleans Square. Here the priorities are the Haunted Mansion and Pirates of the Caribbean. Visit them and move on to Splash Mountain, in Critter Country.
- Meander through the shops of New Orleans Square, and then stop for a leisurely dinner at a nearby eatery. Riverbelle Terrace, the French Market, and the full-service Blue Bayou and Café Orleans are all excellent options.
- Select a spot riverside about 45 minutes ahead for the evening's performance of Fantasmic! (if it is scheduled).
- Wait for the crowds to disperse at show's end, and make your way to Big Thunder Mountain Railroad for one last ride before the park closes.

A Second Day in
Disney's California Adventure

- If you don't have a reservation for Ariel's Princess Celebration Breakfast at Ariel's Grotto, be sure to grab breakfast before arriving at the park.
- Cut through Hollywood Pictures Backlot and head straight for the Twilight Zone™ Tower of Terror. Then move over to Paradise Pier.
- Thrill-seekers will flip for California Screamin' and gamers will swoon over Toy Story Mania!
- Take a lunch break at Burger Invasion, Pacific Wharf Cafe, of Wine Country Trattoria; or, if the park is open late, head back to your hotel to relax or splash in the pool (remember to get your hand stamped before exiting, so that you can return to California Adventure later in the day). Another option is to spend the afternoon in Downtown Disney—the restaurants and shops will all be open by noon.
- Your California adventure picks up again with Soarin' Over California, followed by a trip to It's Tough to be a Bug!, then on to Grizzly River Run (if you don't mind getting soaked).
- Stop for the parade if you haven't seen it already, and then make your way toward Hollywood Pictures Backlot.
- Wander through the Backlot, enjoying the impromptu entertainment, take in Turtle Talk with Crush and the Toy Story Zoetrope inside Disney Animation, and catch the next showing of Muppet*Vision 3-D. Consider taking Aladdin fans to see his musical spectacular a second time.
- Line up at least 30 minutes early for the evening's performance at the Hyperion Theater.
- If time permits after the show, revisit some of your favorite attractions or search for last-minute souvenirs at the large shops in the park's Sunshine Plaza (near the main entrance).

Fingertip Reference Guide

BARBERS AND SALONS

Hair may be cut or coiffed at Marika's Hair Salon at the Hilton Anaheim (777 Convention Way; 714-703-1367) or at Bella Hair Salon & Spa at the Annabella Hotel (1030 W. Katella Ave.; 714-535-2659).

CAR CARE

The Anaheim office of the Automobile Club of Southern California (ACSC) is located at 420 N. Euclid Ave.; 714-774-2392. For ACSC emergency roadside service, call 800-400-4222; *www.aaa-calif.com.*

DRINKING POLICIES

While there's a strict no-alcohol policy at Disneyland Park, drinking is an option at many of the dining spots in its sister park, Disney's California Adventure, as well as at Downtown Disney. Alcohol may also be purchased at the lounges and restaurants of the three Disney hotels. The legal drinking age in California is 21.

LOCKERS

Lockers of various sizes are available just outside the main entrance of the parks; inside Disneyland on Main Street (behind the Market House); and inside Disney's California Adventure (DCA) across from Guest Relations. Prices are $7, $10, $11, or $12 per

HOT TIP!

To avoid the sometimes maddening congestion at the Main Street locker location, consider stowing your stuff at the lockers near the picnic area, just outside Disneyland Park's turnstiles.

day, depending on the locker's size. These storage facilities make it convenient to intersperse frolicking on the attractions with shopping; just make your purchases and stash them in a locker. Availability is limited, and during busy periods all the space can be taken well before noon. Disney's California Adventure guests may stash items in lockers for free while they ride Grizzly River Run. They are off to the side of the attraction's entrance.

LOST AND FOUND

At any given time, a survey of the shelves of Lost and Found might turn up cameras, umbrellas, strollers, handbags, lens caps, sunglasses, radios, jewelry, and even a few crutches, false teeth, and hubcaps. Once, a wallet containing $1,700 in cash was turned in. The Disneyland Resort will return lost items to guests who fill out a report.

If you find a lost item, you'll be asked to fill out a card with your name and address; if the object isn't claimed within 60 days, you have the option of keeping it. This system encourages honesty, so if you lose something, check at the Lost and Found. (Inquire at City Hall in Disneyland.) If you lose something at a hotel, contact the front desk.

MAIL

Postcards are sold in gift shops all over Anaheim, in many shops and souvenir stands on Disney property, and at the three Disney hotels. Stamps are sold in both theme parks and at all three Disney hotels.

Cards and letters that are deposited in the mailboxes in the theme parks are picked up and delivered to the U.S. Post Office once a day, early in the morning. All items are postmarked Anaheim, not Disneyland. (By the way, don't forget to arrange for your own mail to be held by the post office or picked up by a neighbor while you're on vacation.) Due to the heavy volume, expect delivery to take a bit longer than usual. (There's a lot to write home about in these parts!)

Post Office: The U.S. Post Office closest to the Disneyland Resort is Holiday Station, about a half mile from the parks (1180 W. Ball Rd.; Anaheim; 714-533-8182). It's open from 8:30 A.M. to 5 P.M. weekdays only.

MEDICAL MATTERS

Blisters are the most common complaint received by Disney's First Aid departments, located at the north end of Main Street, adjacent to Lost Children in Disneyland, and by Mission Tortilla Factory in the Pacific Wharf area of Disney's California Adventure. So be forewarned, and wear comfortable, broken-in shoes (bring a back-up pair, too)—and pack Band-Aids, just in case.

If you have a serious medical problem while on-property, contact any Disney cast member. He or she will get in touch with First Aid to make further arrangements. First Aid, staffed by registered nurses, will store breathing machines and crutches for guests. It will not dispense medication to anyone under 18 without the consent of a parent or chaperone.

It's a good idea to carry an insurance card and any other pertinent medical information. Those with chronic health problems should carry copies of all their prescriptions, along with their doctor's telephone number.

Prescriptions: The pharmacy at CVS, about a mile from Disney, is open 8 A.M. to 10 P.M. Monday through Friday, Saturdays 9 A.M. to 7 P.M., and Sundays 10 A.M. to 6 P.M. (1660 W. Katella Ave., at Euclid; Anaheim; 714-530-0500). Another CVS, about three miles away, is open 24 hours daily (12031 Brookhurst St., at Chapman, Garden Grove; 714-530-5280).

Refrigerator Facilities: In the parks, insulin and antibiotics that must be refrigerated can be stored for the day at First Aid. (It does not store breast milk for nursing mothers, however.) Outside the parks, there are refrigerators in many of the area's hotels and motels. If your room doesn't have one, a fridge can usually be supplied at a nominal charge. Or the hotel or motel can store insulin in its own refrigerator. Inquire in advance.

MONEY

Cash, traveler's checks, personal checks, Disney Dollars, American Express, Visa, MasterCard, Disney gift cards, the Disney

Rewards Visa, and the Discover Card are accepted as payment for admission to the theme parks, for merchandise purchased in shops, and for meals (except at souvenir and food carts, where it's strictly cash or Disney Dollars). Checks must be imprinted with the guest's name and address, drawn on a U.S. bank, and accompanied by proper ID—that is, a valid driver's license or passport. Department store charge cards are not acceptable identification for check-writing purposes. Disney hotel guests who have left a credit card number at check-in can charge most expenses in the parks to their hotel bill.

Disney Dollars: Accepted as cash throughout the parks, Disney Dollars are the equivalent in value of U.S. dollars. They are sold at the main entrances of the parks, as well as at City Hall in Disneyland, at select shops on-property, and at most Disney Stores nationwide. Kids love to use them; they also make good inexpensive gifts and souvenirs, and may be accepted as cash at Disney Store locations.

Disney Gift Cards: Available for purchase at many merchandise locations, these may be redeemed throughout the Disneyland Resort (though there are some exceptions at Downtown Disney and vendors not equipped to accept credit cards).

Financial Services: Automated teller machines (ATMs) are located at each park's main entrance; in Disneyland at the Bank of Main Street, by the Fantasyland Theatre, in the Frontierland Stockade, and in the Starcade; in California Adventure at the Entry Plaza, by the Bay Area near Golden Dreams, beside Cocina Cucamonga, near Burger Invasion, and by Malibu-Ritos; in Downtown Disney by Häagen-Dazs; and in all three Disneyland Resort hotels.

It's possible to cash a personal check made out to Disneyland for up to $100 at the main entrance to each park or City Hall; proper identification is required. The ATMs at the main entrance accept credit cards for cash advances. Note that the presence of a bank on Main Street is a tad deceiving. The bank offers no financial services.

American Express Cardmember Services: American Express cardholders can cash personal checks up to $1,000 per week ($200 in cash and the rest in traveler's checks) with a personal American Express card, or up to $2,500 per week ($500 in cash and the rest in traveler's checks) with a Gold Card. They can also get a cash advance of $500 on their Optima Card (with a valid PIN number). All services are offered at American Express Travel Services, at 763 S. Main St., Suite 190, Orange; 714-541-3318.

This office can also exchange foreign currency (for a fee [$5 for members, $7 for nonmembers], regardless of the amount) and replace lost or stolen cards or traveler's checks within 24 hours. Call 800-528-4800 to get a security code for cards and 800-221-7282 to get a claim number for checks. Hours are usually 9 A.M. to 6 P.M. Monday through Friday and 9 A.M. to 4 P.M. Saturday.

Many Anaheim banks sell American Express traveler's checks, usually for a one percent fee. There is no fee for travelers checks purchased with non-bank-issued Amex cards at the Travel Services office.

Foreign Currency Exchange: In addition to the American Express Travel Services mentioned above, foreign currencies can be exchanged (for a fee) at the Travelex office in Downtown Disney; 714-502-0811. Paper currency only.

PETS

Except for service animals, pets are not allowed in Disneyland or Disney's California Adventure. However, any nonpoisonous creatures can be boarded in the Disneyland Pet Care Kennel, which is located by the entrance to the Disneyland park. Reservations are not necessary (the kennel rarely reaches capacity). Pets may be boarded for the day (no overnight stays). In addition to proof of rabies and distemper vaccinations, guests have to show proof of hepatitis and leptospirosis vaccinations for dogs over four months of age. Without proof of all four vaccinations, the dog will not be permitted entrance to the kennel. At press time, it cost $15 per day, per pet. Cash or Disney Dollars only. To inquire about kennel rates during

HOT TIP!
Internet savvy? Disneyland offers (free) monthly podcasts for your listening pleasure. Go to *www.disneyland.com/podcast* to download the informative "behind-the-magic" shows.

your visit, call 714-781-7290.

Disney personnel do not handle the animals, so the pet owners themselves must put their animals into the cages and take them out again. Guests are encouraged to drop by to visit with and walk their pets several times a day. Kennel attendants are not responsible for walking any animals in their care.

Note: During busy seasons there may be a morning rush, starting about 30 minutes before the theme parks open, so you may encounter some delay in arranging your pet's stay.

Outside the Disneyland Resort: If you want to board your pet nearby, contact Animal Inns of America, 10852 Garden Grove Blvd.; Garden Grove, CA 92643; 714-636-4455; *www.animals.com*.

Some hotels and motels in the Disneyland area accept well-behaved (preferably small) pets, but most do not allow guests to leave animals in the room unattended. One exception is the pet-friendly Hilton Anaheim (714-750-4321). There is no charge for pet guests here. The hotel is about a 20- to 25-minute walk to Disneyland.

To find out about other possibilities for pets, contact the Anaheim/Orange County Visitor & Convention Bureau; 714-765-8888 or search "pets" at *www.anaheimoc.org*.

PHOTOGRAPHIC NEEDS

The Main Street Photo Supply Co. inside Disneyland can answer questions and recharge most batteries (or you can bring your own charger and plug it in there). Disney's California Adventure offers similar services. For anything more serious, rent a camera and have a factory-authorized shop do the work on your camera when you return home. If you've lost your lens cover, it's worth checking at Lost and Found (see page 33); they may not have your cap, but they often have extras.

For a selection of film and digital camera supplies, go to Kani's Camera, 1428 E. Katella Ave.; 714-633-6035; *www.kaniscamera.com*.

Try not to take your camera on rough or bumpy rides. Stash it in a locker or with a non-riding member of your party.

RELIGIOUS SERVICES

Catholic: St. Justin Martyr; 2050 W. Ball Rd.; 714-774-2595; *www.saintjustin.org*; about two miles from Disneyland. Weekday masses are held at 6:30 A.M. and 8:30 A.M. (English); Saturday at 5:30 and 8:30 P.M. (English) and 7 P.M. (Spanish); and Sunday at 6:45 A.M., 8 A.M., 11 A.M., 12:30 P.M., and 5:30 P.M. (English) and 9:30 A.M. and 7 P.M. (Spanish). Holy day masses are at 6:30 A.M. and 8:30 A.M. (English), and 7 P.M. (bilingual); holy day eve, 5:30 P.M. (English).

Episcopal: St. Michael's Episcopal Church; 311 W. South St.; 714-535-4654; about seven blocks from Disneyland. Sunday services are at 8 A.M. and 10:15 A.M. (English) and at 8 A.M. and 12:30 P.M. (Spanish).

Jewish: Temple Beth Emet; 1770 W. Cerritos Ave.; *www.tbe-anaheimoc.org*; 714-772-4720; a few blocks from Disneyland. Services are held on Fridays at 6:30 P.M., the last Friday of each month at 8 P.M., and 9 A.M. Saturdays.

Lutheran: Prince of Peace Lutheran Church; 1421 W. Ball Rd.; 714-774-0993; *www.popanaheim.com*; about one mile from the Disneyland Resort. Sunday services are at 8 A.M. and 10:45 A.M. (traditional), 9:15 A.M. (contemporary), and noon (Korean).

Non-denominational: The Kindred Community Church; 8712 E. Santa Ana Canyon Rd.; 714-282-9941. Services are held on Sunday at 9 A.M. It's about 11 miles from Disneyland; *www.kindredcommunitychurch.org*.

United Methodist: West Anaheim United Methodist Church; 2045 W. Ball Rd.; 714-772-6030; approximately two miles from Disneyland. Sunday services are at 10:30 A.M.

SHOPPING FOR NECESSITIES

It's a rare vacationer who doesn't leave some essential at home or run out of it mid-trip. Gift shops in almost all the hotels stock items no traveler should be without, but they usually cost more than in conventional retail shops. One good source is CVS Pharmacy, about a mile from the Disneyland Resort; 1660 W. Katella Ave. at Euclid; 714-530-0500.

Inside the theme parks, aspirin, bandages, suntan lotions, and other sundries are sold at a variety of shops; just ask a cast member to direct you to the closest one. Some items are also available at each park's First Aid location and Baby Care Center. A shop at each Disneyland Resort hotel also offers a wide selection of sundries.

SMOKING POLICIES

State law bans smoking anywhere inside restaurants, bars, and cocktail lounges, but most establishments provide patios for puffing and often heat them on chilly evenings. At the Disney theme parks, smoking is allowed in designated smoking areas. Check a park guidemap for exact locations. All hotels at the Disneyland Resort are completely smoke-free.

TELEPHONES

Local calls from most pay phones in Southern California cost 35–50 cents. Most hotels in the same area charge an average of a dollar or more for local, toll-free, and credit-card calls made from your room.

For long-distance calls, policies vary from hotel to hotel, but charges are always higher than they would be for direct-dial calls made from a pay phone. It makes the most sense to use a calling card when dialing long-distance from a room phone.

Phone Cards: Disney offers AT&T prepaid phone cards in values of $10 and $20. They can be purchased from machines in Disneyland and Disney's California Adventure, and at the Disneyland and Grand Californian hotels.

Weather Hotlines: For weather info, call 714-550-4636, ext. 2515; *www.nws.noaa.gov* or *www.weather.com*.

Wireless Phones: To ensure a dose of uninterrupted magic for you and those around you, turn off your cell phone while visiting the parks. You'll be glad you did.

TIPPING

The standard gratuities around Anaheim are about the same as in any other city of its size. Expect to tip bellhops about $1 per bag. Generally, tip cabdrivers 15 percent; outstanding shuttle or tour bus drivers, $1. Valets usually get $1–$2 when you pick up the car. In restaurants, a 15 to 20 percent gratuity is the norm. If you are pleased with the condition of your room, it is customary to leave a gratuity of $2–$5 per day for the housekeeper (leave a note with the tip to avoid confusion). Note that room-service bills often include a gratuity.

Accommodations

The welcome sign is always out at the Disneyland Resort hotels, where themed meals, amenities, and decor are definitely in character and add to the fun of a Disneyland vacation. And the resort's Grand Californian Hotel & Spa takes staying at Disneyland to a new level of luxury.

In addition to the three hotels within the Disneyland Resort, there are more than 40 properties in Orange County, known as Disneyland Good Neighbor hotels, that the Walt Disney Travel Company has handpicked to round out their Disney lodging options. We've selected a bunch of these recommended hotels, based on services and proximity to Disneyland, to highlight in this chapter.

If the sole purpose of your trip is to visit Disney, plan to stay in Anaheim, either on Disneyland property or at one of the surrounding hotels. Once you arrive and check in, you won't need your car again until you leave. Free transportation to and from the parks is provided by monorails and trams serving the Disneyland Resort, and by buses serving neighboring hotels, motels, and inns. If struck with a bit of wanderlust, know that Anaheim is within range of a host of Southern California destinations, including movie studios, museums, beaches, and more.

We've provided a variety of options in Anaheim, from old-fashioned to contemporary, simple to sublime. We've also included a selection of Orange County's seaside escapes and charming bed-and-breakfast inns, for those interested in venturing beyond the Disney region.

Disneyland Resort Hotels

PHOTO BY JILL SAFRO

Fans of the Disneyland Resort are faced with a difficult decision. It isn't whether or not to stay on-property (that's recommended if it's within the budget), but which of the three hotels to choose. Some factors to consider:

The whimsical pool area, arcade, and character meals make the classic Disneyland Hotel appeal to the kids in the family (and the kid in us all).

Meanwhile, Disney's Paradise Pier Hotel boasts a sunny facade to complement Disney's California Adventure. Inside, the Disney influence is subtle, though it's possible to dine with characters.

The design team has really outdone itself with the Grand Californian Resort and Spa. Located inside Disney's California Adventure, the hotel's theming and style touch every detail, right down to the floorboards.

Whichever hotel you choose, one thing is certain—a stay on-property is sure to complete the overall Disney experience. From a resort information TV channel to wake-up calls from Mickey Mouse himself, every detail reminds you that you're in Disney's land.

Exclusive Benefits: Several perks are reserved for guests staying on-property. Perhaps the most significant of these is early entry into the parks (at no extra cost) on select mornings. There's also preferred admission (with a ticket) to a park if it reaches capacity.

One of the most convenient perks is the ability to charge almost any expense incurred at a Disney theme park back to the hotel room, if a credit card imprint was taken at check-in. Purchases can be charged to the room from the time of check-in until 11 A.M. on the day of departure.

Shoppers may also enjoy the benefit of having purchases delivered to their hotel's Bell Services Desk, where they can pick up their packages the next day—rather than having to carry them through the parks all day.

Other on-property perks include in-lobby screenings of Disney's animated classics (at all Disneyland Resort hotels) and wake-up calls from Mickey. Courtesy pick-up is available for guests with disabilities to and from Paradise Pier in Disney's California Adventure park.

Check-in and Check-out: Check-in begins at 3 P.M., but guests who arrive early can check in, store their luggage at the Bell Desk, and go have fun. A photo ID is required at check-in. Check-out is at 11 A.M., and, again, bags can be stored until guests are ready to depart. Express check-out is available by leaving a credit card imprint at check-in.

> ## HOT TIP!
> Rooms equipped for guests with disabilities are available at the three Disney hotels, all of which are completely non-smoking. No exceptions.

Prices: Rates for standard guestrooms range from about $235 to $480. They vary according to hotel, view, and season. Room tax is 15 percent.

Deposit Requirements: A deposit equal to one night's lodging is required within 21 days from the time the reservation is made. Reservations are automatically canceled if a deposit is not received in that time period. Reservations booked fewer than 21 days prior to arrival are held for about a week without deposit. Deposit payment can be mailed in the form of check or money order, or can be guaranteed by a credit card over the phone (in which case the card is not actually billed until check-in).

Cancellation Policy: The deposit will be refunded if the reservation is canceled at least 72 hours before the scheduled arrival.

Additional Costs: Room rates at all three hotels are based on double occupancy. While there is no charge for kids under 18 sharing their parents' room, extra adults will each cost $15 extra per night. Note that there is no fee for sleeping bags, or cribs.

A $10 per day resort service fee includes overnight parking, use of the fitness centers, weekday newspaper delivery, high-speed

Internet access, and local telephone calls. Valet parking is available for $14 per day.

Discounts: Annual Pass bearers are rewarded with special rates and discounts throughout the Disneyland resort. There may be discounts available to Southern California residents, members of the military, and teachers—be sure to ask when you make your reservation. Disney's Visa cardholders can earn reward dollars when they use the card. These dollars can be redeemed at Disneyland, Walt Disney World, and the Disney Cruise Line. If you're not a Disney Visa cardholder and would like to become one, flip to the back page of this book. Our coupon can help you get a $50 bonus.

Packages: The Walt Disney Travel Company offers packages that feature a stay at one of the Disneyland hotels. See "Travel Packages" in *Getting Ready to Go*, or contact the Walt Disney Travel Company at 714-520-5050.

PHOTO BY JILL SAFRO

DISNEYLAND HOTEL: This fanciful resort adjacent to the Downtown Disney District was the first hotel erected at the Disneyland Resort. The family-friendly property features a Peter Pan–inspired outdoor area with a 5,000-square-foot swimming pool that incorporates a 100-foot waterslide, a pirate ship, and (waiting beside the ship) a comical sculpture of Tick Tock, the hungry crocodile from Disney's classic movie *Peter Pan*. A small, winding shoreline, flower gardens, rock formations, and a wedding gazebo add to the property's picturesque terrain.

The hotel has 969 rooms, including 61 suites (one of which has a Pirates of the Caribbean theme), located in three separate towers. Most tower rooms have two double beds, and many can accommodate up to five people (one of them on a daybed). All the interior tower rooms have glass doors that open (there is a rail, but no balcony) and are ideal for relaxing or enjoying a snack by. The

11-story Dreams Tower looks toward Downtown Disney and Disney's California Adventure on one side and the main pool on the other. The 14-story Wonder Tower's rooms provide city views as well as windows overlooking the waterfall and koi pond. The 11-story Magic Tower offers rooms with pool views, but only on one side; guests on the other side look out over city rooftops, with Disneyland to the right, offering the best view of the fireworks.

A monorail stop is a short walk away, in neighboring Downtown Disney, which means extremely easy access to Disneyland (it drops guests off in Tomorrowland), a nice convenience for guests who relish a break in their park-going with a trip to a hotel pool; to the small beach or to Team Mickey's Workout, a gym that features weight machines and aerobic exercise equipment. The workout room is included in the resort service fee. Guests may access it with their room keys.

Guests also enjoy Horseshoe Falls, a 165-foot-wide cascade that visitors can walk beneath. Nearby, a tranquil pool is filled with Japanese koi fish. The large arcade, a big draw for younger guests, is located in the shopping area beside the waterfall. Note that the classic fountain show, Fantasy Waters, was retired a few years ago.

In the lobby of the Magic Tower, a large shop called Fantasia sells Disney souvenirs. Goofy's Kitchen, hosted by Chef Goofy and his Disney pals, is an extremely popular buffet open for breakfast and dinner; Steakhouse 55 offers breakfast and dinner in an elegant setting; and Hook's Pointe & Wine Cellar features a mesquite grill "surf and turf" cuisine and offers Never Land pool views. The Coffee House, Captain's Galley, and Croc's Bits 'n' Bites provide snacks and quick meals for guests on the go. Room service is available. (For more information about hotel dining, see the *Good Meals, Great Times* chapter.)

The convention and meetings area, adjacent to Goofy's Kitchen and linked to the lobby via a photo-lined passageway, deserves a look for its Disney-related artwork, including a floor-to-ceiling collage of Disney collectibles and milestones. Created entirely from old toys, souvenirs, name tags, and other assorted memorabilia, it commemorates the colorful and unique history of Disneyland. The photo hall of fame depicts celebrities, members of royalty, and political figures who have visited the resort.

The hotel can provide safe-deposit boxes, currency exchange, and child-care referrals. An ATM is on the premises. Airport buses bound for the John Wayne (Orange County) and Los Angeles airports make regular stops at the hotel, as do tour buses, city and county buses, and buses traveling to and from downtown Los Angeles.

Rates run from about $255 to $345, depending on the view and season, plus $15 for each extra adult beyond two (no charge for kids under 18 staying in their parents' room); no charge for rollaways or cribs. Concierge-level rooms start at $470. Suites range from $600 to $3,620. (The higher amount is for the Pirates of the Caribbean Suite and Mickey Mouse Penthouse.) It is possible to get a Mickey Mouse or princess themed room connected to a standard room. Sold as pairs, they start at $605. Self-parking is included in the daily resort fee ($17 per day for valet); others pay $6 per hour, with a $30 maximum for 24 hours.

Disneyland Hotel; 1150 Magic Way; Anaheim, CA 92802; 714-956-6425 (to make reservations) or 714-778-6600 (front desk); *www.disneyland.com.*

DISNEY'S GRAND CALIFORNIAN HOTEL & SPA: This 745-room hotel is in a prime

location—smack-dab in the middle of the Disneyland Resort. (Thanks to the Disney Vacation Club, the resort will be expanded to include about 200 new rooms, 44 suites, and 50 villas by the end of 2009.) It even has its own private entrance to Disney's California Adventure theme park and easy access to the Downtown Disney District.

A border of trees surrounds the six-story hotel, built as a tribute to the Arts and Crafts tradition of the early 1900s—a style made famous by the striking designs of architect Frank Lloyd Wright. Rich cedar and redwood paneling decorates the cavernous lobby, where display cabinets filled with original art and quality reproductions introduce guests to that rich period of art. The lobby's great hearth has a perennially lit fire. Furnishings throughout the hotel have warm colors and intricate textures. Even the hotel staff wears period costumes.

Each of the 705 deluxe guestrooms and 40 suites features a 32-inch flat-panel TV, a DVD player, a tiny safe, weekday newspaper delivery, desk with two-line telephone, a computer and fax–accessible, high-speed internet data port, iron and board, and small (unstocked) refrigerator. The bathroom has marble surfaces, a makeup mirror, and hair dryer.

Most of the guestrooms in the hotel feature two queen beds, though 80 have a king bed, and 160 have one queen bed plus a bunk bed with a trundle (these rooms sleep five). The carved wooden headboards are designed to resemble vines on a trellis, the bedspreads have a stained-glass-like design, and Bambi appears subtly in the shower curtain pattern.

Guest services include 24-hour room service, laundry and dry cleaning, and a full-service business center. The concierge level offers upgraded amenities and services. Guests can relax at the Fountain Pool or frolic in Redwood Pool (the two are adjacent), with its themed slide; or they can enjoy the two whirlpools, children's pool, clothing boutique and gift shop, and a child-activity center known as Pinocchio's Workshop. The luxurious Mandara Spa features treatment rooms and a couples suite accented with Balinese-inspired art and textiles. The spa includes a fitness center, steam rooms, and a nail spa.

Among the varied dining options are the award-winning Napa Rose, which features California cuisine and wines, and Storyteller's Cafe, open for breakfast, lunch, and dinner in an Old California setting and the backdrop for

a character-hosted breakfast with a buffet in addition to an à la carte menu. A quick-service eatery, Whitewater Snacks, supplies coffee, fast food, and baked goods; the poolside bar is good for a quick meal or snack. The Hearthstone Lounge doubles as a breakfast spot each morning, dispensing coffee and pastries to guests heading into the park.

The hotel can provide safe-deposit boxes and currency exchange. An ATM is on the premises. Airport buses bound for Orange County and Los Angeles airports stop here, as do tour buses, city and county buses, and buses traveling to and from Los Angeles.

Rates for regular rooms run about $350 to $480, depending on the view and season, plus $15 for each extra adult (no charge for children under 18 staying in their parents' room); concierge rooms start at about $610; presidential suites start at about $3,420. There are no rollaway beds, but a themed sleeping bag with a pad can be supplied; no charge for cribs. Self-parking is included in the daily resort fee, as are local calls, daily newspaper delivery, and fitness center access; valet parking is $17.

Disney's Grand Californian; 1600 S. Disneyland Drive; Anaheim, CA 92803; 714-956-6425 (for reservations and additional information) or 714-635-2300 (front desk); *www.disneyland.com.*

DISNEY'S PARADISE PIER HOTEL: This property's facade reflects the ambience and breezy, carefree California style of the Paradise Pier district of the park, which it overlooks. The smallest of the Disneyland Resort hotels, it is popular with business people and families alike.

The hotel's two high-rise towers—one 15 stories, the other 14 stories—are juxtaposed to create a central atrium, which cradles the lobby and a larger-than-life character sculpture. Mickey's familiar silhouette shows up extensively in the hotel's decor—in the artwork, the ceramics, and even the upholstery.

Each of the 489 rooms, including 20 suites, features Disney-themed furnishings, one king-size bed or two queen beds, plus a twin daybed in the sitting area (a particular convenience for families). The rooms on the cabana level open onto a large recreation area that also includes a sundeck, swimming pool, slide, whirlpool, children's play area, and snack bar. If you plan to spend a lot of time in or beside the pool, consider a concierge-level room on the third floor for direct access.

The spacious and well-stocked Mickey in Paradise shop, a coffee bar with its own Mickey cappuccino machine, and two restaurants are on the ground level of the hotel. Disney's PCH Grill offers dishes inspired by boardwalk-style favorites and a popular character breakfast, Lilo & Stitch's Aloha Breakfast (buffet and à la carte options). The hotel's other restaurant, Yamabuki, has a full sushi bar (refer to *Good Meals, Great Times*). Room service offers PCH Grill specialties. The

hotel also has an exercise room, a small concierge lounge, and an ATM. A glass-enclosed elevator provides a bird's-eye view of both the lobby and Disney's California Adventure.

Guests at the hotel have access to the Hotel Guest Entrance from the Grand Californian Hotel & Spa into Disney's California Adventure. The hotel is also connected to the Disneyland Resort and Downtown Disney by a landscaped walkway. Guests can also get to Disneyland by taking the monorail from the Downtown Disney station. Both Disneyland and Disney's California Adventure theme parks are within a 10- to 15-minute walk.

Regular rates run from about $235 to $305, depending on the view and the season (no charge for kids under 18 sharing their parents' room), plus $15 per extra adult; no charge for rollaways or cribs. Concierge rooms start at about $320. Suites range from about $585 to $1,830. Self-parking is included in the daily resort fee, as are local calls, weekday newspaper delivery, and exercise room access; valet parking is $17.

Disney's Paradise Pier Hotel; 1717 S. Disneyland Dr.; Anaheim, CA 92802; 714-956-6425 (reservations) or 714-999-0990 (front desk); *www.disneyland.com.*

Disneyland Good Neighbor Hotels

With fewer than 2,300 rooms available at the Disneyland Resort and tens of thousands of guests pouring through the parks each day, it's no wonder that a majority of visitors stay off Disney property. To make it easier for guests to narrow down their off-property choices, the folks at Disney have selected local hotels and motels that meet their standards and anointed them "Disneyland Good Neighbor" properties. Before receiving the Disney seal of approval, hotels are supposedly graded on amenities, services, decor, guest satisfaction, price, and location. Note that all Good Neighbor properties sell Disneyland tickets.

Ranging from national chains to smaller operations, the Good Neighbor hotels proliferate along Harbor Blvd., which flanks the resort on the east. From Harbor, it's easy to walk to the Disneyland Resort. A few properties are on Ball Rd., the resort's northern boundary. Below Katella Ave., which borders the resort to the south, side streets lead to the Anaheim Convention Center and the city's major convention hotels. Divided into the categories of Suite, Superior, Moderate, and Economy, there are more than 40 Good Neighbor hotels in all. In the following pages we describe some of our favorites. For the Good Neighbor properties not described here, see "The Rest of the Best" on page 47.

Prices: Expect to pay $99 to $299, or more, per night for a hotel room for two adults and two children (kids usually stay in their parents' room for free), $69 to $262 for a motel room, and $40 to $70 for tent or RV camping. Prices drop a bit in winter; they are highest in the summer and over holidays. The room tax in Anaheim is 15 percent.

Additional Costs: When comparing accommodation costs, consider hidden zingers, like parking. Big hotels usually charge for it ($11 to $20 a day; more for valet service). Many also charge an additional fee when more than four people occupy a room. Inquire about telephone rates when you check in— hotel surcharges are notoriously huge.

Savings: You can save money by staying in a hotel that offers complimentary breakfast and shuttle service to Disneyland. Discounts are sometimes offered to those who belong to an automobile or retirement association.

Individual Needs: What's essential for one vacationer—and worth the extra cost—might seem frivolous to another: room service, on-site restaurants, live music, a suite, a kitchen, concierge service and amenities, large swimming pool, exercise room, or a place that accepts pets.

Packages: The Walt Disney Travel Company offers packages in conjunction with each of the Good Neighbor hotels—representing potentially big savings for travelers. Refer to "Travel Packages" in the *Getting Ready to Go* chapter of this book, or simply contact the Walt Disney Travel Company directly at 714-520-5060.

Note: The following recommended establishments accept major credit cards and offer nonsmoking rooms and rooms for travelers with disabilities, unless otherwise indicated. Call the properties directly to inquire about deposit requirements and cancellation policies. Rates given were correct at press time but are subject to change and should always be confirmed by phone.

Suite Hotels

RESIDENCE INN BY MARRIOTT ANAHEIM MAINGATE: At first glance, the buildings with tile roofs could easily be mistaken for a condominium complex. The well-maintained grounds are landscaped with hibiscus, bougainvillaea, lemon, sweetgum, and pepper trees, plus park-style benches and, we're convinced, the only remaining orange tree still standing in the city of Anaheim.

Inside the inn, the living room–like lobby is inviting, with chairs, cocktail tables, fireplace, and television. Facilities include a fitness center, a swimming pool that's open 24 hours, a kids' pool, a whirlpool, and a single court for tennis, basketball, or volleyball. There is also a guest laundry and a fitness center.

The suites are spacious and feature a 25-inch television; pay-per-view movies and

Nintendo; a breakfast bar; and a fully equipped kitchen with a dishwasher, stove, microwave, and full refrigerator. Several room configurations are available.

Complimentary services include grocery delivery (though guests must pay for the actual groceries), housekeeping, a full breakfast buffet daily, and a social hour Monday through Wednesday from 5 P.M. to 7 P.M. The hotel will accept pets for a flat charge of $100. Anaheim Resort Transit provides bus transportation for a fee.

There are five levels of suite available. Each comes with either a king or two queen beds and all have sofa beds. Rates range from $139 for a studio to $329 for the multi-room Penthouse Family Suite. Lower, long-term rates are also available. There is no extra charge for cribs. Rollaway beds are no longer provided by this hotel, but Aerobeds are available.

Residence Inn by Marriott Anaheim Maingate; 1700 S. Clementine St.; Anaheim, CA 92802; 714-533-3555 or 800-331-3131; or *www.anaheimri.com.*

Superior Hotels

ANAHEIM MARRIOTT: Next to the Anaheim Convention Center and the Hilton, the Marriott is a favorite among conventioneers. Most of the 1,031 rooms, located in two towers and two four-story wings, have balconies. Each has one king-size bed or two doubles and cable TV. The hotel restaurants—JW's Steakhouse and Cafe Del Sol—are quite popular. For a quick bite, drop by the Pizza Hut or Starbucks Marketplace on the premises.

There is a partially covered pool surrounded

PHOTO BY KEITH GROSHANS

by lounge chairs, as well as a whirlpool and a health club. Guests enjoy poolside and lobby bars, and concierge services.

The hotel is a couple of long blocks from the Disneyland Resort—for most it is not within walking distance. Shuttle service to the Disney theme parks is provided by Anaheim Rapid Transit for a fee; transportation to area airports may also be arranged.

Rates for two start at $189 (there is no charge for children under 18 sharing their parents' room); suites start at $785; $20 per additional adult. Rollaway beds and cribs are free. Special packages are available. Self-parking costs $20 per day; valet parking is $27 per day. Note that pets are no longer accepted at this hotel.

Anaheim Marriott; 700 W. Convention Way; Anaheim, CA 92802; visit the hotel's Web site at *www.marriotthotels.com/laxah*; or call 714-750-8000 or 800-228-9290.

HILTON ANAHEIM: The 15-story glass exterior of Southern California's largest hotel reflects the Anaheim Convention Center, just steps away, and the three-story atrium lobby invites the outdoors (and swarms of conventioneers) inside. The Hilton has 1,572 rooms, including 93 suites, decorated in soft, light colors and California art. Atop the hotel, the Executive Level provides special services and amenities, as well as complimentary continental breakfast and hors d'oeuvres in its lounge.

The hotel's outdoor recreation center, on the fifth floor, features a heated swimming pool, four whirlpools, and three levels of sundecks and greenery. There is a Starbucks Marketplace on the premises. Other dining options include the Casablanca-style Cafe Oasis, serving three meals a day; and Pavia, with Northern Italian cuisine and live entertainment. Don't overlook The Sushi Bar, The Gazebo, and Hastings Sports Lounge. Note that restaurants tend to be especially crowded at lunchtime and during convention breaks.

Add to that a business center and two levels of shops. The 25,000-square-foot Sports and Fitness Center has exercise equipment, a pool, basketball court, whirlpool, steam room, sauna, exercise classes, spa facials, body treatments, and massage.

The Orange County Walk of Stars, the sidewalk entrance to the hotel, highlights notables such as Gene Autry, Steve Martin, and Buzz Aldrin. Rates for a double room range from $99 to $309, plus $20 per extra adult (no

charge for kids under 18 when sharing their parents' room); suites run a bit higher. Ask about packages. There's no charge for cribs, but rollaway beds cost $20 a night. Self-parking costs $15 per day, valet parking $19. Pets are permitted.

Hilton Anaheim; 777 Convention Way; Anaheim, CA 92802; 714-750-4321 or 800-801-8241; *www.hilton.com*.

HYATT REGENCY ORANGE COUNTY: The hotel, located in Garden Grove, is four (long) blocks south of Disneyland. Its dramatic, 17-story atrium encloses palm trees and greenery and houses the California Grill restaurant, Starbucks, Pizza Hut Express, a gift shop, and Networks Lounge. Each of the 654 guestrooms features either a king-size bed or two queen beds and cherry-wood furniture that complements the modern interior design.

Amenities include coffeemakers, hair dryers, iron with board, plus satellite TV. The one- and two-bedroom suites also have a living room, refrigerator, and microwave. Suites can accommodate between 4 and 6 people.

Kids' Suites include a room for the little ones, complete with bunk beds, activity table, and the Disney Channel. The parents' room has a king bed, 25-inch TV, fridge, and microwave.

The hotel's impressive recreational facilities, located on the South Tower's third-story roof, include a heated pool, a whirlpool, a fitness center, and two tennis courts. Another outdoor pool and whirlpool are on the ground floor of the North Tower. Free transportation to the Disneyland Resort is provided, and airport shuttle service is available.

Room rates run $109 to $225 (no charge for

children under 18 occupying their parents' room), plus $25 for each additional adult; $139 to $325 for suites. There is no charge for cribs. Self-parking is $15 per day; valet parking, $17.

Hyatt Regency Orange County; 11999 Harbor Blvd.; Garden Grove, CA 92840; *www.orangecounty.hyatt.com*; 714-750-1234 or 800-233-1234.

SHERATON ANAHEIM HOTEL: With its turrets and Tudor design, this 489-room hotel looks more like a castle, surrounded by grounds that incorporate three peaceful courtyards, a rose garden, fountain, pond, and small waterfall. The recently renovated lobby boasts a stone fireplace in a comfortable, contemporary setting. The hotel also has a restaurant, cocktail lounge, and combination deli and gift shop called the California Deli. The staff gets high marks for their enthusiasm.

The hotel has 463 rooms and 26 suites—all with signature "Sweet Sleeper Beds." The rooms—all large (490 square feet)—have two queen- or one king-size bed, cable television, in-room movies, voice mail, irons, ironing boards, hair dryers, and coffeemakers. Each suite has a sitting area with a sofa bed and refrigerator.

The hotel has an arcade, heated pool, whirlpool, exercise room, guest laundry, and conference rooms. It provides room service, a business center, and frequent complimentary shuttle service to the Disneyland Resort. Airport transportation is available. Rates for doubles run from $145 during off-season to $275 during peak season (no charge for children under 18 sharing their parents' room); $325 for suites; rollaways are $10; no charge for cribs. Be sure to request the best available rate when confirming pricing.

Sheraton Anaheim Hotel; 900 S. Disneyland Dr.; Anaheim, CA 92802; 714-778-1700 or 800-325-3535; *www.sheraton.com/anaheim*.

Moderate Hotels

ANABELLA HOTEL: Architectural elements of this Spanish-style property reflect the rich history of California missions. Whitewashed adobe walls and curved roof tiles are graced by palm trees and lush, blossoming plants. Thick arches welcome guests into public areas featuring covered walkways and a fountain. Even the shape of the outdoor whirlpool echoes this theme in its rose window design.

Standard and deluxe rooms sleep up to four; Carita Suites sleep up to three, while

Mission and Kids' Suites sleep up to five with an additional sleeper sofa or bunk beds. All rooms have granite baths, refrigerators, hair dryers, coffeemakers, cable TV, and on-demand movies. In a separate building, the Club Anabella Concierge Rooms also come with robes and slippers, flat-panel TVs, a newspaper, and a complimentary continental breakfast. Wireless Internet service is available for a fee.

There are two pools, one for adults only. The Bella Nail & Hair Salon offers a variety of services, including pedicures, manicures, and facials. At the Tangerine Grill & Patio, guests can enjoy breakfast, lunch, dinner, or a cocktail in the dining room or outside. Other amenities include a fitness center, a business center, and a guest laundry.

Rooms range from $99 to $199; suites from $149 to $299; and Concierge rooms from $169 to $389. The daily charge for rollaways is $20; for cribs, $10. Self-parking is also $10 per day. Guests can walk to the Disneyland Resort in 10–15 minutes, but the hotel recommends using Anaheim Resort Transit.

The Anabella Hotel; 1030 W. Katella Ave.; Anaheim, CA 92802; 714-905-1050 or 800-863-4888; *www.anabellahotel.com.*

ANAHEIM CAMELOT INN & SUITES:

Directly across the street—and a relatively short walk away—from the Disneyland Resort, this hotel, with its shingled roof, clock tower, turrets, and tidy window boxes, looks like something out of a Bavarian village. Each of the 121 rooms and suites has a microwave, refrigerator, coffeemaker, hair dryer, and an iron with board. The inn offers complimentary continental breakfast. It also has a fourth-floor terrace pool (with a view of Disneyland's Matterhorn), a whirlpool, two gift shops, and a guest laundry facility.

Although there's no in-house restaurant, many places to eat, including Millie's Restaurant & Bakery, are within walking distance. Millie's also provides room service to all guestrooms. In-room dining is available daily from 7 A.M. to 10 P.M.

Deluxe standard rooms, most with two queen-size beds, range from $119–$159 year-round; one-bedroom suites range from $199 to $249 and accommodate up to six people, but they have only one bath. Rollaways are $15 plus tax; cribs are free. Anaheim Resort Transit provides transportation to the Disneyland Resort for a fee. There is no shut-tle service, but it is possible to walk to the Disneyland Resort entrance via Harbor Boulevard.

Anaheim Camelot Inn & Suites; 1520 S. Harbor Blvd.; Anaheim, CA 92802; call 714-635-7275 or 800-828-4898; or visit *www. camelotinn-anaheim.com.*

ANAHEIM FAIRFIELD INN BY MARRIOTT:

Fronted by palms and pines, this handsome, affordable 467-room hotel is situated across from the Disneyland Resort. All of its rooms are accented with Disney artwork. The rooms are in two towers (one tower is nine stories high; the other, eight). Each room features a king-size bed or two queen beds, child-size sleeper sofa, cable TV, an iron and board, hair dryer, refrigerator, and coffeemaker. The hotel is served by a family-style eatery called Millie's Restaurant & Bakery.

Other facilities include a heated pool, whirlpool, gift shop, Seattle's Best Coffee, and Pizza Hut. The rooms may be occupied by up to five people, and rates range from about $119 to $199; cribs are available.

Anaheim Fairfield Inn by Marriott; 1460 S. Harbor Blvd.; Anaheim, CA 92802. Call 714-772-6777 or 800-228-2800, or visit the hotel website at *www.marriott.com/laxoc.*

BEST WESTERN PARK PLACE INN & MINI SUITES:
This three-story, 199-room inn is located across from Disneyland Resort's pedestrian entrance. The lobby is spacious, with a high ceiling and several cozy seating areas, a fireplace, and windows looking out onto Harbor Blvd.

A gift shop sells Disney souvenirs. Room configurations include a king-size bed and sleeper sofa, two queen-size beds and a sleeper sofa, or two double beds. All rooms are equipped with a refrigerator, microwave, iron with board, and coffeemaker (coffee is included at no additional cost).

Among the facilities are a pool with an adjacent whirlpool, and a guest laundry. Rates, which include continental breakfast at the inn or pancakes at adjacent Captain Kidd's, run $104 to $144 for a standard room that sleeps up to four; mini suites run $124 to $164 (and sleep up to six). Rollaway beds cost $20; cribs are free.

Best Western Park Place Inn & Mini Suites; 1544 S. Harbor Blvd.; Anaheim, CA 92802; 714-776-4800 or 800-854-8175, ext. 4; or visit the hotel's Web site at *www.bestwestern.com.*

BEST WESTERN STOVALL'S INN: What makes the inn unique is its topiary garden. The property features 288 guestrooms, complimentary continental breakfast, fitness room, business center, and a pair of pools (one is heated), two whirlpools, a wading pool, and a gift shop. Room configurations include two queen, one king, or two double beds and a bathroom with a separate sink, and plenty of counter space. Refrigerators are included for free.

Room rates for up to five people run $69 to $149. Rollaways are $12; cribs are free.

Best Western Stovall's Inn; 1110 W. Katella Ave.; Anaheim, CA 92802; call 714-778-1880 or 800-854-8177, ext. 3; or visit *www.bestwestern.com.*

CANDY CANE INN: There's a lot to like about this sweet, two-story hotel: fountain out front, relaxed ambience, wrought-iron touches, and flowers everywhere. Located just down the street from the Disneyland Resort's main entrance (a manageable walk for adults and non-toddlers), the Candy Cane Inn is family-run and well-maintained.

Each of the 172 rooms, most of which face a courtyard, has a refrigerator, dual-line phone with voice mail, coffeemaker, iron, hair dryer, and two queen beds with down comforters, dust ruffles, and European pillow shams. Add to that the guest laundry, swimming pool, gazebo-covered whirlpool, and fitness center. A complimentary continental buffet breakfast is served daily. Premium rooms also have microwaves, free movie rentals, in-room breakfast, turndown service, and late check-out. Sightseeing services are available, as well as complimentary shuttle service to and from the Disneyland Resort. Transportation to local airports can be arranged. Parking is free.

Rates for a double room with two queen-size beds range from $99 to $174, depending on the season. Rollaways, available only in deluxe and premium rooms, are $10; no charge for cribs. The inn is located across the street from a small shopping area with fast-food eateries.

Candy Cane Inn; 1747 S. Harbor Blvd.; Anaheim, CA 92802. Call 714-774-5284 or 800-345-7057, or visit *www.candycaneinn.net.*

HOWARD JOHNSON ANAHEIM: This property has some of the lushest landscaping of any place in Anaheim, except for the Disney hotels, and that's a major reason to stay here. Flowers and trees proliferate; a central fountain anchors the four two-story units. The

hotel is close to Disneyland Resort and local eateries. For a fee, Anaheim Resort Transit offers shuttle service to and from Disneyland.

The 317 rooms are divided among six buildings on seven acres. Most have two queen beds, and all have a refrigerator, Sony PlayStation, and free high-speed Internet access. The rooms are relatively spacious, though the bathrooms are a bit small.

There are two pools (one is Castaway Cove, a pirate-themed mini water park including a toddler's wading pool and fountain play area), and a large whirlpool. Facilities include two laundry rooms, gift shop, and arcade. The hotel's partner restaurant, Mimi's Café, is next door. Babysitting can be arranged. Rates range from $99 to $179, depending on the season. There is no charge for parking. Rollaways are $7; cribs are free.

Howard Johnson Anaheim; 1380 S. Harbor Blvd.; Anaheim, CA 92802; 714-776-6120 or 800-422-4228; *www.hojoanaheim.com.*

SHERATON PARK HOTEL AT THE ANAHEIM RESORT: This newly renovated 14-story tower is easy to spot, and the 490 rooms and six suites have full or small balconies that provide a view of the pool or the Disneyland Resort (and a view of the fireworks). All rooms offer either one king or two queen beds, pay-per-view movies, irons, coffeemakers, and hair dryers.

A large gift shop is on the premises, as is a lobby bar, coffee shop, a Southwestern-themed restaurant, snack shop, and a sports bar. The hotel also has a fitness center, large pool, whirlpool, and a poolside bar.

Shuttle service is available (provided by Anaheim Resort Transit for a fee) to the Disneyland Resort. Room rates run $149 to $299 for doubles, depending on occupancy and season; suites start at $550. Rollaways cost $15 extra; cribs are available free of charge.

Sheraton Park Hotel at the Anaheim Resort; 1855 S. Harbor Blvd.; Anaheim, CA 92802; 714-750-1811 or 800-325-3535; or visit *www.sheraton.com/anaheimresort.*

> **HOT TIP!**
> If you stay in the 1300 to 1500 block of Harbor Blvd., you can cross the street and walk to the parks from your hotel. Of course, once you reach Disneyland Resort property, it's another 5- to 15-minute walk to get to the parks' turnstiles.

TROPICANA INN & SUITES: This establishment is right at the pedestrian crosswalk into the Disneyland Resort. Each of its 194 rooms has a TV, coffeemaker (with coffee), refrigerator, microwave, hair dryer, iron, in-room movies, and either a king-size bed or two queens. Each morning, a free refreshment (coffee, juice, and pastry) is served in the hospitality room.

The inn has no restaurant, but an on-site shop sells fruit, fried chicken, breakfast items, and other food; a gift shop sells souvenirs. IHOP, Millie's Restaurant & Bakery, and other eateries are within walking distance. Millie's provides room service. It's about a ten-minute walk to Disneyland. Anaheim Resort Transit provides shuttle service for a fee.

The inn has a heated outdoor pool and guest laundry. Room rates start at $139. Suites accommodate up to eight people. Suite rates range from $159 to $229. Some suites come with kitchens.

Tropicana Inn & Suites; 1540 S. Harbor Blvd.; Anaheim, CA 92802; 714-635-4082 or 800-828-4898; *www.tropicanainn-anaheim.com.*

The Rest of the Best

Here's a roundup of the remaining Good Neighbor hotels. They have amenities and rates similar to those described in this chapter. However, some are a bit far from the Disneyland Resort.

Note: Hotels and motels boasting "Good Neighbor" status are subject to change during the year; visit *www.disneyland.com* for updates.

Suite Hotels
- Anaheim Marriott Suites; 12015 Harbor Blvd.; Garden Grove; 714-750-1000
- Embassy Suites Anaheim-North; 3100 E. Frontera St.; Anaheim; 714-632-1221
- Embassy Suites Anaheim-South; 11767 Harbor Blvd.; Garden Grove; 714-539-3300
- Hampton Inn & Suites Los Angeles/Anaheim-Garden Grove; 11747 Harbor Blvd.; Garden Grove; 714-703-8800
- Hilton Suites Anaheim/Orange; 400 N. State College Blvd.; Orange; 714-938-1111
- Homewood Suites by Hilton Anaheim-Main Gate Area; 12005 Harbor Blvd.; Garden Grove; 714-740-1800
- La Quinta Inn & Suites Anaheim Disneyland; 1752 Clementine St.; Anaheim; 714-635-5000
- Residence Inn by Marriott Anaheim/Garden Grove; 11931 Harbor Blvd.; Garden Grove; 714-591-4000
- Staybridge Suites; 1855 S. Manchester Ave.; Anaheim; 714-748-7700

Superior Hotels
- Crowne Plaza Anaheim Resort; 12021 Harbor Blvd.; Garden Grove; 714-867-5555

Moderate Hotels
- Anaheim/Orange Hawthorn Suites; 720 The City Dr.; Orange; 714-740-2700
- Best Western Anaheim Inn; 1630 S. Harbor Blvd.; Anaheim; 714-774-1050
- Best Western Pavilions; 1176 W. Katella Ave.; Anaheim; 714-776-0140
- Best Western Raffles Inn & Suites; 2040 S. Harbor Blvd.; Anaheim; 714-750-6100
- Carousel Inn & Suites; 1530 S. Harbor Blvd.; Anaheim; 714-758-0444
- Clarion Hotel Anaheim Resort; 616 Convention Way; Anaheim; 714-750-3131
- Courtyard by Marriott Anaheim Buena Park; 7621 Beach Blvd.; Buena Park; 714-670-6600
- DoubleTree Hotel Anaheim/Orange County; 100 The City Dr.; Orange; 714-634-4500
- Hilton Garden Inn Anaheim/Garden Grove; 11777 Harbor Blvd.; Garden Grove; 714-703-9100
- Holiday Inn-Anaheim Resort; 1915 S. Manchester Ave.; Anaheim; 714-748-7777
- Holiday Inn Hotel & Suites; 1240 S. Walnut; Anaheim; 714-535-0300
- Portofino Inn & Suites; 1831 S. Harbor Blvd.; Anaheim; 714-782-7600
- Radisson Hotel Maingate-Anaheim; 1850 S. Harbor Blvd.; Anaheim; 714-750-2801

Economy Hotels
- Jolly Roger Hotel; 640 W. Katella Ave.; Anaheim; 714-782-7500
- Ramada Maingate—At the Park; 1650 S. Harbor Blvd.; Anaheim; 714-772-0440
- Ramada Plaza Anaheim Resort; 515 W. Katella Ave.; Anaheim; 714-991-6868
- Travelodge Anaheim International Inn; 2060 S. Harbor Blvd.; Anaheim; 714-971-9393

On the Coast

When it comes to upscale and elegant lodging, Orange County's coastal resorts are especially tempting—and they're only about a half-hour drive from the Disneyland Resort. Imagine spending the day in the park and then returning to your hotel for a stroll on the beach at sunset. Most coastal hotels do not offer regularly scheduled shuttle service to the Disneyland Resort (or anywhere else, for that matter), so you will need a car.

Laguna Beach

INN AT LAGUNA BEACH: Perched dramatically on a cliff overlooking Laguna Beach, the inn is within walking distance of Heisler Park, Main Beach, the Laguna Art Museum, and many galleries, shops, and cozy cafes. Completely nonsmoking inside, the recently renovated inn has 70 rooms, 52 of which have ocean views.

Each room is furnished with a ceiling fan, air-conditioning, a TV, DVD (with selections from a video library), coffeemaker, hair dryer, an iron, a small refrigerator, bathrobes, CD player, feather beds, and free Wi-Fi service. Rooms come with one king, one queen, or two queen beds and a shower or bathtub in various configurations. Some rooms also have a sleeper sofa. Four corner deluxe rooms, two of which are quite large, provide stunning views of the coastline. Beach towels and umbrellas are in the room and may be used for the length of your stay.

There is one swimming pool and a whirlpool. Continental breakfast is complimentary and is delivered to your room; the inn treats guests to cookies and refreshments from 5 P.M. to 9 P.M. daily. On-site parking is available for $14 a day.

Rates in summer run from $215 to $299 for village-view rooms and $350 to $569 for ocean-view rooms. The rest of the year, expect to pay $139 to $289 for village-view rooms and $249 to $509 for ocean view.

Inn at Laguna Beach; 211 N. Coast Hwy.; Laguna Beach, CA 92651; 800-544-4479; *www.innatlagunabeach.com.*

SURF & SAND RESORT: Perched beside 500 feet of sandy beachfront less than a mile from the shops, galleries, and restaurants of Laguna Beach, this stylish hotel has 152 rooms and 13 suites, almost all with king-size beds and private balconies. The accommodations fill four buildings.

Rooms are decorated with furnishings the color of sand dunes, all with in-room movies (for a fee), CD-DVD players with attachments for iPods, flat-screen TVs, robes, and hair dryer.

The five-story Seaview building, which overlooks the pool and beach, has the biggest and the priciest rooms here (the one- and two-bedroom suites are larger and cost more). Because of its location, guests staying in the three-story Surfside building may have the sensation of being afloat when the surf rolls in. The Towers building is also right on the water, while the Catalina building is set a little further back.

HOT TIP!
Stay in Laguna if small inns and early-morning walks along the beach appeal to you. Choose Newport if you prefer resort hotels and nightlife. It's easier to get rooms in Newport than in Laguna on summer weekends.

Splashes Restaurant has in- and outdoor seating, serves breakfast, lunch, and dinner, and features primarily Mediterranean cuisine. Adjacent to it, Splashes Lounge is popular at sunset; both have direct access to the beach. The hotel also has a medium-size pool (beach access, as well), a shop, and a spa. The Aquaterra Spa purports to blend the "healing therapeutic essences of the ocean and land." Room service and concierge service are available.

Where to Rent a Beach Bungalow

Newport Beach is simply brimming with cottages, condominiums, and duplex apartments waiting to be your beach home away from home. Some include patios with barbecue facilities, and many are conveniently situated right on the sand, within easy strolling distance of local restaurants and shops. For additional information, contact the Newport Beach Conference & Visitors Bureau; 949-719-6100 or 800-942-6278; *www.newportbeach-cvb.com.*

A member of Preferred Hotels & Resorts Worldwide, the Surf & Sand is situated across the road from several art galleries and is approximately a 40-minute drive south from the Disneyland Resort.

Rates for doubles range from $495 to $695, depending on the location, time of year, and time of week; suites start at $900. The hotel offers valet parking for $27 a day; self-parking may be possible on the street, but spaces are tough to come by.

Surf & Sand Resort; 1555 S. Coast Hwy.; Laguna Beach, CA 92651; 949-497-4477 or 888-869-7569; *www.surfandsandresort.com.*

Dana Point

RITZ-CARLTON, LAGUNA NIGUEL: This magnificent deluxe resort sits on 18 acres, high on a bluff that overlooks the Pacific Ocean and Orange County's southern coast. The views from the lounge and from many of the 367 guestrooms and 29 suites are sensational. On a clear day you can see Catalina Island, 37 miles away, and at night the sound of the surf lulls you to sleep.

In addition to a two-mile stretch of sandy beach (which is open to the public), the hotel has two pools and two whirlpools, a nearby 18-hole golf course designed by Robert Trent Jones, Jr., four tennis courts, and table tennis. The Ritz-Carlton Spa and ocean-front fitness center offers yoga and Pilates classes, a sauna, exercise room, and salon.

The Eno bar features wine tastings with cheeses and chocolates from around the world. Restaurant 162$'$ offers three meals a day, as well as a Friday night seafood buffet and Sunday champagne brunch. Afternoon tea is served Thursday–Saturday, and room service is available around the clock. Other hotel amenities include concierge service and a shuttle to and from the golf course and beach.

Rates for doubles range from $525 to $875, depending on location and view (or $774 to $3,000 for Club rooms, with the addition of five culinary treats throughout the day). Suites start at $975. There is no charge for cribs, but rollaways are $50 per day. Parking is valet only, $30 a day for overnight guests, $25 for other visitors. The hotel is about a 40-minute drive south from the Disneyland Resort.

Ritz-Carlton, Laguna Niguel; One Ritz-Carlton Dr.; Dana Point, CA 92629; 949-240-2000 or 800-241-3333; *www.ritzcarlton.com.*

Newport Beach

BAY SHORES ON THE PENINSULA: The inn has that special ambience unique to small, family-run places. Guests are encouraged to hang out in deck chairs on the roof; check out free DVDs; use the complimentary umbrellas, boogie boards, pails, and beach toys; and grab fruit, coffee, or tea from the kitchen whenever the urge strikes. The three-story building has an elevator, a sundeck, breakfast room, and free parking. There's no pool or restaurant on the property, but the bay, ocean, and popular Crab Cooker restaurant are just a stroll away. The property is nonsmoking.

Most of the 25 rooms are furnished with a queen bed, though some have one king or two queen beds. All feature hair dryers, as well as air-conditioning, though the last is hardly necessary, given the constant ocean breeze. Double-paned windows muffle noise from the street. The Bay Suite has one full, one twin, and one queen bed (plus a pull-out couch in the living room), a balcony with a bay view, a kitchen, two baths, and a fireplace. Two Annex Suites contain two queen beds but no kitchen or view. Each suite sleeps 4 to 6.

Rates include a breakfast of fresh muffins, eggs, bagels, toast, and hot or cold cereal; they range from $160 to $294 for a double room, depending on the season. Annex Suites run $240 to $470; the Bay Suite is $399 to $650. Friday and Saturday nights require a two-night minimum; holidays require a three-night minimum. Rollaways and cribs are not available. The hotel is about 20 minutes from the Disneyland Resort. It does not have rooms for travelers with disabilities.

Bay Shores on the Peninsula; 1800 W. Balboa Blvd.; Newport Beach, CA 92663; 949-675-3463 or 800-222-6675; *www.thebestinn.com*.

HYATT REGENCY NEWPORT BEACH: This local landmark (it was one of the first resort hotels in the Newport area), with a terra-cotta exterior and French doors and windows, exudes a California-Mediterranean air of laid-back luxury. Its 403 guestrooms come in several settings: some wrap around a courtyard, others look onto the golf course or Newport Bay, while others face one of the hotel's attractive pools. There are also four villas, each with three bedrooms, three baths, a fireplace, and a private yard with a pool.

Besides a nine-hole golf course, three large swimming pools, and three whirlpools, the hotel has volleyball and shuffleboard courts, a spa, a health-and-fitness center, and 26 acres of lush, landscaped grounds. Guests have privileges at the adjoining private Palisades Tennis Club, which has 16 courts that are lighted for night play. The Sol restaurant serves three meals in a garden-like setting and on a terrace. Sunday brunch features fresh seafood, carved meats, sushi, and a selection of tempting desserts.

The hotel provides complimentary transportation to Balboa Island, Fashion Island, and John Wayne Airport, where shuttle service to the Disneyland Resort is available. Rates for doubles start at $169; suites start at $450. There is no charge for children under 18 sharing their parents' room; $22 daily per extra adult; no charge for rollaways or cribs. Self-parking is $16, valet parking, $22. Pets are no longer allowed. The hotel is about a half-hour drive south from Disneyland.

Hyatt Regency Newport Beach; 1107 Jamboree Rd.; Newport Beach, CA 92660; *http://newportbeach.hyatt.com*; or 949-729-1234 or 800-233-1234.

NEWPORT BEACH MARRIOTT HOTEL & SPA: The attributes of this 532-room property are many, but foremost among them are the views of Balboa Bay and the Pacific Ocean, the eight tennis courts (lighted for night play), two good-size swimming pools, four whirlpools, and the convenient location across the street from Newport Center Fashion Island, with its nearly 200 boutiques, department stores, and eateries.

The hotel boasts a fine restaurant with an open-air terrace, plus a pleasant bar. It also has concierge service, a gift shop, free transportation to John Wayne Airport, and a health club that is free to all hotel guests. Underground self parking is available for $16 a day; valet is $22 per day. The guestrooms (the result of a 60-million-dollar renovation effort) are located in two towers and in two low-rise wings; room configurations feature one king or two double beds.

Rates run $289 to $399 for doubles and $550 and up for suites; no charge for cribs or rollaways. Rooms accommodate up to five guests at a time. The hotel is approximately a half-hour drive south from the Disneyland Resort.

Newport Beach Marriott Hotel & Spa; 900 Newport Center Dr.; Newport Beach, CA 92660; 949-729-3500 or 800-228-9290; *www.marriott.com*.

ACCOMMODATIONS

Bed & Breakfast Inns

Economical, intimate, congenial. These are a few reasons fans give for choosing to stay in B&Bs. Guestrooms are often furnished with antiques, they may have fireplaces or fabulous ocean views, and private baths have become the norm. B&Bs get the day off to a fine start by supplying a filling breakfast in a serene setting. Most of Orange County's B&Bs are clustered along the coast.

BLUE LANTERN INN: On a bluff overlooking the Pacific, this upscale guesthouse has a slate roof, leaded glass doors, and cobblestoned pathways lined with flowers. Each of the 29 rooms features casual California decor, a fireplace, large bathroom with whirlpool tub, refrigerator, coffeemaker, television, DVD player, phone, high-speed Internet access, and robes. Some have a private patio or balcony, with views of the Dana Point Harbor or the ocean. The staff provides turndown service.

Complimentary breakfast is served in the sunroom, as are wine and hors d'oeuvres later in the day. Guests chat and play games around a fireplace in the lobby's sitting area or in the library. Teddy bears proliferate in the public areas (and are for sale); the guestrooms, on the other hand, are more sophisticated and nearly bear-free. The inn has an exercise room; it also makes bikes available to guests.

Rates for doubles range from $175 to $500. It's one block west of the Pacific Coast Highway, well within walking distance of several restaurants, and about a half-hour drive from the Disneyland Resort. Because of the location, it's a particularly good choice for those who plan to visit points in both Anaheim and San Diego.

Blue Lantern Inn; 34343 Street of the Blue Lantern; Dana Point, CA 92629; 949-661-1304 or 800-950-1236; *www.bluelanterninn.com.*

CASA LAGUNA INN & SPA: This has got to be one of Southern California's best-kept secrets, tucked atop a hill overlooking the ocean, just south of Laguna's galleries and restaurants. More enclave than inn, it has five patios, where guests enjoy a full, made-to-order breakfast and afternoon refreshments and hors d'oeuvres—unless they choose to socialize in the inn's landmark Mission House (built in 1920). Also on the grounds is a heated pool landscaped with exotic flowers, and a bell tower with an observation deck.

The 22 rooms and suites are individually decorated with a mix of turn-of-the-century furnishings in wicker and wood. Each one has a private bathroom with shower (some have a whirlpool tub), air-conditioning, high-speed Internet access, cable TV, CD and DVD player (with use of available disks), telephone, and small refrigerator. There is a spa that offers massage and body treatments and a room for accessing the Internet. The one-bedroom

Cottage, which dates from 1932, features original stained glass, a sitting room with a fireplace, a living room area, and a private wraparound deck. The Cottage and some suites have kitchens. All suites (and some rooms) have fireplaces.

The courtyard-room rates are $150 to $250; the ocean-view rooms, $200 to $340; suites, $260 to $590; and the Cottage, $450 to $590. Kids under 2 stay for free in the Capistrano Suite. There are no rooms for guests with disabilities. Parking is free. The inn is about a 30-minute drive south from the Disneyland Resort.

Casa Laguna Inn & Spa; 2510 S. Coast Hwy.; Laguna Beach, CA 92651; 949-494-2996 or 800-233-0449; *www.casalaguna.com.*

DORYMAN'S INN: Across the street from the ocean in a charming part of Newport Beach, this combination restaurant and B&B is elegant, romantic, and Victorian. Each of the 11 guestrooms is beautifully appointed with French and American antiques, a queen- or king-size bed, a fireplace, and modern amenities, including Italian marble showers that double as sunken tubs, a pedestal sink or one tucked into an oak cabinet, plus a television and a telephone. Half the rooms overlook the ocean and one has a whirlpool tub. Rose petals may be ordered for a luxurious, romantic touch.

The inn has lamp- and skylighted passageways, wood paneling, a breakfast room, and a patio (three rooms open directly onto it) that is perfect for sunbathing, and sunrise and sunset watching. Rates range from $429 to $499 and include breakfast and parking. Take the elevator to the second floor, where the reception area and the rooms are. Note that the

entire facility is nonsmoking and there are no rooms for guests with disabilities. The inn is a half-hour drive south from Disneyland.

Doryman's Inn; 2102 W. Oceanfront; Newport Beach, CA 92663; 949-675-7300; *www.21oceanfront.com.*

LEMON TREE HOTEL: This low-rise, yellow and white gem off State College Boulevard has rustic wooden handmade furniture from Guadalajara and a communal barbecue on the grounds. Run by two Aussie couples, there is a tiled fountain and courtyard, pool, Jacuzzi, gym, and guest laundry. The 83 rooms include king, double queen (sleeps four), studios and one-and two-bedroom furnished apartments. Rooms offer a microwave, fridge, cable TV, iron, and coffee maker. Some rooms have mirrored closets, others, a wooden armoir. Apartments have full kitchens. The executive and two-bedroom apartments each have an outdoor patio and plasma television. A light continental breakfast is served. Wireless Internet is available and there is free computer access in the lobby.

Rates for king, double queen, and king and queen studios range from $79 to $99, apartments range from $99 to $189. Disney theme park tickets are available here.

Lemon Tree Hotel, 1600 East Lincoln Ave., Anaheim, CA 92805; 866-311-5595 or 714-772-0200; *www.hotelaaa.com.*

MISSION INN BED & BREAKFAST: Nestled in an 80-year old Valencia orange grove adjacent to Mission San Juan Capistrano, this inviting inn has 20 cozy and contemporary rooms with floral bedding. Two suites and four rooms have fireplaces. To keep the relaxed feel, owners request that all guests be at least 12 years old. Free Wi-Fi access, refrigerators, cable TV, hairdryers, irons and boards, and CD players in every room. Expanded European breakfast and afternoon snack are included. There is also a heated swimming pool.

Rates range from $175 for standard rooms, $195 for rooms with fireplaces and rooms facing the patio, and $225 to $235 for a suite. The Amtrak and Metrolink train depot is within easy walking distance. Twenty miles south of John Wayne Orange County Airport and sixty miles from Los Angeles and San Diego International Airports.

Mission Inn Bed & Breakfast, 26891 Ortega Highway, San Juan Capistrano, CA 92675; 877-271-1416; *www.missioninnsjc.com.*

Disneyland Park

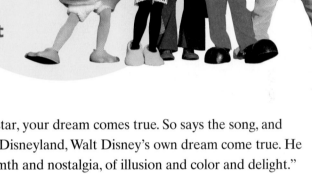

When you wish upon a star, your dream comes true. So says the song, and it's always possible in Disneyland, Walt Disney's own dream come true. He envisioned "a place of warmth and nostalgia, of illusion and color and delight." The result: a place where imagination is given free rein, grins and giggles are encouraged, and everyone can see the world through a child's eyes.

The undisguised pleasure on the faces of park-goers reveals that they have fallen under the spell of a turreted pink castle; the oompah of a band marching down Main Street, U.S.A.; the sound of a train conductor's voice calling "All aboard!"; a close-up encounter with Mickey and Minnie; or a nighttime spectacle more fantastic than the most elaborate dream.

Those who first entered Disneyland as kindergartners now return with their own children—or even grandchildren—to find the park of their memories unchanged in spirit and heart. Attractions have come and gone since the park opened in 1955, of course, and whole new "lands" have been added.

But the enchantment guests experience when they walk through the portals of "The Happiest Place on Earth" remains constant. That may well be Disneyland's most enduring accomplishment.

Main Street, U.S.A.

1. Disneyland Railroad Station
2. Main Street Cinema
3. Main Street Vehicles
4. The Walt Disney Story, Featuring "Great Moments with Mr. Lincoln"

Adventureland

5. Enchanted Tiki Room
6. Indiana Jones Adventure
7. Jungle Cruise
8. Tarzan's Treehouse

Critter Country

9. Splash Mountain
10. The Many Adventures of Winnie the Pooh

Mickey's Toontown

11. Chip 'n' Dale's Treehouse
12. Disneyland Railroad Station
13. Donald's Boat
14. Gadget's Go Coaster
15. Goofy's Bounce House
16. Mickey's House
17. Minnie's House
18. Roger Rabbit's Car Toon Spin

Frontierland

19. Big Thunder Mountain Railroad
20. Golden Horseshoe Stage
21. Mark Twain Riverboat
22. Tom Sawyer Island
23. Sailing Ship Columbia

New Orleans Square

24. Disneyland Railroad Station
25. Haunted Mansion
26. Pirates of the Caribbean

Tomorrowland

27. Astro Orbitor
28. Autopia
29. Disneyland Monorail
30. Disneyland Railroad Station
31. Honey, I Shrunk the Audience
32. Innoventions
33. Space Mountain
34. Star Tours
35. Buzz Lightyear Astro Blasters
36. Finding Nemo Submarine Voyage

Fantasyland

37. Alice in Wonderland
38. Casey Jr. Circus Train
39. Dumbo the Flying Elephant
40. Fantasyland Theatre
41. It's a Small World
42. King Arthur Carrousel
43. Mad Tea Party
44. Matterhorn Bobsleds
45. Mr. Toad's Wild Ride
46. Peter Pan's Flight
47. Pinocchio's Daring Journey
48. Sleeping Beauty Castle
49. Snow White's Scary Adventures
50. Storybook Land Canal Boats

– – – Parade Route

N ←

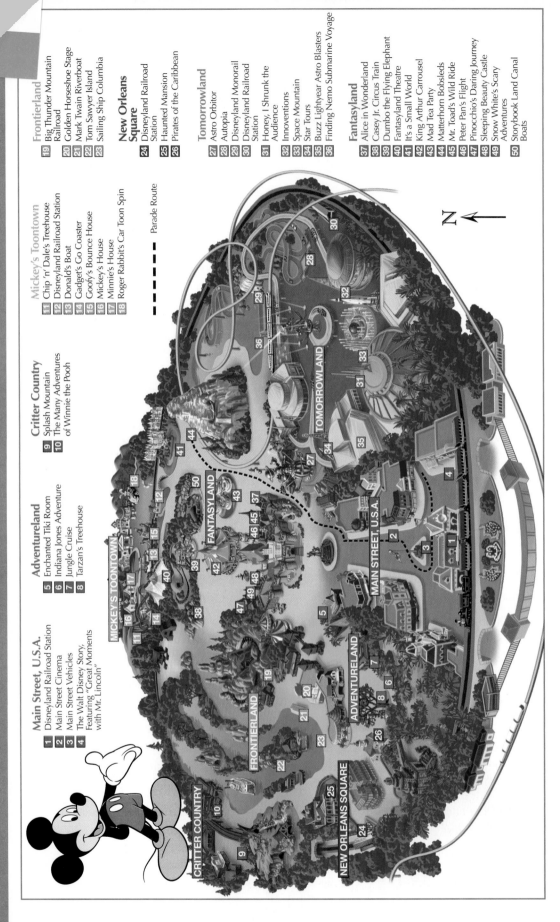

Getting Oriented

Disneyland Park's layout—a basic hub-and-spokes configuration—is simple, but it was innovative when the park opened in 1955. The design makes getting around easy, though it's not altogether effortless, since the numerous nooks, crannies, and alleyways can be a bit confusing at first.

The hub of the theme park's wheel is Central Plaza, which fronts Sleeping Beauty Castle. From it extend five spokes leading to eight "lands": Main Street, U.S.A.; Adventureland; Frontierland; New Orleans Square; Critter Country; Fantasyland; Mickey's Toontown; and Tomorrowland.

As you face Sleeping Beauty Castle, the first bridge to your left takes you to Adventureland; the next one, to Frontierland and New Orleans Square. To your right, the first walkway goes to Tomorrowland, and the next one—known as Matterhorn Way—leads directly into Fantasyland and on to Mickey's Toontown. If you cross the Castle's moat and walk through the archway, you'll also end up in Fantasyland. Critter Country occupies its own cul-de-sac extending north from New Orleans Square.

Study the map at left to familiarize yourself with the layout of Disneyland before you actually set foot in it. When you arrive at the park, ask for a park Times Guide, which includes information about the times and locations of the day's scheduled entertainment, as well as where and when to see the characters. It also supplies a list of special services available in the park.

PARKING

Guests are directed to park in Disney's Mickey and Friends parking structure or in one of three lots: Pinocchio, on Disneyland Drive beside the Disneyland Hotel; Simba, behind and adjacent to Disney's Paradise Pier Hotel; and Timon, a remnant of the original Disneyland parking lot off Harbor Boulevard. (Disney's California Adventure stands on what used to be the rest of that lot.) If one parking area is full, a cast member will direct you to one that isn't. Courtesy tram service transports guests from the parking deck and the Timon lot only.

Parking areas open an hour before the park does, but getting a space can take a half hour if there's a long line of park-goers, all with the same idea of getting a head start on the day.

Parking Fees: Guests arriving in regular passenger vehicles pay $11 to park. (The fee for vans and RVs is $13; for buses, $18.) You may leave the lot during the day and return later the same day at no additional charge. (Hold on to your parking stub as proof of payment.)

Lost Cars: Even if you take careful note of where you parked, you might have trouble remembering the exact spot when you return later. Hundreds more vehicles will likely be parked around yours. If this happens, contact a cast member and tell him or her approximately when you arrived. With that information, parking lot personnel can usually figure out the car's general location, and someone will then comb the lanes for it on a scooter.

GETTING AROUND

The Disneyland Railroad's five narrow-gauge trains make a 20-minute loop around the perimeter of the park, stopping at stations in Main Street, U.S.A.; New Orleans Square; Mickey's Toontown; and Tomorrowland. Horse-drawn streetcars, horseless carriages, and a motorized fire engine make one-way trips up and down Main Street.

To travel outside Disneyland Park, consider the sleek monorail, which glides between Tomorrowland and Downtown Disney. From Downtown Disney, you can walk to any of the three on-property hotels—the Disneyland Hotel, Disney's Paradise Pier Hotel, and Disney's Grand Californian Hotel & Spa. Disney's California Adventure park is just a few steps from the entrance to Disneyland (the two parks require separate admission, unless you have a Park Hopper Ticket; see page 57 for ticket pricing).

Park Primer

BABY FACILITIES

The Baby Care Center, on Main Street, U.S.A., by First Aid, provides changing tables, high chairs, toddlers' toilets, and a nursing area. Baby bottles can be warmed here, and baby powder, diapers, formula, and food are sold. There are no napping facilities or babysitting services.

FIRST AID

First Aid is located at the north end of Main Street, next door to the Main Street Photo Supply Co. A registered nurse is on duty during park operating hours.

GUIDED TOURS

No fewer than four behind-the-scenes tours originate from the Guided Tour Gardens, just left of City Hall. They are *Welcome to Disneyland*, *A Walk in Walt's Footsteps*, *Discover the Magic*, and *Holiday Time at Disneyland*. Park admission is required for all tours. Prices and schedules vary from tour to tour. For details, turn to page 21 of this book's *Getting Ready to Go* chapter.

HOURS

Disneyland is open daily. Monday–Thursday hours are generally from about 10 A.M. to 8 P.M., Friday and Sunday from about 9 A.M. to 10 P.M., Saturdays from 8 A.M. to 11 P.M., with extended hours during the summer months and holiday periods. For specific Disneyland Park hours, call 714-781-4565, or visit *www. disneyland.com.*

During the busy summer and Christmas holiday seasons, it's especially wise to arrive first thing in the morning so that you can visit the popular attractions before the lines get long. If you arrive at Disneyland too late, the parking structure and surrounding lots could be more crowded than usual; this is almost always the case in the summer months and during the last week of December.

For more timing tactics, see "Hot Tips" in this chapter and "Crowd Patterns" in the *Getting Ready to Go* chapter.

INFORMATION

Cast members at Disneyland Information Centers in City Hall and at Central Plaza can answer any questions you might have (or help plot your day so that you can make the most efficient use of your time and see what attractions truly interest you). Specifics on special services and safety considerations have been compiled in Disneyland's guidemap; ask for it when you enter the park.

Information Board: An invaluable resource for planning the day, the Information Board is set up permanently at the north end of Main Street, U.S.A. Located by a grassy spot near the Plaza Pavilion and the entrance to Adventureland, it lets you know how long the waits are for most of the popular attractions, what (if anything) is not operating that day, and where and when park entertainment will take place. The board is updated every hour. Cast members who are stationed there will also answer specific questions and provide information about the restaurants and hotels in the Disneyland Resorts. They can help guests locate their favorite Disney characters in the park, too.

MONEY MATTERS

Cash and traveler's checks are accepted at all food and merchandise locations throughout Disneyland. American Express, MasterCard,

Visa, JCB Card, and the Discover Card are accepted at all shops, cafeterias, fast-food eateries, snack bars, and full-service establishments (cash and Disney Dollars only at most park vending carts).

Personal checks with your name and address printed on them, drawn on U.S. funds, and accompanied by a government-issued photo ID, are also accepted as payment for meals and merchandise.

Disneyland Resort hotel guests may charge almost any purchase made in the theme park back to their hotel bill if they gave a credit card number at check-in. Keep in mind that this service is not available at most Downtown Disney locations.

Guests may purchase Disney Dollars in $1, $5, and $10 denominations from any park entrance ticket booth and City Hall. Disney Dollars are accepted at the three Disney hotels, Downtown Disney, California Adventure, and throughout Disneyland. They can be redeemed for real currency at any time. Though one might expect the Bank on Main Street to be, well, a bank, it is not. It is a processing center for annual passes. No financial services are offered at this address.

There are several ATMs here. The first one, encountered when first entering the park, is located beside the Bank on Main Street.

PACKAGE STORAGE

There's no need to lug bags around. You can store bulky purchases at the Newsstand at the entrance to Disneyland (on the right as you exit the park).

SAME-DAY RE-ENTRY

Guests who wish to leave the park and return later the same day may do so by getting their hand stamped upon exiting. The stamp will survive numerous hand washings. Keep in mind that you will need both your park ticket and a hand-stamp for re-entry.

SMOKING POLICY

At Disneyland Park, smoking is only permitted in designated smoking areas; refer to a park guidemap for specific locations. It is prohibited inside all attractions, waiting areas, shops, and indoor and outdoor dining areas.

STROLLERS & WHEELCHAIRS

Strollers and wheelchairs may be rented for about $7 inside the turnstiles of Disneyland Park, with a $20 deposit and major credit card.

Electric Convenience Vehicles (ECVs) cost $35 for the day, with a $20 deposit and major credit card. Lost strollers may be replaced at the main entrance and at The Star Trader shop in Tomorrowland.

SECURITY CHECK

All guests entering Disney theme parks are subject to a security check. Backpacks, parcels, purses, etc., are searched by security personnel before guests are permitted to enter.

Expect car trunks to be searched when entering Disney parking facilities.

Guests checking into Disneyland Resort hotels are asked to present a valid government-issued photo ID.

Ticket Prices

Although prices are always subject to change, the following will give you an idea of what you can expect to pay. Note that prices and ticketing structure are likely to change in 2009. For current prices, call 714-781-4565, or visit *www.disneyland.com.**

	Adults	Children**
One-Day Ticket (one park)	$66	$56
One-Day Ticket	$91	$81
Two-Day Ticket (hopper)	$132	$112
Three-Day Ticket	$189	$159
Four-Day Ticket	$214	$183
Five-Day Ticket	$234	$204
Six-Day Ticket	$239	$209
Two-Park Deluxe Annual Passport		$259
Two-Park Premium Annual Passport		$379

*Discounts may be available through the Web site.

**3 through 9 years of age; children under 3 free

Main Street, U.S.A.

This pretty thoroughfare represents Main Street America in the early 1900s, complete with the gentle clip-clop of horses' hooves on pavement, melodic ringing of streetcar bells, and strains of nostalgic tunes such as "Bicycle Built for Two" and "Coney Island Baby."

The sounds of brass bands, a barbershop quartet, and ragtime piano fill the street. An old-fashioned steam train huffs into a handsome brick depot. Rows of picturesque buildings line the street. Authentic gaslights, which once lit up Baltimore and St. Louis, flicker at sundown in ornate lampposts lining the walkways, and the storefronts—painted in a palette of pastels—could not be more inviting. Walt Disney was a master of detail: throughout Main Street, even the doorknobs are historically correct.

To make the buildings appear taller, a set designer's technique called forced perspective was employed. The first floor is seven-eighths scale (this allows guests to enter comfortably); the second story is five-eighths scale; and the third, only half size. The dimensions of the whole are small enough for the place to seem intimate and comforting, yet the proportions appear correct. (Forced perspective was also used to make the Matterhorn and Sleeping Beauty Castle seem taller than they are.)

The shops that line Main Street, U.S.A., draw guests back repeatedly during their Disneyland visit (see the "Shopping" section of this chapter and you'll understand why).

The following attractions are listed in the order in which you'll encounter them while walking from the main entrance up Main Street to the Central Plaza, toward Sleeping Beauty Castle.

Birnbaum's Best

Stamps like this one indicate the attractions that we find superlative in one (and usually more) of the following ways: state-of-the-art technology, theming, beauty, novelty, thrills and spills (make that splashes), and overall whimsy. Each "Birnbaum's Best" promises to deliver a dynamite Disneyland experience!

CITY HALL: Before strolling up Main Street, stop briefly at the Information Center at City Hall, on the west side of Town Square, to find entertainment schedules, make dining reservations, or get advice to help you plan your Disneyland day. City Hall is also a great meeting place if members of your party separate and plan to congregate later.

PHOTO BY JILL SAFRO

FIRE STATION: Next door to City Hall, this was Walt Disney's home away from home during the construction of Disneyland. His apartment, on the top floor, is decorated just as he left it, but is not open to the public. A light burns in the window in his memory. Kids love—and are welcome—to climb on the fire wagon parked inside the Firehouse. It's a realistic copy of a train from the early 1900s and provides a great photo opportunity.

BANK OF MAIN STREET: If you're looking to exchange foreign currency or purchase Disney Dollars, you can do so at City Hall, but not here. This "bank" is a processing center for annual passes. (There is an ATM outside for those in search of cash.)

DISNEYLAND RAILROAD: Walt Disney loved trains so much he actually built a one-eighth-scale model of one, the Lilly Belle, in the backyard of his home. So it was only natural that his first theme park include a railroad—five narrow-gauge steam trains that circle Disneyland park in about 20 minutes,

HOT TIP!
The Disneyland Railroad is wheelchair-accessible at New Orleans Square, Mickey's Toontown, and Tomorrowland stations.

making stops in Main Street, U.S.A.; New Orleans Square; Mickey's Toontown; and Tomorrowland.

Main Street just wouldn't be Main Street without the sound of the trains chugging in and out of the station and the conductors calling, "All aboard!"

Two of the locomotives were built at the Walt Disney Studios, while three had other lives before coming to Disneyland. Guests who ride the train between Tomorrowland and Main Street, U.S.A., are in for a couple of surprises. In 1958, Walt Disney added a diorama of the Grand Canyon, depicted from its south rim on a seamless, handwoven canvas that is 306 feet long and 34 feet high, and covered with 300 gallons of paint. The fauna and foliage depict deer, a mountain lion, a golden eagle, wild turkeys, skunks, porcupines, and desert mountain sheep, surrounded by quaking aspens and piñons and ponderosa pines, with a snowfall, a storm, a sunset, and a rainbow thrown in for good measure. The accompanying music is the "On the Trail" section of American composer Ferde Grofé's *Grand Canyon Suite*.

Adjacent to the Grand Canyon, yet eons away, the Primeval World diorama—a scene of misty swamps, deserts, rain forests, erupting volcanoes, and 46 prehistoric creatures—inspired by Disney's 1940 film *Fantasia*—opened in 1966, after an interim stop at the Ford Pavilion at the New York World's Fair.

DISNEYLAND—THE FIRST 50 MAGICAL YEARS: Unveiled during the "Happiest Celebration on Earth," this special collection of exhibits from Disneyland's early days has extended its stay inside the Main Street Opera House. Among the focal points is a scale model of the park circa opening day 1955, plus the original pencil aerial schematic of Disneyland created by Walt Disney and legendary Disney Imagineer Herb Ryman. Note that the attraction normally featured here—"Great Moments with Mr. Lincoln: A Journey to Gettysburg"—will return sometime in 2009.

MAIN STREET VEHICLES: Main Street's motorized fire wagon, horseless carriages, and horse-drawn streetcars give the thoroughfare a real touch of nostalgia, while at the same time giving guests a lift from one end of the street to the other. The fire truck is modeled after those that might have been discovered on an American Main Street in the early 1900s, except that it has seats where the hose was meant to be carried.

The horse-drawn streetcars, inspired by those in 19th-century photographs, carry 30 passengers each. Most of the horses that pull the cars are Belgians (characterized by white manes and tails and lightly feathered legs) and Percheron draft horses.

Save Time in Line!

For those of us who'd prefer not to waste time standing in line for theme park attractions, Disney's Fastpass is nothing short of a miracle. Basically, the system allows guests to forgo the task of waiting in an actual line for a number of theme park attractions.

How? Simply by walking up to the Fastpass booth (located near the entrance of participating attractions) and slipping their park ticket into the Fastpass machine.

In return, guests get a slip of paper with a time printed on it (in addition to the safe return of their park ticket). That time—for example, 4:05 P.M. to 5:05 P.M.—represents the "window" in which guests are invited to return to the attraction and practically walk right on—without standing in a long line!

Once you use your Fastpass to enter an attraction (or the time on it has passed), you can get a new Fastpass time for another attraction. It's also possible to get a Fastpass for a second attraction two hours after the first one is issued.

For example, if one pass was issued at 2 P.M. you can get a Fastpass for another attraction at 4 P.M. Sound confusing? It won't be once you've tried it.

Disney's Fastpass service is free and available to everyone bearing a valid theme park ticket. It should be available during peak times of the day and all peak seasons. We've placed the Fastpass logo (FP) beside the listings for all of the attractions that were participating at press time. However, since more attractions are scheduled for inclusion, check a park map for an up-to-the-minute listing of Fastpass attractions.

Note that all Disney attractions continue to offer the option of standing in a traditional line. If you happen to enjoy the standing-in-line experience, by all means, go for it. Otherwise, take our advice: Fastpass is the way to go!

MAIN STREET CINEMA: This small, standing-room-only theater features classic, early Mickey Mouse cartoons.

PENNY ARCADE: This place is now more of a candy shop than arcade, but the air of nostalgia remains. Those who have frequented it in the past will be happy to find Esmeralda front and center, as before, ready as always to tell your fortune. The arcade still has Mutascopes, machines that feature hand-cranked moving pictures and require a penny to operate. Fans of the classic electrocution machine will be sad to know that it is M.I.A.

PHOTO BY JILL SAFRO

Save some change for the arcade's nine penny presses. You insert a penny (plus a few other coins to pay for the service), and the penny will be flattened and imprinted with the image of Sleeping Beauty Castle or the face of one of the Disney characters.

CENTRAL PLAZA: Main Street, U.S.A., ends at Central Plaza, the hub of the park, and four of the park's lands are directly accessible from here. At its center stands the Walt and Mickey Partners statue. It's one of the park's most popular picture spots.

One of Disneyland's two Information Centers is located here, near the entrance to Adventureland. Besides the information desk, there is a handy Information Board, updated hourly, that posts wait times for many attractions, which attractions offer Fastpass, what (if anything) is not operating that day, and where and when park entertainment will take place.

PLAZA GARDENS: Visiting performers fill the small stage here in the afternoons, and guests dance to live bands Saturday evenings year-round and Friday evenings in summer. This is a fine spot to bring a snack and relax.

Adventureland

For someone who grew up in Marceline, Missouri, around the turn of the 20th century, as Walt Disney did, the far-flung regions of the world must have seemed most exotic and exciting. So it's not surprising that when he was planning his new park, he designated one area, called Adventureland, to represent all the (then) remote and mysterious corners of the world.

The original South Seas–island ambience all but disappeared with the opening of the Indiana Jones Adventure in 1995, and Adventureland became a 1930s jungle outpost. Today, the entrance to the Jungle Cruise is a walk-through headquarters, with period photographs and radios playing big-band music interrupted by news flashes about Professor Jones's latest exploits and discoveries. Shops here now sell wares that appeal to modern-day adventurers.

WALT DISNEY'S ENCHANTED TIKI ROOM: Introduced in 1963, this was the first of the park's Audio-Animatronics attractions and the precursor of more elaborate variations, such as "Great Moments with Mr. Lincoln" and the above-mentioned Dr. Jones. Housed in a vaguely Polynesian complex situated at the entrance to Adventureland, the 15-minute show was recently given a spiffy face-lift.

The stars are four feathered emcees (José, Michael, Pierre, and Fritz), backed up by a sextet of pastel-plumed, long-eyelashed parrots, and an eclectic chorus of orchids, carved wooden tiki poles, tiki drummers, singing masks, bird-of-paradise flowers, macaws, Amazon parrots, toucans, fork-tailed birds, cockatoos, and several other species.

The 225 performers all sing and drum up a tropical storm with so much animation that it's hard to resist a smile. Their repertoire includes "In the Tiki, Tiki, Tiki Room" (the show's theme song), "The Hawaiian War Chant," "Let's All Sing," and "Aloha to You."

JUNGLE CRUISE: The spiel delivered by the skipper on this seven-minute river adventure has its share of corny jokes, but your navigator may turn out to be a natural comic with a funny delivery. Just remember that the bad jokes are all part of the fun.

As jungle cruises go, this one is as much like the real thing as Main Street, U.S.A., is like life in a real small town—long on loveliness and short on the visual distractions and minor annoyances that constitute the bulk of human experience. There are no mosquitoes and no Montezuma's revenge. And the Bengal tiger and two king cobras at the ancient Cambodian ruins, and the great apes, gorillas, crocodiles, alligators, elephants, hippos, and lions in the water and along the shores represent no threat to passersby—though according to maintenance crews, they are almost as much trouble as real ones. Of course, there's no telling how guests will take the attraction's newest residents: a pack of peeved piranhas. Or vice versa. Good luck with that!

Movie buffs should note that Bob Mattey, who helped develop these jungle creatures, also worked on the giant squid for the Disney film *20,000 Leagues Under the Sea*, the man-eating plants in many Tarzan movies, and the menacing mechanical shark in *Jaws*.

The large-leafed upright tree in the Cambodian ruins section of the attraction is a Sacred Fig (*Ficus religiosa*), the same species of tree under which Buddha received enlightenment in India many centuries ago.

TARZAN'S TREEHOUSE: The 70-foot-high *Disneydendron semperflorens grandis*, or "large, ever-blooming Disney tree," which cradled the Swiss Family Treehouse from 1962 to mid-1999, now embraces another lofty dwelling: Tarzan's Treehouse, inspired by the book by Edgar Rice Burroughs and Disney's 1999 animated feature *Tarzan*. Overlooking the Jungle Cruise and the Temple of the Forbidden Eye (the setting for Indiana Jones's misadventures), this moss- and vine-covered "high-rise apartment" shelters Tarzan; his adoptive mom, the ape Kala; and his companion, Jane.

An interactive play area at the base of the tree has been designed around the scientific equipment that Jane and her father brought to the jungle. (Guests are welcome to experiment with some of it.) Nearby, a makeshift wooden staircase crafted from shipwreck salvage and a weathered suspension bridge provide easy access to the treehouse itself.

Jane's drawings, displayed throughout the compound, reveal the amazing story of Tarzan's survival and coming-of-age in the wild. (But could there be trouble in paradise? That lout of a leopard, Sabor, is lurking in the tree!) By the time guests plant their feet on terra firma once more, they will have hit new heights, not unlike a certain high-flying hero himself, and gotten acquainted with some of the characters—human and animal—who have shared in his exploits.

BIRNBAUM'S BEST — INDIANA JONES™ ADVENTURE: FP

Hidden deep within the dense jungles of India, the Temple of the Forbidden Eye was built long ago to honor the powerful deity Mara. According to legend, Mara could "look into your very soul" and grant the "pure of heart" one of three gifts: unlimited wealth, eternal youth, or future knowledge. But legend also issues a stern warning: "A terrible fate awaits those who gaze upon the eyes of Mara!" Dr. Jones would only comment, "Records indicate that many have come, but few have returned."

Now you can take an expedition through the ancient temple ruins in this attraction based on the George Lucas/Steven Spielberg film trilogy. The whole experience, including the pre-show and queue area, can easily take more than an hour (without a Fastpass), though the ride itself lasts about 3½ minutes. You follow the jungle path through Dr. Jones's cluttered encampment, then enter the temple via the path marked by his original team. In the queue area, a newsreel tells of Jones's latest expedition. What it does not reveal is that he has entered the temple and disappeared.

Following in his footsteps, you will see warning signs that indicate there still may be booby traps that have not yet been disarmed. (The fun is in paying no heed to the warnings and letting the spikes fall where they may.) Inside the temple, guests board 12-passenger vehicles reminiscent of 1930s troop transports. One person takes the wheel and serves as the expedition driver, but not until all are securely fastened in their seats for the twists and turns ahead. Hold on to your hat!

The search for Indiana Jones is on, and an encounter with the fearsome Mara is unavoidable. The trip reveals a world of mummies, glowing fires, falling lava, worrisome snakes, and poisonous darts.

Surprises lurk around every bend, and escape is only temporary (just as in the movies), as you suffer an avalanche of creepy crawlies, traverse a quaking suspension bridge, and, best of all, find yourself face-to-face with a gigantic rolling ball that threatens to flatten everyone in its path. At the end of the ride, Indy himself is waiting for you, with a flippant parting remark such as "That wasn't so bad," or "Next time you're on your own."

Thanks to the wizardry of Disney Imagineers, no two rides are exactly the same, so each time you enter the Temple of the Forbidden Eye, the experience will be slightly different.

Note: Pregnant women and guests who suffer from heart conditions, motion sickness, weak backs, and other limitations should not ride. Kids must be at least 3 years old and at least 46 inches tall to board; those under 7 must be accompanied by an adult. Spooked by snakes? There are more than a few in here. They're not real, but still rather creepy. Just a warning.

New Orleans Square

Though New Orleans Square did not figure in the Disneyland layout until 1966, it's certainly among the park's most evocative areas. This would be true even if it were home only to the superb Haunted Mansion and Pirates of the Caribbean. But there's also its picturesque site on the shores of the Rivers of America, and its architecture, a pastiche of wrought iron, pastel stucco, French doors, and beckoning verandas.

Not to be missed are the pleasant open-air dining spots; the romantic Blue Bayou restaurant overlooking the moonlit lagoon stretch of Pirates of the Caribbean; the unique assortment of shops; and the music—lively jazz and Dixieland, performed in traditional New Orleans style.

As you sit here on a warm evening, snacking on fritters and hot chocolate, images of Disneyland-as-amusement-park evaporate.

Just as Main Street, U.S.A., makes the theme park a great place to shop, New Orleans Square makes it a fine spot to spend a few relaxing hours. Those click-click sounds emanating from the railroad station are the Morse code version of the actual speech Walt Disney gave on the opening day of Disneyland back in 1955.

The attractions that are described on the following pages are listed in the order in which you would encounter them while strolling from east to west in Disneyland's New Orleans Square.

BIRNBAUM'S ★**BEST**★ **PIRATES OF THE CARIBBEAN:** The most swashbuckling adventure you'll find at Disneyland, this 16-minute boat ride transports guests through a series of sets portraying a rowdy pirate raid on a Caribbean village. Bursting with cannon fire, stolen loot, a gluttonous feast, and a raucous band of unruly mercenaries, Pirates of the Caribbean has entertained more people than any theme park attraction in history. It was the last attraction built under Walt Disney's direct creative supervision.

The experience begins with a short excursion through a bayou, where will-o'-the-wisps glow just above the grasses. Fireflies twinkle nearby, while stars spangle the twilight-blue sky overhead. The attention to detail nearly boggles the mind. The Audio-Animatronics

cast includes drunken pigs whose legs actually twitch in their soporific contentment, singing marauders, and wily wenches. The observant will note a couple of new rapscallion residents. Yep, that beloved scallywag Captain Jack Sparrow has dropped anchor here, as has his nefarious nemesis, Captain Barbossa.

While it's by no means the most politically correct attraction on property (far from it, actually), the theme song, "Yo-Ho, Yo-Ho (A Pirate's Life for Me)" manages to transform what is actually a picture of some blatant buccaneering into a rousing time for all. A must— again and again.

BIRNBAUM'S ★BEST★ **HAUNTED MANSION:** In a British radio interview, Walt Disney once explained how sorry he felt for those homeless ghosts whose hauntable mansions had fallen to the wrecker's ball. Feeling that these lost souls sorely needed a place of their own, he offered this Haunted Mansion, unquestionably one of Disneyland's top attractions. From its stately portico to the exit corridor, the special effects are piled on to create an eerie, but never terrifying, mood. Just frightfully funny.

Judicious applications of paint and expert lighting effects heighten the shadows that play ghoulishly on the walls outside. The jumble of trunks, chairs, dress forms, and other assorted knickknacks in the attic are left appropriately dirty, and extra cobwebs, which come in convenient liquid form, are strung with abandon. The eerie music and the slightly spooky tones of the Ghost Host often set small children to whimpering, and soon their Mickey Mouse

PHOTO BY KEITH GROSHANS

ears have been pulled tightly over their eyes. Still, the spirits that inhabit this house on the hill—999 in all—are a tame lot for the most part, though they are always looking for occupant number 1,000.

HOT TIP!
Haunted Mansion Holiday kicks off in October and runs through December. It features Jack Skellington from Tim Burton's *The Nightmare Before Christmas*, as well as holiday decor galore. Silly, seasonal sight gags abound.

What makes the seven-minute attraction so special is the attention to, and abundance of, details—so many that it's next to impossible to take them all in during the first, or even the second or third, time around. In the Portrait Chamber, a roomful of fearsome-looking gargoyles that adjoins the chandeliered and lace-curtain-adorned foyer, it's fun to speculate on whether the ceiling moves up or the room moves down. (It's one way here and the opposite way at the mansion's counterpart at Walt Disney World's Magic Kingdom.)

Once in your Doom Buggy, look for the bats' eyes on the wallpaper, the tomb-sweet-tomb plaque, and the rattling suit of armor in the Corridor of Doors. Can you spot a Hidden Mickey in the haunted dining room?

Then there are the dead plants and flowers and broken glass in the Conservatory, where a hand reaches out of a half-open casket; the terrified cemetery watchman and his mangy mutt in the Graveyard; the ghostly teapot that pours spectral tea; the ectoplasmic king and queen on the teeter-totter; the bicycle-riding spirits; the transparent musicians; and the headless knight and his supernatural Brunhilde. Nice stuff all.

The mansion was constructed in 1963, based on studies of houses around Baltimore; the attraction itself opened in 1969. The song "Grim Grinning Ghosts" was composed especially for the Haunted Mansion attraction.

Frontierland

This is the America experienced by the pioneers as they pushed westward: rough wilderness outposts, dense forests, rugged mountains delineating the skyline, and rivers lapping at the shore.

The sights in Frontierland are just about as pleasant as they come at Disneyland, and the atmosphere as relaxing. That's especially true in the afternoon, when the riverboat *Mark Twain*, with its elaborate wooden lacework trim, pulls majestically away from its dock for a cruise along the Rivers of America.

The following Frontierland attractions are described in the order in which visitors encounter them while moving counterclockwise from the Central Plaza gateway toward Big Thunder Mountain.

FRONTIERLAND SHOOTIN' EXPOSITION:

This shooting gallery, set in an 1850s town in the Southwest Territory, is completely electronic. Eighteen rifles are trained on Boothill, a mining town complete with a bank, jail, hotel, and stables. They fire infrared beams that trigger silly results whenever they strike the red, reactive targets. The most challenging target is the moving shovel, which, when struck, causes a skeleton to pop out of a grave.

Note: Disneyland tickets do not include use of the arcade. Pay 50 cents for 20 shots—then fire away.

BIRNBAUM'S BEST **BIG THUNDER MOUNTAIN RAILROAD:** FP Hold on to your hats and glasses, because this here's the wildest ride in the wilderness. Inspired by peaks in Utah's Bryce Canyon, Big Thunder Mountain is entirely a Disney creation. The name comes from an old Indian legend about a sacred mountain in Wyoming that thundered whenever men tried to excavate its gold. The attraction took five years of planning and two years of construction, and it cost about as much to build as the rest of the original Disneyland attractions put together—$16 million.

As roller coasters go, this one is relatively tame. It's short on steep climbs and precipitous drops that put hearts in throats and make stomachs protest, but long on tight curves that provoke giggles of glee. Adding to the appeal of this thrill ride is the scenery that the runaway mine train passes along the way: a pitch-black bat cave, giant stalactites and stalagmites, a waterfall, a natural-arch bridge that affords fine views over the Big Thunder landscape, and mine walls ready to cave in.

The queue area sets the scene of the quaint mining town, with two hotels, a newspaper office, dance hall, saloon, and general store. If you listen closely, you may hear a local barmaid flirting with a miner to the tune of "Red River Valley" or "Listen to the Mockingbird."

FP = Fastpass attraction (see page 60)

As you proceed toward the loading area, notice the brownish stone walls on each side of you. They were created from a hundred tons of real gold ore from the former mining town of Rosamond, California, which also yielded the ten-foot-tall stamp mill designated Big Thunder Mine 1880.

For the best of both worlds, ride twice — once by day, to see the scenery, and again after dark, for the pleasure of hurtling through the cool night (you might catch a glimpse of the Fantasmic! show).

Note: Pregnant women and guests who have heart conditions, motion sickness, weak backs, and other limitations should not ride. Children must be at least 3 years old and a minimum of 40 inches tall to board. Kids under 7 years old must be accompanied by an adult.

MARK TWAIN RIVERBOAT: One of the original Disneyland attractions and the first paddle wheeler built in the United States in half a century, this five-eighths-scale vessel circumnavigates Tom Sawyer Island. Along the way, it passes the River Belle Terrace, the Royal Street Veranda, the docks for the Tom Sawyer Island Rafts, piney Critter Country, a water-fall, abandoned railroad tracks, and lovely dense woods full of the alders, cottonwoods, maples, and willows that might have been found along the Missouri frontier more than a century ago. Moose, elk, and (real) ducks complete the passing scene.

On a busy day, this 14-minute ride offers a pleasant respite from the crowds. And if you manage to get one of the few chairs in the bow, the *Mark Twain* also provides a rare opportunity to put your feet up.

PHOTO BY JILL SAFRO

GOLDEN HORSESHOE SALOON: Tongue-in-cheek humor and western flair are the key ingredients in the musical and specialty acts featured at this entertainment venue. The hall itself is resplendent with chandeliers, polished floors and banisters, and a long brass railing. Walt Disney kept a private box here, just to the left of the stage, on the upper level.

Billy Hill & the Hillbillies, brothers who

mix bluegrass music and wacky comedy, are regular performers at the Golden Horseshoe Stage (for specifics, see page 90). Performance times vary. Check a guidemap's entertainment schedule or drop by City Hall when you arrive at the park.

There is no assigned seating inside; all of the seats are good, though those up front or on the balcony are perhaps the best.

SAILING SHIP COLUMBIA: A full-scale replica of the ten-gun, three-masted "Gem of the Ocean," the *Columbia* operates seasonally and on higher-attendance days at Disneyland. The original ship, constructed in Plymouth, Massachusetts in 1787 and christened the *Columbia Redivivia* ("freedom reborn"), was the first American craft to circumnavigate the globe. (Back then, that took three years to do.)

Disney's *Columbia*, dedicated in 1958 and renovated in 1984, was the first of its kind to be built in more than a century, and it circumnavigates the Rivers of America in 15 minutes. It has a steel hull and a deck planked with Douglas fir, and measures 110 feet from stem to stern, with an 84-foot mainmast. Usually moored at Fowler's Harbor, opposite the Haunted Mansion, the ship towers majestically over the treetops below.

Below Decks: The *Columbia*'s maritime museum, open only when the ship is operating, illustrates the way sailors lived on the original vessel during its later voyages, as reported in the ship's log and in letters between the captain and the owners.

PIRATE'S LAIR ON TOM SAWYER ISLAND: Yes, you read that right—there's been a pirate invasion in Frontierland! The formerly peaceful getaway that was pre-pirate Tom Sawyer Island has been transformed into a piratey paradise, complete with hidden treasure, creepy caves, shipwrecks, swordplay, and . . . pirates, of course. (They encourage budding buccaneers to take the Pirate Oath, so be forewarned.)

The only way to reach the island, which sits in the middle of the Rivers of America and was at one time the highest point in Disneyland, is by raft (which is piloted by a pirate). Once there, guests have many areas to investigate. Among them is Smuggler's Cove, which incorporates the island's beloved bridges and invites guests to man the bilge pumps in an effort to raise some sunken treasure. Then there's the Castle Rock lookout point, complete with spy-

glasses and peepholes (perfect for spying on scallywags or fellow theme park guests); Will Turner's Blacksmith Shop offers a glimpse at some of his works-in-progress; Dead Man's Grotto is a dark and labyrinthine set of caves sporting some spooky-yet-snazzy special-effects. Purists are pleased by the preservation of Tom and Huck's Tree House—but for many, the highlight here is meeting that rollicking rogue, Captain Jack Sparrow himself.

Small signs point to places of interest on the island, and even though the footpaths are decidedly well-trodden, any time spent here is worthwhile, and could encompass some of your happiest moments at Disneyland.

Note: Tom Sawyer Island closes early to allow for Fantasmic! preparation. Check at the dock for excursion times, particularly the last departure.

Disneyland Park Fastpass Attractions

Long lines got you down? Not to worry—most of the major Disneyland attractions now offer Fastpass. (For an explanation of this time-saving, line-skipping system, turn to page 60.) Here's a list of those "E-ticket" crowd-pleasers (keep in mind that attractions may be added to the list at any time—check a park guidemap for last-minute inclusions):

ADVENTURELAND
Indiana Jones Adventure

CRITTER COUNTRY
Splash Mountain

FRONTIERLAND
Big Thunder Mountain Railroad

MICKEY'S TOONTOWN
Roger Rabbit's Car Toon Spin

TOMORROWLAND
Star Tours; Autopia; Space Mountain

Critter Country

PHOTO BY KEITH GROSHANS

Lush, shady forests of pines, locusts, white birches, coastal redwoods, and evergreen elms surround Critter Country, one of the most pleasant corners of Disneyland. In 1972, this land debuted as Bear Country, the backwoods home of the since departed Country Bear Playhouse. From 1956 through 1971, the area was called the Indian Village, complete with teepees and a dance circle, and was part of Frontierland.

In 1989, the zone welcomed foxes, frogs, geese, rabbits, crocodiles, and many of the other critters that make up the Audio-Animatronics cast of Splash Mountain. To make the new furry residents feel at home, Disney Imagineers rechristened the area Critter Country. Observant guests will spot scaled-down houses, lairs, and nests tucked into hillsides and along the river.

BIRNBAUM'S **★BEST★** **SPLASH MOUNTAIN:** **FP** The fourth peak in Disneyland's mountain range of thrill rides— along with Big Thunder Mountain, the Matterhorn, and Space Mountain—Splash Mountain is unlike the other three attractions, where passengers ride roller coaster–style cars down tubular steel tracks. In this nine-minute ride, they board hollowed-out logs and drift on a waterborne journey through backwoods swamps and bayous, down waterfalls, and finally (here's where the speed picks up) over the top of a steep spillway at the peak of the mountain into a briar-laced pond five stories below.

HOT TIP!
If you want to get soaked on Splash Mountain, sit in the front of the car; the spray has less of a dampening effect in the back. Though nobody stays dry!

Splash Mountain is based on the animated sequences in Walt Disney's 1946 film *Song of the South*, and the principal characters from the movie—Brer Rabbit, Brer Fox, and Brer Bear—appear in the attraction courtesy of Audio-Animatronics technology. In fact, Splash Mountain's stars and supporting cast of 103 performers number almost as many as those in Pirates of the Caribbean, which has 119 Audio-Animatronics characters.

Comparisons to Pirates of the Caribbean are particularly apt, as Splash Mountain was consciously designed to be a "How do we top this?" response to the popular, long-running pirate adventure. Splash Mountain breaks new ground on several counts. Besides setting a record for total number of animated characters, it also boasts one of the world's tallest and sharpest flume drops (52½ feet at a 47-degree angle). It's one of the fastest rides ever operated at Disneyland Park.

One other twist makes Splash Mountain unique in the annals of flumedom: After hurtling down Chickapin Hill, the seven-passenger log boats hit the pond below with a giant splash—and then promptly sink underwater (or seem to), with just a trace of bubbles left in their wake.

Splash Mountain's designers didn't only borrow the attraction's characters and color-saturated settings from *Song of the South*. They also included quite a bit of the film's Academy Award–winning music. In fact, the song in the attraction's finale, "Zip-a-Dee-Doo-Dah," has become something of a Disney anthem over the years. The voice of Brer Bear is performed by none other than Nick Stewart, the same actor who spoke the part in the film when it was released in 1946.

Keep in mind: The hotter the day, the longer the lines, so go early or late.

Note: You must be at least 40 inches tall and 3 years old to ride the Splash Mountain attraction. Children under 8 must be accompanied by an adult.

DAVY CROCKETT'S EXPLORER CANOES:

Of all the boats that circle the Rivers of America, these 35-foot fiberglass craft may offer the most fun, at least for the stalwart. They are real canoes, and, no, they are definitely not on tracks. Though the helmsman and the sternman may be strong enough to handle the rowing, guests' contributions are also vital when it comes to completing the 2,400-foot voyage.

Note: This attraction operates only on certain days, and it closes at dusk. Check at the landing for excursion times.

HOT TIP!

Davy Crockett's Explorer Canoes is an attraction that operates seasonally. In other words, they might not be open during your visit. To learn if the canoes will be bobbing in the Rivers of America during your trip, visit *www.disneyland.com* before you leave home.

THE MANY ADVENTURES OF WINNIE THE POOH:

There's a cuddly critter in town and he goes by the name of Winnie the Pooh. In this colorful attraction, everyone's favorite honey-lovin' cub treats Disneyland guests to a wild and whimsical 3½-minute tour of his home turf.

The attraction features a most unlikely form of transportation: beehives! They whisk (and bounce) guests through the Hundred Acre Wood, where the weather's most blustery. The wind is really ruffling the feathers of one of the locals. It seems Owl's treehouse has been shaken loose and just may topple to the ground—and onto the beehives below.

Similar sight gags abound, from a bubble-blowing Heffalump (hey, this is Disneyland) to a treacherous flood that threatens to sweep Tigger, Piglet, and the rest of the gang away. When Pooh saves the day, it's time to celebrate—and everyone is invited to the party.

Note that, like many of the Fantasyland attractions, this Critter Country ride has a few scenes that take place in near darkness. Some youngsters may find these moments a bit unsettling. (If they can handle the likes of Mr. Toad's Wild Ride and Pinocchio's Daring Journey, they should be fine in the Hundred Acre Wood.)

Fantasyland

Walt Disney called this a timeless land of enchantment. We couldn't agree more. Village lanes twist between houses built of half-timbers, brick, stone, and stucco, often embellished with brightly colored folk paintings. The skyline, dominated by the peak of the Matterhorn, bristles with chimneys and weather vanes, turrets and towers. At the center of it all, as if deposited here by an itinerant carnival, is the King Arthur Carrousel.

When Walt Disney created Snow White's Scary Adventures, Mr. Toad's Wild Ride, and Peter Pan's Flight, the black light and glow-in-the-dark paints he used (so popular during the psychedelic sixties) were great novelties. But in recent decades, the palette of available hues and the spectrum of special-effects techniques have taken quantum leaps forward, and Fantasyland has benefited from these remarkable advances. Thanks to fiber optics, rear projection, holography, and other advanced special-effects techniques (developed in the course of constructing Epcot at Walt Disney World and Tokyo Disneyland), it has become even more of a visual treat.

Note: Parents of young children should be aware that some of Fantasyland's attractions take place in the dark. These include Peter Pan's Flight, Mr. Toad's Wild Ride, Alice in Wonderland, Snow White's Scary Adventures, and Pinocchio's Daring Journey.

Attractions are described here as you come upon them when moving roughly counter-clockwise from Sleeping Beauty Castle.

SLEEPING BEAUTY CASTLE: Rising above the treetops at the end of Main Street, U.S.A., it could be a figment of your imagination or a mirage created by Tinker Bell's pixie dust. Closer inspection proves this architectural confection is as real as the swans in the moat surrounding it. A composite of medieval European castles, primarily in the French and Bavarian styles, Sleeping Beauty Castle, the gateway to Fantasyland, is constructed of concrete, with towers that rise 77 feet above the moat. Trimmed in 22-karat gold leaf, it appears shiny even on gray days. The structure seems larger than it really is due to the use of forced perspective, down to the bricks.

From the Central Plaza, you're actually looking at the back of the castle; Walt Disney decided it was prettier that way and had the builders turn it around. The drawbridge, lowered when the park first opened in 1955, is like a real one—though it's been raised (and lowered again) only once since then. That historic event took place in 1983, at the rededication ceremony for the "new" Fantasyland.

Outside the castle, juniper is planted around the water's edge; it's one of the few green plants that the swans won't eat. One of the two graceful trees to the right of the drawbridge bears hundreds of tiny yellow flowers in spring, and the other is covered with fragile lavender flowers for several weeks in early summer.

ARIEL'S GROTTO: The Little Mermaid spends most of the day in a grotto just a few steps north of her father's garden. Here she visits with guests, who often ask her to sign their autograph books or pose for a photograph. She's happy to oblige. You can take as many shots as you like with your own camera or purchase any of the shots taken by one of Disneyland's photographers via Disney's PhotoPass program. For details on PhotoPass, see page 12.

TRITON GARDEN: This tiny oasis, located between the castle and the entrance to Tomorrowland, is filled with landscaped walkways, tide pools, rock outcroppings, and succulent plants. But the big lure at Triton Garden is the jets of water that leap from rock to rock and catapult over the bridge. Kids can't resist matching wits with them. At night, the interplay of lights, colors, and fountain spray transforms the garden into a particularly pretty spot.

PHOTO BY KEITH GROSHANS

SNOW WHITE WISHING WELL & GROTTO: Tucked off Matterhorn Way, at the eastern end of the moat around Sleeping Beauty Castle, this is one of those quiet corners of the park easily overlooked by guests. If you stand by the wishing well, you might hear Adriana Caselotti, the original voice of Snow White, singing the lovely melody "I'm Wishing," written for Disney's Oscar-winning 1937 film.

While Snow White sings, jets of water rise and fall in the waterfall fountain on the other side of the walkway, and a quartet of small fish rises up from the bottom of the pool at the base of the cascade to swim around in little circles. Any coins tossed into the well go to charity. FYI: This is a very popular spot for guests to "pop the question."

BIRNBAUM'S
★BEST★ **PETER PAN'S FLIGHT:** This attraction is one of the park's loveliest—and most popular. Based on the story by Sir James M. Barrie about the boy who wouldn't grow up, by way of Walt Disney's 1953 animated feature, the ride's special effects soar to celestial heights.

Pirate ships carry travelers through the clouds and into a sky filled with tiny fiber-optic stars.

Water ripples and gleams softly in the moonlight; the lava on the sides of a volcano glows with almost the intensity of the real thing. After an ephemeral few minutes, the ships seem to drift through a waterfall and back into reality, an unloading area that is all the more jarring after the magic of the trip through Never Land.

Of the approximately 350 miles of fiber optics found throughout Fantasyland, the majority are used in this ride. The twinkling London scene is an enlarged model of an authentic map of the city.

BIRNBAUM'S
★BEST★ **MR. TOAD'S WILD RIDE:** Based on the 1949 Disney film *The Adventures of Ichabod and Mr. Toad*—which was inspired by Kenneth Grahame's classic novel *The Wind in the Willows*—this simple, zany attraction is housed in an English manor bristling with ornate chimneys that really smoke. The wild, low-tech ride is experienced from the perspective of the eccentric but lovable Mr. Toad.

Of course, he is as inept a driver as you'd expect a toad to be. During the excursion, you crash through the fireplace in his library; burst through a wall full of windows; careen through the countryside; charge headlong into a warehouse full of TNT; lurch through the streets of London; then ram into a pub and veer out again. During the two-minute journey, you'll also be berated by a judge in court, nearly collide head-on with a railroad train, and be banished to a fiery inferno.

Did You Know?

There is a shadow of Sherlock Holmes (complete with pipe and cap) in the second-story window of the manor that houses Mr. Toad's Wild Ride.

ALICE IN WONDERLAND: Traveling in oversize caterpillars, visitors fall down the rabbit hole and embark upon a bizarre adventure in that strange world known as Wonderland. They come face-to-face with Tweedledum and Tweedledee, a garden filled with singing roses, the Cheshire Cat, the Queen of Hearts and her playing-card soldiers, the White Rabbit, and other characters from Lewis Carroll's beloved story *Alice in Wonderland*.

At the end of the nearly four-minute ride, the giant "un-birthday" cake explodes, providing a suitable climax to this sweet interlude.

MAD TEA PARTY: The sequence in Walt Disney's 1951 release *Alice in Wonderland* in which the Mad Hatter hosts a tea party for his "un-birthday" is the theme for this attraction—a group of colorful oversize teacups whirling wildly on a spinning tea table. Festive Japanese lanterns hang overhead. The park's original thrill ride back in 1955, it lasts only 1½ minutes, so if the line is long, come back later.

Note: The teacups may look mild, but it's a good idea to let a reasonable interval pass after eating before you take one for a spin.

BIRNBAUM'S BEST **MATTERHORN BOBSLEDS:** Though it's 100 times smaller than the actual peak, Disney's version of the Matterhorn is still a credible reproduction. The use of forced perspective makes the snowy summit look much loftier than the approximately 147 feet it does reach. Even the trees and shrubs help create the illusion. Those at the timberline are far smaller than the ones at the bottom.

The ride itself, like the more sophisticated Space Mountain and Big Thunder Mountain Railroad attractions, has to be counted among the most thrilling at Disneyland. At the time the Matterhorn Bobsleds were dedicated, in 1959, they were considered an engineering novelty because their dispatch system allowed more than one car to be in action at once. The ride was also the world's first tubular steel roller coaster. This classic is also considered to be Disney's first thrill ride.

The adventure begins with a long climb into the frosty innards of the mountain, then makes a speeding, twisting, turning descent through a cloud of fog and past giant icicles and ice crystals. The wind howls as you hurtle toward a brief but inevitable encounter with the Abominable Snowman. The speed of the downhill flight away from the creature seems greater than it really is because much of the journey takes place inside tunnels. Splashdown is in an alpine lake.

Note: Pregnant women, children under 3, and guests who suffer from weak backs, heart conditions, motion sickness, or other physical limitations should not take the ride. Guests must be at least 40 inches tall.

STORYBOOK LAND CANAL BOATS: This seven-minute cruise through Monstro the Whale and past miniature scenes from classic Disney animated films is not one of Disneyland's major attractions, yet few who take the trip deny that the journey is one of the park's sweetest, filled with intricate, evocative settings. No detail was spared, from the home of the Three Little Pigs to the Old English village of Alice in Wonderland (where the White Rabbit boasts his very own mailbox) to the London park that Peter Pan and Tinker Bell flew over with Wendy, John, and Michael Darling on their way to Never Land.

PHOTO BY JILL SAFRO

Other storybook locales include the marketplace where Aladdin met Princess Jasmine, the Seven Dwarfs' home and jewel mine, and Cinderella's castle. At the end of the cruise, the boat drifts past Geppetto's village, Prince Eric and Ariel's castle, and King Triton's castle.

BIRNBAUM'S ★BEST★ IT'S A SMALL WORLD: The background music for this attraction is cheerful and sing-song, sometimes maddeningly so. It does grab your attention, starting with the cheery facade, embellished with stylized representations of the Eiffel Tower, the Leaning Tower of Pisa, Big Ben, the Taj Mahal, and other landmarks. The 30-foot-tall clock with the loud ticktock and the syncopated swing is frosting on the architectural cake. The whirring of gears that marks every quarter hour alone warrants a trip to the attraction's plaza.

Boats carry guests into a land filled with more than 300 Audio-Animatronics dolls representing children from 100 regions of the world. It's a pageant for the eyes, even if the ears grow weary. (If you find yourself humming "It's a Small World" for the next several hours, you can blame Richard M. and Robert B. Sherman, the Academy Award–winning composers of the music for *Mary Poppins*, among many other Disney scores.)

Topiary figures in the shapes of a giraffe, elephant, rhinoceros, lion, horse, and other friendly beasts bid guests a fond farewell at the end of the ride.

Note that It's a Small World is transformed inside and out between Thanksgiving and New Year's to become as close to a winter wonderland as you're likely to find in Southern California. The dolls even sing "Jingle Bells" along with "It's a Small World."

CASEY JR. CIRCUS TRAIN: One of the key sequences in the movie *Dumbo*, in which an engine named Casey Jr. pulls a circus train up a steep hill, became the inspiration for this 3½-minute train ride that circles Storybook Land. The Storybook Land Canal Boats are better for viewing the landscaping and miniature details there, but it's worth a ride inside one of the wild-animal cage cars. Each train has two of them—plus a real caboose. Listen as the engine chugs, "I think I can," and then, "I thought I could," as it negotiates the hill.

DUMBO THE FLYING ELEPHANT: As beloved a symbol of Fantasyland as Sleeping Beauty Castle, this ride reminds all who see it of the baby elephant immortalized in the 1941 Disney film. Dumbo discovers, after drinking from a bucketful of champagne, that his inordinately large ears, which have been such a source of embarrassment, actually enable him to fly.

A mechanical marvel, Dumbo the Flying Elephant is full of filigreed metalwork, with cogs, gears, and pulleys galore. Brass pipes spew water from the base, and music is supplied by a vintage band organ housed in a small, ornate structure nearby. That figure atop the ride is Timothy Mouse, who became Dumbo's manager after the little elephant was hired to be a star by the same circus folk who once teased him. The topiary figures pay tribute to the little guy with the floppy ears.

SNOW WHITE'S SCARY ADVENTURES:

Ornamental stone ravens perch on carved stone skulls atop a stone tower, and hearts pierced through with swords lie at the base of the twisted pillars that support this brooding building. All this might lead you to expect an attraction as frightfully elaborate as the Haunted Mansion. It isn't. That said, the two-minute ride includes several fairly jarring scenes. In one, the Queen changes into a scary old hag before your eyes; in another, this wicked witch has the nerve to tempt you with a poisoned apple.

After passing a brief and joyful scene in the Seven Dwarfs' cottage, the cars travel through a creepy dungeon, visit a workshop where the Queen labors over her bubbling cauldron, and then venture into the Frightening Forest, where moss-draped trees point talon-like branches at passersby. The visit to the jewel mines, where the Seven Dwarfs labor, is more beautiful than scary, because of the emeralds, rubies, and sapphires glowing benignly in the darkness.

It all ends in true storybook fashion: As the evil Queen attempts to roll a stone down the side of a mountain to crush the dwarfs below, she gets struck by lightning (via a strobe effect) and tumbles over the edge of a cliff, leaving Snow White, the handsome prince, and their seven sidekicks to live happily ever after, as depicted in the mural near the exit. The music is taken from rare recordings used to create the film's original soundtrack.

Note: This attraction can be too intense for small children.

PINOCCHIO'S DARING JOURNEY:

Based on Disney's 1940 animated feature, this is a three-minute morality play of sorts, with Jiminy Cricket serving as host and guide. Pinocchio, who is the creation of the toymaker Geppetto, pays a visit to Pleasure Island and then discovers the right way to live.

As the ride vehicles move from the cheerful land of popcorn and Ferris wheels to the seamy world of Tobacco Road, Pleasure Island hues are replaced by drab shades of brown and gray. Here, little boys are turned into donkeys and sold to the salt mines.

Pinocchio escapes that fate, nearly becomes supper for Monstro the Whale, and winds up back home in the care of Geppetto—another happily-ever-after ending. The final scene, in which the Blue Fairy turns into a cloud of sparkles and then disappears, leaving a smattering of pixie dust on the floor, is partially accomplished via fiber optics.

Note: This attraction may be a bit frightening to toddlers (not to mention those of us who may be spooked by the concept of turning into a donkey).

KING ARTHUR CARROUSEL:

Guests come upon this graceful park landmark as they stroll toward the Sleeping Beauty Castle passageway into Fantasyland. One of the few attractions in the park that is an original rather than a Disney adaptation, the carrousel contains 68 horses—all movable, as Walt Disney wished. Carved in Germany over a century ago, no two alike, they are as pampered as the live Belgian horses on Main Street. The ornamentation on them is gold, silver, and copper leaf.

The faces on the inside and outside of the carrousel are gold leaf. The shields on the lances supporting its big overhead canopy are those of the Knights of the Round Table and other, less illustrious, crests. Nine hand-painted panels on top of the carrousel's main face re-create the story of Sleeping Beauty.

PHOTO BY KEITH GROSHANS

Mickey's Toontown

Disneyland lore tells us that when Mickey Mouse burst onto the movie scene in 1928 in *Steamboat Willie*, the first synchronized-sound cartoon, his success was so great that his busy schedule demanded he practically live at the Walt Disney Studios. Thirty cartoons later, in the early 1930s, he was one tired mouse, so he moved into a quiet residence in a "toon only" community south of Hollywood. Over the years, many toon stars gravitated to Mickey's Toontown, as it quickly became known. Minnie Mouse, Pluto, Goofy, Roger Rabbit, Chip, Dale, and Gadget all live here, and Donald Duck docks his boat, the *Miss Daisy*, on Toon Lake.

> ## HOT TIP!
> There are no full-service restaurants in Toontown, just a few fast-food places with window service, and limited outdoor seating. So don't plan on having a big meal here.

One afternoon in the early 1950s, while Mickey and his close friend Walt Disney were relaxing on Mickey's front porch, Walt revealed his idea for a theme park that would appeal to "youngsters of all ages." Mickey suggested that he build it next to the secret entrance to

Toontown, and the rest is history. Disneyland opened to the public in 1955, but little did anyone realize when they were drifting through It's a Small World that they were right next door to Mickey's Toontown.

In 1990, Mickey and his friends decided to open up their neighborhood and their homes to non-toons, and in preparation, all of Toontown received a new coat of ink. The grand opening took place in January 1993, marking the first new "land" to debut at Disneyland since Critter (originally Bear) Country opened in 1972.

Legend aside, the development of Toontown was a real challenge: to create a three-dimensional cartoon environment without a single straight line. Yet as topsy-turvy as it is, Mickey's Toontown is a complete community, with a downtown area, including a commercial center and an industrial zone, plus a suburban neighborhood. The best part is that everything is meant to be touched, pushed, and jumped on. Kids do just that, while adults relish the attention to detail and the assortment of gags. Much of what's here is interactive, from the mouse-hole covers to the public mailboxes.

This booming toontropolis is home to ten attractions, two shops, and three fast-food eateries. The rides are described in the neighborhood sections that follow; the shops, in the "Shopping" section later in this chapter; and the eateries, in the *Good Meals, Great Times* chapter of this book.

Guests enter this colorful land by walking under the Toontown train depot. The attractions are listed as they are encountered when strolling counterclockwise.

Downtown Toontown

In Toontown's "business" zone, an animated taxi teeters off the second-floor balcony of the Cab Co. A runaway safe has crashed into the sidewalk, and crates of rib-ticklers, ripsnorters, slapsticks, and wisecracks wait for passersby to lift the lids. At the Fireworks Factory, a plunger sets off quite a response when pressed; it's a good thing the Toontown Fire Department is located right next door.

Lift the receiver of the police phone outside the Power House (home to all sorts of electrifying gizmos—open the door at your own risk), and you might hear a voice over the toon police car radio, announcing, "Someone put mail in the box, and the box doesn't like it. Please respond post haste." Or step on the mouse-hole cover near the post office, and you might hear, "How's the weather up there?" or, "Is it time to come out now?"

You never know what to expect once inside Toontown—but it's all bound to be "goofy."

ROGER RABBIT'S CAR TOON SPIN: FP
This chaotic, rollicking ride combines the technology of the Mad Tea Party teacups (cars here spin 360 degrees) and the tracks of

PHOTO BY JILL SAFRO

Fantasyland attractions, such as Mr. Toad's Wild Ride. Benny the Cab and Roger Rabbit join the dizzying chase, which takes guests through the back alleys of the toon underworld made famous in the film *Who Framed Roger Rabbit.* The mission of each car is to save Jessica Rabbit from the evil weasels while avoiding the dreaded Dip.

ROGER'S FOUNTAIN: In this funny fountain, a statue of Roger Rabbit is suspended in midair, afloat on a column of water erupting from a broken fire hydrant that he has seemingly crashed into. He's still holding the steering wheel from the cab he was driving. Surrounding the hydrant, four floating cab tires serve as inner tubes for fish spouting arcs of water into the air.

POST OFFICE: Each kooky mailbox actually speaks in the voice of the character whose mail it receives—Mickey Mouse, Minnie Mouse, Roger Rabbit, Jessica Rabbit, Donald Duck, and Goofy. It can be quite a cacophony.

Outside, the letter box pipes in with comments like, "Don't just stand there—mail something!"

Toon Square

Located between the downtown area and the residential section of Toontown, this district is home to local businesses and institutions, including the Toontown Skool, the Department of Ink & Paint, and the 3rd Little Piggy Bank. Toontown's three eateries—Clarabelle's Frozen Yogurt, Pluto's Dog House, and Daisy's Diner—stand side by side on the square.

CITY HALL: Toon residents emerge from this municipal building and proceed to the bandstand out front to greet guests, entertain with their antics, and provide more relaxing photo opportunities than are often available elsewhere in Disneyland.

When a character is about to arrive, the colorful "Clockenspiel" above City Hall comes to life: Mallets ring bells, toon hands pull whistles, and figures of Roger Rabbit and Mickey Mouse pop out of cannons, blowing horns that, in turn, produce bouquets of flowers.

GOOFY'S GAS: From the looks of it, any traveler would think twice about refueling at

this station. On the other hand, it does house Toontown's public restrooms and telephones, and that's an important location to know (though we don't recommend making any important business calls here).

Pedestrians can now refuel here, too. A candy stand, called Goofy's Tuneup Treats, (open seasonally) offers sweet snacks. It's also a convenient locale to purchase souvenirs. The funny water fountain beside the station dispenses refreshing H_2O.

Mickey's Neighborhood

The homes in this district sit at the base of the 40-foot-tall Toon Hills, which have their own version of the famous Hollywood sign. The attractions are described as a guest would pass them while walking counterclockwise from Mickey's Fountain.

MICKEY'S FOUNTAIN: A statue of the world's most famous mouse stands at the center of a pool surrounded by toon-style musical instruments, creating a whimsical centerpiece for the Toontown residential area.

MINNIE'S HOUSE: It's hard to miss Minnie's house. This lavender-and-pink creation has a sweetheart theme for the sweetheart inside. Here guests can peek at Minnie's living room with its chintz sofa and sophisticated magazines (*Cosmousepolitan* and *Mademouselle*) on the coffee table.

There are messages from Goofy and Mickey on the answering machine in the hallway. Guests are invited to create new fashions for Minnie on the computer in her dressing room.

In Minnie's kitchen, a cake in the oven rises when a knob is turned, pots and pans clank

out a melody when the stove is switched on, and the dishwasher churns when a button is pushed. The Cheesemore refrigerator is stocked with an assortment of dairy products, including Golly Cheeze Whiz, and the shopping list left on the outside of the fridge hints at this mouse's cheeses of choice. Be sure to check out the cookies on her kitchen table (and be prepared for a little trick, courtesy of Ms. Mouse).

As you leave Minnie's House, you'll pass the wishing well in her yard. Don't think you're hearing things: It's been known to share a few parting thoughts.

MICKEY'S HOUSE: A path leads from Minnie's backyard to the front door of Mickey's House. The welcoming yellow dwelling with a tile roof, huge green door, and green shutters is home to the toon who started it all. Not only is Mickey's face on the mailbox out front, but his welcome mat is in the instantly recognizable shape of three circles— his head and ears.

HOT TIP!
Toontown closes one hour before the rest of Disneyland Park on nights when the park is presenting a fireworks show.

In the living room stands a player piano and a curio cabinet filled with all manner of memorabilia, including Mickey's baby shoes and a picture of him with his friend Walt Disney, as well as some of Pluto's treasures—a huge bone and a half-eaten shoe. In the laundry room, the washing machine chugs merrily away, and laundry supplies, such as Comics Cleanser and Mouse 'n' Glo, are at the ready.

From here, make your way through the greenhouse and into Mickey's backyard, where you'll see Pluto's doghouse and a garden with mysteriously disappearing carrots.

DISNEYLAND PARK

MICKEY'S MOVIE BARN: Ever industrious, Mickey has transformed the old barn in back of his house into a workplace, and guests are welcome to visit him here. The first stop is the Prop Department, where costumes and props from some of his famous cartoons are stored.

In the Screening Room, a bumbling Goofy projects movie clips from a few "remakes" currently in progress, among them *Steamboat Willie* and *The Sorcerer's Apprentice*. Mickey is hard at work on a soundstage, but happy to take a break. Guests enter in small groups for a photo and auto-graph session with the "famouse" star.

Note: You can't get to Mickey's Movie Barn without going through his house. This attraction is a must for die-hard fans of the Mouse.

CHIP 'N' DALE TREE-HOUSE: Just past Mickey's House stands the home of that jolly chipmunk duo, Chip and Dale. Styled to look like a redwood tree, this high-rise accommodates kids, but not adults. A spiral staircase leads to the lofty perch, whose windows provide a fine view of Toontown.

GADGET'S GO COASTER: Gadget is the brilliant inventor from the TV cartoon *Chip 'n' Dale's Rescue Rangers*. So it's only fitting that some of her handiwork is within view of their treehouse. Gadget, the ultimate recycler, has created this coaster from an assortment of giz-mos that once served other purposes. Giant toy blocks are now support beams for the

tracks; hollowed-out acorns have become the cars of the train; and bridges have been created from giant combs, pencils, paper clips, and such. The thick steel tracks give the impression of a tame ride, but there are a few thrills, right up to the final turn into the station. This experience is exciting but brief (1 minute), so if the line is long, save it for later.

Note: Kids must be at least 3 years old before they can ride Gadget's Go Coaster. Those under 7 must be accompanied by an adult. Pregnant women are advised to skip the trip. It may be a small coaster, but it's wilder than one might expect.

MISS DAISY: Donald Duck's house-boat, named for his fair-feathered friend, is docked in Toon Lake, adjacent to Gadget's Go Coaster. Parents can relax in a shaded seating area near a waterfall while their children explore the boat, which looks a whole lot like its owner.

See if you can recognize Donald's eyes in the large portholes of the pilothouse, his jaunty blue sailor's cap in the roof of the cabin, and his face in the shape of the hull. Would-be sailors can climb the small rope ladder or the spiral staircase up to the pilothouse to steer the wheel that turns the compass or to toot the boat's whistle.

GOOFY'S PLAY HOUSE: Located beside the *Miss Daisy*, this playground is just for kids. The garden outside Goofy's house boasts an odd assortment of delights: giant stalks bear-ing popcorn guarded by a Goofy-style scare-crow, spinning flowers, a leaky garden hose, and a patch with watermelons and pumpkins. Inside, young visitors can peek into Goofy's cupboards, climb on his furniture, and tickle the keys of the piano (doing so yields "goofy" sound effects rather than musical notes). Across the street is Goofy's Gas. It's not a real filling station, but is a great place to take little ones for a pit stop (it's a restroom).

TOON PARK: This tiny enclave next to Goofy's Play House supplies a safe play area for toddlers. Adjacent seating gives parents and other guests an inviting place to rest and enjoy the youngsters' antics.

Tomorrowland

PHOTO BY JILL SAFRO

When Walt Disney was alive, the future seemed simple: We would all dress in Mylar and travel in flying saucers. The Tomorrowland he created in the fifties was set in the distant year of 1987, part Buck Rogers and part World's Fair. The latest incarnation of Tomorrowland, rededicated in May 1998, is based on a classic vision of the future, one that looks at it from the perspective of the past. The result is an innocent and hopeful place (imagine, for instance, a planet that renews itself!), one more in keeping with the rest of Disneyland than with the sterile, less positive future world often depicted in contemporary films.

Visit Tomorrowland today, and you enter a visually engaging terrain, where the palette of colors is not otherworldly but warm and earthy. Futuristic boulders and dreamlike architecture coexist with apple, orange, lemon, and pomegranate trees that line pathways created from gray, mauve, and burgundy bricks. This landscape fires the intellect as much as the imagination.

Galileo Galilei, Leonardo da Vinci, Jules Verne, H. G. Wells, and certainly Walt Disney would have felt at home here. Aldous Huxley probably wouldn't have.

Four of Tomorrowland's newer attractions are also at Walt Disney World, in Florida: Honey, I Shrunk the Audience; Innoventions; Astro Orbitor; and Buzz Lightyear's Astro Blasters (known in Florida as Buzz Lightyear's Space Ranger Spin). Other well-loved Tomorrowland attractions remain, among them Space Mountain, Star Tours, and Autopia.

A replica of the Moonliner, a Tomorrowland icon from 1955 to 1966, sits on a pedestal near the site of its predecessor. Sleek monorail trains still glide to and from the Downtown Disney district, while traditional Disneyland Railroad trains continue to chug their way into the Tomorrowland station, a reminder that the past is indeed prologue.

The following attractions are described as you encounter them when proceeding counterclockwise from the Main Street entrance to Tomorrowland.

ASTRO ORBITOR: Towering above the entrance to Tomorrowland, this big whirligig with spinning orbs and speeding starships is a fitting symbol for Tomorrowland. Astro Orbitor, modeled on a drawing made by Leonardo da Vinci almost five centuries ago, is the successor to Rocket Jets, which gave Disneyland guests a lift for 30 years. Each ride vehicle accommodates two passengers (or two adults and one small child), who can maneuver it up and down while spinning clockwise for 1½ minutes, reveling in sweeping views of Tomorrowland, Central Plaza, and Sleeping Beauty Castle.

Note: The minimum age to ride is 1 year. Young children have to be in the company of an adult.

BIRNBAUM'S ▸BEST◂ **BUZZ LIGHTYEAR ASTRO BLASTERS:** 🄵🄿 The evil Emperor Zurg is up to no good—and it's up to that Space Ranger extraordinaire Buzz Lightyear and his Junior Space Rangers (that means you) to save the day.

So goes the story line of Tomorrowland's brand-new video game–inspired spin through toyland. The adventure is experienced from a toy's point of view. Guests begin their 4½-minute tour of duty as Space Rangers at Star Command Action Center. This is where Buzz gives his team a briefing on the mission that lies ahead. Then it's off to the Launch Bay to board the ride vehicles. The ships feature dual laser cannons, glowing lights, and a piloting joystick.

In addition to Buzz and the evil Emperor, you may recognize some other toy faces swirling about—the little green, multi-eyed alien squeaky toys, best known for their awe of "the claw." The squeakies have been enlisted to help in the fight against Zurg.

HOT TIP!
To maximize your scoring potential at the Buzz Lightyear attraction, aim for targets that are lit up, moving, or far away. They yield the most points.

Once Junior Space Rangers blast off, they find themselves surrounded by Zurg's robots, who are mercilessly ripping batteries from toys. As Rangers fire at targets, beams of light fill the air. For every target hit, you will be rewarded with sight gags, sound effects, and points. The points, which are tallied automatically, are accumulated throughout the journey. Although the vehicles follow a rigid "flight" path (they're on a track), the joystick allows riders to maneuver the ships, arcing from side to side or spinning in circles while taking aim at their surroundings.

When the star cruiser arrives at Zurg's spaceship, it's showdown time. Will good prevail over evil? Or has time run out for the toy universe? And will you score enough points to be a Galactic Hero? (Most people improve their scores with a little practice.)

PHOTO BY JILL SAFRO

BIRNBAUM'S BEST **STAR TOURS:** FP Inspired by George Lucas's blockbuster series of *Star Wars* films, this is one of the most intriguing attractions at Disneyland. It offers guests the opportunity to ride on droid-piloted StarSpeeders, the exact same type of flight simulator used by military and commercial airlines to train pilots. Once aboard the spacecraft, guests embark on a harrowing flight into deep space and encounter giant ice crystals and laser-blasting fighters. It goes without saying that seat belts are definitely required.

During the pre-show, guests watch as the *Star Wars* characters R2-D2 and C-3PO, here employees of a galactic travel agency, bustle about in a hangar area, servicing the Star Tours fleet of spacecraft.

Riders board the 40-passenger craft for what is intended to be a leisurely trip to the Moon of Endor. The flight is out of control from the start, as the rookie pilot proves that Murphy's Law applies to the entire universe. The sensations are extraordinary.

Note: Passengers must be free of back problems, heart conditions, motion sickness, and other physical limitations to ride. Guests under 40 inches tall and kids younger than 3 may not ride. Pregnant women are advised to skip this one.

STARCADE: There are easily 200 games in this "pay as you play" arcade—incorporating motorcycles, race cars, skateboards, snowboards, bicycles, snow skis, horses, spacecraft, and tanks. Most represent whatever happens to be hottest at the moment. Costs range from 25 cents to $4 per game. There are $1, $5, and $10 change machines, as well as a cashier, on the premises.

BIRNBAUM'S BEST **HONEY, I SHRUNK THE AUDIENCE:** The latest in 3-D film techniques link up with state-of-the-art chicanery when Rick Moranis, Marcia Strassman, and the kids reprise their roles from the movie *Honey, I Shrunk the Kids*. In this 18-minute misadventure, Professor Wayne Szalinski manages to unleash all sorts of mayhem.

In the pre-show area, guests watch a movie about the development of the Imagination Institute. Then they are welcomed to the Institute and given an overview of what will happen inside, where Professor Szalinski is to receive the Inventor of the Year award and

demonstrate some of his latest inventions.

On the way into the 575-seat theater, guests receive "protective goggles" (3-D glasses) to shield their eyes in case any flying debris comes their way during the demonstrations. One misguided mishap leads to another when the Shrinking Machine and then the Dimensional Duplicator go on the fritz. The theater is accidentally shrunk, and when the professor's young son picks it up to show his mom, the audience is left shaken up but screaming for more.

To add to the mix, in-your-face experiences are provided by a gargantuan dog, a menacing viper, an army of mice (don't say we didn't warn you), and a monster cat that morphs into a lynx and then into a lion. Eventually, everyone and everything returns to normal, sort of.

Note: Honey, I Shrunk the Audience is known to frighten small children and more than the occasional grown-up (especially those afraid of snakes or mice).

INNOVENTIONS: This two-level pavilion housed in the former Carrousel Theater is Tomorrowland's largest attraction. In it, guests can see how today's emerging technologies can improve their lives. Guests hop aboard a slowly rotating base at one of five themed "pods" and receive a quick introduction from the wisecracking, Audio-Animatronics Tom Morrow. That's followed by a show featuring breakthroughs in transportation, music, electronics, and more.

Guests are free to explore the world of Innoventions at their own pace, stepping on and off the moving base to watch live demonstrations, visit the new Innoventions Dream House, and enjoy a "hands-on" experience with new products (none of them for sale) at their leisure. Exhibits may be swapped out at any time.

Note: Parents, hold on to kids, or the rotating floor might deposit them in a different area from yours. There is no time limit at Innoventions; experience it at your own pace.

TOMORROWLAND AUTOPIA: FP The only attraction from the original Tomorrowland, Autopia was dubbed "The Freeway of the Future" back in 1955. Kids have always loved guiding the small sports cars around the twisting roadways (for them, a top speed of seven miles per hour is thrilling). Now pint-size motorists and their parents encounter a souped-up version of the original ride.

The Tomorrowland and Fantasyland roadways now comprise a single attraction (yes, there were two Autopias; the one in Fantasyland opened in 1959 to accommodate spillover crowds). Guests now enter through a single boarding area in Tomorrowland and watch an entertaining pre-show on a large video screen that presents the world from a car's point of view. Drivers (and one passenger per vehicle) travel in restyled cars through 21st-century terrain, experiencing a series of happy roadside surprises along the way. At the ride's end, they may receive a commemorative driver's license as a memento. A shop proffers auto-related toys and assorted souvenirs. This attraction is quite popular with those who've not yet reached "driver's ed" age.

Note: Kids must be at least 52 inches tall and at least 7 years old to drive alone. Pregnant women and guests with back or neck problems should not ride.

BIRNBAUM'S BEST SPACE MOUNTAIN: FP When Space Mountain first opened in 1977, it quickly rocketed to the top of just about everyone's list of favorite attractions. Well, believe it or not, its popularity soared to new heights when the attraction was "relaunched" in the summer of 2005.

While the classic facade and essence of Space Mountain remain intact, the experience is decidedly 21st century. Brave voyagers board new vehicles in a realistic launch port. After shooting through a disorienting tunnel, riders will have a close encounter with a meteorite. After that, it's all about screeching through the darkness, past spinning stars and whirling galaxies. Add to that an edgy sound

track (which is synchronized to each car) and you've got one out-of-this-world attraction.

If your courage fails you, just ask an attendant to direct you to the nearest "chicken exit."

Note: Pregnant women and guests who have weak backs, heart conditions, motion sickness, or other physical limitations should sit this one out. Children younger than 8 years old must be accompanied by an adult (kids under 3 are not permitted to ride). Guests must be at least 40 inches tall to experience Space Mountain.

DISNEYLAND MONORAIL: Who doesn't love the monorail? The first daily operating monorail in the Western Hemisphere was a novelty when it was introduced at Disneyland in 1959. Today, it's still a thrill to see them gliding through the park. The sleek, Mark VII trains, which were introduced in 2008, were designed to evoke images of their 1959 predecessors. Straddling a concrete beamway, the monorail has rubber tires, which enable it to glide quietly, as well as braking wheels atop the beam and guiding and stabilizing wheels on either side.

The 2½-mile-long "highway in the sky" is a distinctive and integral part of Tomorrowland. The nine-minute round-trip ride takes guests around the periphery of Tomorrowland, across the resort to Downtown Disney and its diverting activities, and then back to Tomorrowland.

For a special experience, inform the cast member on the boarding ramp that you'd like to sit up front in the pilot's cabin. It can usually accommodate up to five passengers. If all the seats are taken, you can always wait for the next monorail and try your luck again.

Note that by boarding the monorail in Tomorrowland, you are actually leaving the Disneyland Park. Be sure to get your hand stamped. You'll need to show it and a valid ticket to re-enter the park.

Trips are all "one way." You'll be asked to disembark at the Downtown Disney station. This is the spot to reboard when you're ready to head back to the Disneyland Park. Know that walking is also an option—as Disneyland and Disney's California Adventure are about a 5-minute stroll away.

The monorail is considered more of an attraction than a mode of transportation. It takes about the same amount of time (maybe less) to walk from the Downtown Disney station to the Disneyland Park.

HOT TIP!

A trip on the monorail yields panoramic views of Disney's California Adventure theme park and its neighbor, the Grand Californian resort. However, it does not stop at either place.

BIRNBAUM'S BEST **FINDING NEMO SUBMARINE VOYAGE:** Uh-oh. It seems that curious little clownfish has wandered off *again*. And this time he's done so in Tomorrowland's submarine lagoon! The good news is the subs that used to take guests to the North Pole now provide the perfect means for monitoring the fin-challenged fish and his high-spirited underwater hijinks.

The submarine adventure begins as a quiet expedition to observe an undersea volcano. But faster than you can say, "all drains lead to the ocean," our frisky friends from *Finding Nemo* start floating and fluttering in front of a personal porthole. The whole gang's here, including Nemo's overprotective dad, Marlin, the faithful-if-forgetful royal blue tang, Dory, that totally awesome turtle dude, Crush, and more. They're on a quest to catch up with their buddy Nemo, and you're invited along for the slightly frenetic, completely kinetic undersea search. Oh, and remember that volcano you were going to observe? It erupts.

Will you survive the sub-shaking volcanic quaking and find Nemo? Yep. They don't call this "the happiest place on earth" for nothing.

This whimsical experience is appropriate for guests of all ages, provided that the guests are claustrophobia free. Some moments may be too intense for some tots.

Tomorrowland Icons

MOONLINER: Beside Redd Rockett's Pizza Port, this two-thirds-scale, 53-foot-high replica of an early Tomorrowland icon stands 50 feet from the site of the original rocket. It is set on a 12-foot pedestal that doubles as a refreshment stand, called The Spirit of Refreshment. Water vapor wafts from its nozzles, but the only things "launched" here are bottled beverages (and then only by request). See page 80 for a photo of the Moonliner.

THE OBSERVATRON: This quirky icon for Tomorrowland towers above the area, constantly beaming electronic messages into space. Every 15 minutes, it comes to life in an orchestrated medley of music and motion.

FP = Fastpass attraction (see page 60)   83

Shopping

Until you get to know Disneyland, you might not expect that anyone would visit just to go shopping. But among Southern Californians, it's a top draw for the quality merchandise and appealing gift items. Mickey Mouse paraphernalia, such as key chains, mugs, T-shirts, hats, and other such souvenirs, is found here in abundance, of course, but there are some surprises, such as character-inspired costumes for kids, Mickey Mouse desk accessories for the office, and upscale items, such as art collectibles, jewelry, and products for the home.

Main Street, U.S.A.

CANDY PALACE: An old-fashioned pageant in pink and white, this shop is alluring at any time of day, but never more than when the candy-makers are at work in the glass-walled kitchen confecting candy canes, chocolate-covered strawberries, caramel apples, toffee, fudge, and other temptations for anyone with a sweet tooth. The products made on the premises are available for purchase, along with a bounty of chocolates, hard candies, and licorice.

CHINA CLOSET: If you're in the market for figurines, picture frames, or snow globes, this is the place to go.

CRYSTAL ARTS: Glasses and pitchers, trays, and other mementos can be engraved (for free) and monogrammed while you wait, or you can purchase them unornamented. The shop also sells glass miniatures, bells, and paperweights.

DISNEY CLOTHIERS, LTD.: Disney character merchandise has always been popular, but if you want something a little more stylish, this is where to find it. The spot caters to fashion-conscious shoppers with a love for Disney gear. Almost every item in the selection of men's, women's, and children's clothing and accessories sold here incorporates Disney characters in some way.

DISNEY SHOWCASE: Specializing in the latest trends (Disney style), this shop also proffers products with a Disneyland theme.

DISNEYANA: Collectors and the simply curious alike will discover rare and unusual Disney merchandise here, such as limited-edition art and hand-painted cels inspired by Disney animated classics. Popular pieces include crystal, bronze, and pewter figurines, and striking porcelain sculptures from the Walt Disney Classics Collection.

Note: Disney Imagineers and artists often drop by the shop to sign reproduction artwork sculptures, or recently published books.

PHOTO BY JILL SAFRO

EMPORIUM: Much like an old-time variety store, this large and bustling shop offers an incredible assortment of wares, and it is home to the popular Disneyland logo merchandise. Decorative figurines, clothing, plush toys, character hats, and a wide variety of souvenirs make up the bulk of the stock.

LE CHAPEAU: This hat shop stocks Mickey Mouse ears in black and various colors. Not only can you get your name stitched on the back, but you can also design your own mouse ear hat.

MAIN STREET MAGIC SHOP: Small but well stocked with gags and tricks—and books about how to pull them off—this shop has the wherewithal to inspire budding illusionists. In the market for an invisible pooch? A magic wand? An ice cube with a bug in it? This place has it all.

MAIN STREET PHOTO SUPPLY CO.: If a roving Disneyland photographer snaps your mug, this is the place to pick up the print. You can also find memory cards, batteries, film, frames, and photo albums.

MARKET HOUSE: This Disney version of an old-fashioned general store sells cookies, licorice ropes, jelly beans, chocolates, and hard candy—all the goodies you would expect to find in a turn-of-the-century store. Kitchen accessories, dinnerware, and gourmet foods, all loaded with Disney character (and characters), are Market House favorites.

PHOTO BY JILL SAFRO

NEW CENTURY JEWELRY: Among the delicate offerings here are 14-karat-gold charms of Tinker Bell, Donald Duck, and Minnie Mouse. The marcasite character jewelry is subtle and sophisticated.

NEW CENTURY TIMEPIECES: Merchandise in all shapes and sizes, including Mickey Mouse watches and alarm clocks, along with other character-laden novelty clocks, beckons from the polished wood cases at this shop.

NEWSSTAND: While no actual news is offered here (No news is good news, right?), this stand stocks postcards and souvenir items.

PENNY ARCADE: Adjacent to the Gibson Girl Ice Cream Parlor is a virtual Coney Island of food and fun. Jars of "penny"-style candy, available by the piece, fill ornate shelves, and scrumptious saltwater taffy, which you won't find anywhere else in the park, is available by the scoop in more than a dozen flavors, including licorice, peppermint, and root-beer float. To add to the carnival atmosphere, old-fashioned arcade games that still cost a penny to play and a Welte Orchestrion line the walls.

SILHOUETTE STUDIO: Working at the rate of about 60 seconds per portrait, Disneyland's silhouette artists truly are a wonder to behold. Individual and group portraits are available.

20TH CENTURY MUSIC COMPANY: This little place carries a rather extensive selection of classic Disney music and DVDs.

New Orleans Square

CRISTAL D'ORLEANS: Glasses and chandeliers, decanters and ashtrays, pitchers and paperweights are typical treasures here. All engraving, and some monogramming, is free.

JEWEL OF ORLEANS: This jewel of a store specializes in one-of-a-kind estate pieces—carefully chosen rings, cameos, watches, brooches, and cuff links—some date from 1850 to 1990, but most are Art Deco, from the 1920s and 1930s. Diamonds, rubies, opals, emeralds, sapphires, pearls, and garnets, all in artistic settings, twinkle from the display counters. Prices range from about $125 to $24,000.

LE BAT EN ROUGE: Need to cross a few Disney villain–related items off your shopping list? You've come to the right place. Also lining the shelves are tchotchkes and thingamabobs with a *Tim Burton's The Nightmare Before Christmas* theme.

LA BOUTIQUE DE NOEL: Filled with the Christmas spirit year-round, this shop is a repository of holiday collectibles. Santa Claus figures, wooden soldiers, Christmas stockings, ornaments, and decorations prove irresistible any time of year. Operating hours may vary.

LA MASQUERADE D' ORLEANS: Informally known as "pin central," this little shop is filled with collector pins, lanyard starter sets, and pin-trading accessories.

L'ORNEMENT MAGIQUE: The whimsical designs of the artist Christopher Radko fill this tiny shop. Cruella De Vil, Winnie the Pooh, the Seven Dwarfs, and Peter Pan have all inspired ornaments, and each year Radko creates a design exclusively for Disneyland. Operating hours may vary.

PIECES OF EIGHT: Wares with a pirate theme are purveyed at this shop beside the Pirates of the Caribbean exit. There are pirate rings, ships' lanterns, stocking caps, and fake knives, swords, and skulls in plastic and rubber. You'll also discover T-shirts, key chains, glasses, and other souvenir items imprinted with the Pirates of the Caribbean logo. For the right price, you can fill up a bag with pirate booty.

PORTRAIT ARTISTS: Sit for a portrait amidst the quaint charm of a New Orleans *rue* (street).

ROYAL STREET SWEETS: Satisfy your sweet tooth (or teeth) at this shop that specializes in sugary treats.

Frontierland

BONANZA OUTFITTERS: This quaint, rustic store has something for the whole pin-trading frontier family: pins, lanyards, and the assorted pin-collecting accoutrements.

PIONEER MERCANTILE: This shop carries all manner of paraphernalia inspired by the pioneer period in American history and this country's folk heroes. Young buckeroos will

Get Your Ears Done Here

Since Disneyland first opened in 1955, there has been no more coveted souvenir of the park than a pair of Mickey Mouse ears personalized with the lucky owner's name—or that of a family member. And never have there been more styles to choose from. They can all be embroidered for no additional charge at both locations of the Mad Hatter, in Fantasyland, Le Chapeau on Main Street, U.S.A., the Gag Factory in Toontown, and at The Star Trader and The Hatmosphere in Tomorrowland. The shops do not embroider company names on hats.

be delighted with the videos and books about the Wild West, and every budding Pocahontas or Pecos Bill will find authentically styled costumes, along with Western character plush toys to be their sidekicks.

WESTWARD HO TRADING COMPANY: It's on the right side as you enter Frontierland from Central Plaza. Hitch up your wagon and come on in. A huge assortment of themed hats stands by. Ideal for kids and kids at heart.

Critter Country

BRIAR PATCH: Situated near Splash Mountain, this small shop offers hats and sundry souvenirs.

POOH CORNER: All manner of Pooh products await, including plush toys, cookie jars, bookends, watches, infants' apparel, children's clothing, sleep shirts, and bedroom slippers. There's a candy kitchen, too.

POOH & YOU PHOTOS: Pooh and his pals can be found in Critter Country. You can take photos with your own camera or purchase any of the shots taken by one of Disneyland's photographers via Disney's PhotoPass program. For details on PhotoPass, see page 87.

Adventureland

ADVENTURELAND BAZAAR: The plush jungle animals corralled here include lions, tigers, and panda bears (oh, my!).

INDIANA JONES ADVENTURE OUTPOST: This outfitter can supply the most daring expeditions with all manner of safari apparel, notably Indy's trademark headgear, as well as other rough-and-ready wear and "artifacts" related to the ever-popular archaeologist and adventurer, Indiana Jones.

SOUTH SEAS TRADERS: This is the spot to browse for surf- and safari-themed items such as T-shirts, shorts, jackets, windbreakers, bags, belts, and a selection of hats.

Fantasyland

DISNEY CASTLE SHOP: Gowns and crowns dazzle the eyes of every young princess who enters this royal boutique, tucked inside Sleeping Beauty Castle, just to the left of the entrance to Fantasyland. From wish-upon-a-star-perfect costumes to jewelry and other courtly keepsakes, this little shop has made more than a few special dreams come true.

FAIRYTALE ARTS: Here guests are turned into princesses, among other things, via the magic of face-painting. There is a fee.

FANTASY FAIRE GIFTS: On Disneyland's parade route, near the entrance to the Fantasyland Theatre, this open-air stand stocks special souvenirs spun from the tales and sights in Fantasyland.

HERALDRY SHOPPE: At this tiny shop in the castle, you can trace your family name through centuries and continents and have its history printed up (a great gift idea). Or choose from hand-painted marble or bronze shields, coat-of-arms certificates, rings, T-shirts, and hats emblazoned with your family crest. There's a small (but impressive) selection of swords for sale, too.

IT'S A SMALL WORLD TOY SHOP: The whimsical structure near the entrance to It's a Small World stocks an assortment of Barbie dolls and accessories, Hot Wheels, and Disney-licensed Mattel toys, dolls, and plush toys featuring the Disney characters.

LE PETIT CHALET GIFTS: As cozy as a warm cup of cocoa on a winter evening, this small Swiss shop, nestled at the base of the Matterhorn, is the repository of traditional Disneyland gifts and souvenirs.

MAD HATTER: Always a great place for hats and plush character caps—and Mouse ears, of course (they'll embroider them for you). The large selection of novelty headgear includes Donald's sailor cap, a hat sporting Goofy's ears, Jiminy Cricket's and Uncle Sam's top hats, and floppy jester caps.

ONCE UPON A TIME—THE DISNEY PRINCESS SHOPPE: At the western end of Sleeping Beauty Castle, this is the main stop at Disneyland for serious toy and costume shopping. Youngsters will go for the inexpensive souvenirs and perhaps cajole parents or grandparents into springing for one of the fantasy costumes. These outfits can transform young guests into Minnie Mouse, Peter Pan, Alice in Wonderland, Buzz Lightyear, or even the nasty Captain Hook. Children's books, videos, games, dolls (including Madame Alexander and Marie Osmond), and the like complete the offerings.

STROMBOLI'S WAGON: Located near the Village Haus restaurant, this stand offers sundry souvenirs—everything from Disney plush toys to Mickey Mouse sunglasses. Some of the smaller items available here include character key chains, pens, buttons, and candy. They stock park guidemaps and Times

Guides, too. The shop is named after one of the villains in *Pinocchio*.

THREE FAIRIES MAGIC CRYSTAL SHOP:

You can create a very personalized souvenir at this unique Disneyland spot: a 2- or 3-D image of yourself etched into a block of crystal. The laser-engraved images make for a mighty memorable keepsake.

Mickey's Toontown

GAG FACTORY: A Laugh-O-Meter outside this shop gives some indication of the fun to be found inside, along with an assortment of character merchandise—plush toys, stationery, souvenirs, T-shirts, novelty headwear, and candy—all featuring the Fab Five (Mickey, Minnie, Donald, Pluto, and Goofy) and their friends. Take a moment to admire the toon architecture, especially the pillars at the back of the store.

PHOTO BY JILL SAFRO

MICKEY & ME PHOTOS: Trying to get your photo taken with Mickey on busy days can be challenging, but if you follow this tip, it's a piece of cake: Mickey can often be found working in the Movie Barn behind his house in Toontown, and he's always happy to stop what he's doing to greet his guests and pose for pictures. You can take as many photos as you like with your own camera (at no charge) or purchase any of the shots taken by a Disneyland photographer via Disney's PhotoPass program. For details on PhotoPass, see page 87. Note that the line to meet the

Mouse is often a long one. But to his legions of loyal fans, it's well worth the wait.

Tomorrowland

AUTOPIA CARS: Racing enthusiasts will enjoy the Autopia-inspired souvenirs offered at this small shop.

LITTLE GREEN MEN STORE COMMAND:

"Sharp" traders know they can find an excellent selection of pins at this spot. Considered the ultimate pin destination at Disneyland, you'll find open and limited-edition pins, lanyards, and pin-trading accessories, as well as lots of items with a *Toy Story* theme.

THE STAR TRADER: The Star Trader is the repository of everything from T-shirts and jewelry to back scratchers and shoehorns, not to mention jewelry, mugs, key chains, candy, and much more—all emblazoned with the likenesses of the Disney characters.

Toys in the likeness of Buzz Lightyear, Woody, and the gang from *Toy Story* can usually be found here, along with hundreds of stuffed animals. In the section over by the Star Tours attraction exit, the *Star Wars* legends have come to collectible life.

Walk of Magical Memories

Now you can own a little piece of Disneyland—10 inches of it, to be exact. For $150 you can purchase and personalize one of the hexagonal bricks that line the esplanade between Disneyland and California Adventure. Inscriptions and Disney logos mark special occasions or salute family names and hometowns. For more information, or to purchase a brick, call 800-760-3566.

Entertainment

Together with Walt Disney World, Disneyland books more entertainment than any other organization in the world. What follows is typical of the variety you can expect. Check a park Times Guide for daily offerings.

Performers & Live Shows

Performers stroll, march, croon, and pluck their way through Disneyland every day—so frequently that all you usually have to do to find them is follow your ears.

Main Street, U.S.A.

ATMOSPHERE BANDS: Look and listen for a variety of musical groups who perform near the Fire House and Sleeping Beauty Castle on select days.

DAPPER DANS: The official greeters of Main Street, U.S.A., this classic singing quartet performs standards in perfect four-part harmony. The colorfully clad performers may be found strolling on the sidewalk or planted beside a storefront.

DISNEYLAND BAND: A presence in the park since opening day in 1955, Disneyland's signature musical group specializes in turn-of-the-century band music, but it can play just about anything. The band performs inside the main entrance when the park opens, in Town Square (at the south end of Main Street), and at other locations. Inquire at City Hall for a show schedule.

FLAG RETREAT: The flag at Town Square is lowered just before sunset each day (times may vary; check at City Hall for specifics) by a team of uniformed Disneyland security cast members. The ceremony is highlighted by performances by the Disneyland Band or the Dapper Dans. The band performs several rousing marches. On the band's day off, the Dapper Dans perform a capella renditions of American classics. "The Star-Spangled Banner" makes for a stirring finale. It is a rewarding experience that captures the essence of what Walt Disney hoped guests would feel as they experienced Main Street, U.S.A. Usually presented daily.

MAIN STREET PIANO PLAYER: Piano players are often on hand to tickle the ivories on the snow-white upright piano on the Corner Café and Plaza Pavilion patios. Daily.

Adventureland

ALADDIN & JASMINE'S STORYTALE ADVENTURES: The story of Aladdin is re-created by Aladdin and Jasmine themselves, with the help of a few "guest stars" picked from the audience. Hosted by two storytellers, Kazeem and Kazoo, the tale unfolds in front of Aladdin's Oasis. Fridays, Saturdays, and Sundays year-round; daily in summer. Check a Times Guide or at the theater for showtimes.

New Orleans Square

JAMBALAYA JAZZ: This group plays down-home New Orleans jazz with plenty of soul. Fetch yourself a mint julep (*sans* alcohol) or a bowl of gumbo and let the music wash over you like the mighty Mississippi.

ROYAL STREET BACHELORS: Their style is early traditional jazz and blues, with a mellow four-beat sound similar to that once commonly heard in the Storyville section of the Crescent City.

Frontierland

BILLY HILL & THE HILLBILLIES: Dishing up a lively mix of bluegrass and comedy on the Golden Horseshoe Stage, these four brothers, all named Billy and all first-rate musicians, never take themselves–or their guests–too seriously.

LAUGHING STOCK CO.: Sheriff Clem Clodhopper has no desire to marry Mayor McGillicuddy's daughter, Sally Mae, but neither of them will take no for an answer. An old-time serial in three parts is played out as the dysfunctional trio finagles to get Sally Mae hitched to someone (anyone), even an unsuspecting park guest. Check a park Times Guide for performance schedule.

HOT TIP!
The park Times Guide offers a current listing of entertainment offerings and schedules. Pick up a copy at the main entrance, City Hall, or at one of the Tip Boards on Main Street. It's free! Note that custodial cast members tend to carry extra copies of Times Guides, too. Just ask.

Fantasyland

ROYAL CORONATION CEREMONY: An immersive area, where "happily ever after happens every day," the Princess Fantasy Faire serves as a training ground for future princesses and knights, as well as offering an opportunity for guests to mingle with a variety of Disney regals. Activities include a Princess Storytelling (in which guests are invited to help tell the tale), a Royal Coronation (offering the inside scoop on reaching regal status), and a Royal Dance (which takes place after the taking the Royal Oath). There's an arts and crafts component, too. Check a park Times Guide for performance schedule.

SWORD IN THE STONE CEREMONY: A lucky child is appointed king or queen of the realm by pulling a magic sword named Excalibur from the stone in front of King Arthur Carrousel. Merlin the Magician presides over the proceedings. Guests are welcome to give it a try when the show is not being performed. Daily.

Tomorrowland

JEDI TRAINING ACADEMY: *Star Wars* fans and Jedi-wannabes can learn the ways of "The Force" right here in Disneyland. A Jedi Master is on hand to teach guests dos and don'ts of using a light saber, as well as help them fend off an unexpected march of Stormtroopers. Expect a special appearance by one notable Dark Lord who'll attempt to lure you to the dark side. Check a park Times Guide for exact times and dates.

TRASH CAN TRIO: Are these entertainers custodians or musicians? They're both! This surprising group of percussionists has the wonderful ability to turn trash cans into musical instruments. Check a park show schedule for times and locations.

Parades

No Main Street is complete without a parade, and Disneyland has plenty. The usual route runs between Town Square and the promenade in front of It's a Small World—or vice versa. The direction and route can vary, so it's wise to ask at the Information Center at City Hall or Central Plaza.

WALT DISNEY'S PARADE OF DREAMS:

Meant to evoke happy memories and spark inspiration, this parade winds its way down Main Street once a day. As it does, gymnasts, trampoline performers, and aerial artists dazzle guests, as do dozens of familiar Disney characters.

It is usually presented each afternoon. Check a park Times Guide for current details and showtimes. *Note that this parade will be replaced in the middle of 2009. Details were not available as this book went to press, but we were assured that the new show will ooze Disney magic.*

Where to Watch the Parades: The best vantage points from which to see the parades are the platform of the Disneyland Railroad's Main Street depot, Town Square near the flagpole, and the curb on either side of Main Street. If you'd like to avoid crowds, any viewing location other than Main Street would be better.

Two other options are the terrace outside the Plaza Inn (but be aware that the seating is limited here) and the tables in the courtyard of the Carnation Cafe, where the view may be partially obstructed. Better still, plan to catch a later parade on nights when more than one are scheduled.

You can also stand on either side of the promenade area in front of It's a Small World, whose multicolored facade provides a whimsical only-at-Disneyland backdrop. Wherever

you decide to station yourself for the parade, plan to arrive about 20 to 45 minutes beforehand to claim your piece of turf.

Fireworks

REMEMBER. . . DREAMS COME TRUE:

This impressive fireworks show, presented nightly in summer, on New Year's Eve, and on other select occasions, ignites the sky with a kaleidoscope of colors over Sleeping Beauty Castle. At about 9:30 P.M. (on Friday, Saturday, and summer nights) Tinker Bell flies in to start the spectacular light show in fantastic fashion. That's followed by the stories of the wishes of classic Disney characters, from Cinderella to Aladdin—all to the accompaniment of a medley of Disney tunes and other musical favorites. More than 200 pyrotechnic shells are fired, one every couple of seconds, in time to the music.

Where to Watch: One of the best areas is about midway down Main Street, U.S.A., near the Main Street Photo Supply Company. (Be sure to face the castle!) Another great spot is near It's a Small World—keep your eye out for a special projection effect that's unique to this area.

Dancing

Bands play several sets in Tomorrowland on Saturdays year-round and nightly during peak seasons. In addition, Plaza Gardens Stage, adjacent to Central Plaza, hosts the popular "Jump, Jive, Boogie, Swing Party" on Saturday evenings throughout the summer. Giddy guests have been known to spin like teacups around the dance floor.

PHOTO BY JILL SAFRO

Special Occasions

Though plenty of special events take place in the park year-round (some require special-admission tickets), Disneyland does not celebrate holidays in a major way, except for the Fourth of July (super-sized fireworks); Halloween, which features an extra-spooky *Nightmare Before Christmas*–themed Haunted Mansion (see page 10); and the period between early November and New Year's, when the entire park glows with holiday themes. (We have witnessed the yuletide holiday decorations in place as early as October.)

The Disneyland Resort officially begins to celebrate the holidays in early November when Santa's Reindeer Round-up, Santa's Beach Blast, and the merriest attraction on Earth—"It's a Small World Holiday"—return for the season.

It's a Small World Holiday celebrates yuletide customs around the world. The singing dolls add "Jingle Bells" to their repertoire in numerous languages, and the clock on the whimsical facade dons a Santa hat.

Main Street, U.S.A., is decked out in traditional red and green, including hundreds of poinsettias and a huge white fir decorated with thousands of lights and ornaments, and surrounded by oversize holiday packages.

On two nights at the beginning of the season, a candlelight procession ending at Town Square takes place. Special music is provided by a large choir, and a holiday story is read by a well-known entertainer. (**A Christmas Fantasy Parade**, a Disney holiday favorite, takes place throughout the holiday season.)

Live entertainment and a fireworks show on **New Year's Eve** (no special ticket required) provide the grand finale for this festive and fun holiday season.

For more information about seasonal happenings in the park, see the *Getting Ready to Go* chapter; for specifics on upcoming special events, call the Guest Relations office (714-781-7290).

Where to Find the Characters

Look for the Disney characters in Town Square on Main Street, U.S.A., as well as in Mickey's Toontown, where they live. The Little Mermaid greets guests at Ariel's Grotto, just north of Triton Garden. Other princesses hold court at the Princess Fantasy Faire in Fantasyland. Pooh and his pals congregate in Critter Country. In Adventureland, Tarzan sometimes hangs out at Tarzan's Treehouse, while Aladdin and Jasmine often stop to chat outside Aladdin's Oasis.

Cast members at the Information Board can help locate characters. Also refer to the *Good Meals, Great Times* chapter of this book, and your Disneyland Times Guide.

Imagination Runs Wild in Fantasmic!

These 22 minutes of magic, music, live performances, and special effects light up the Rivers of America nightly on weekends, holidays, and throughout the summer season. More than 50 performers put on an unforgettable show in a dazzling display of pyrotechnics, lasers, fiber optics, and giant props.

In this tale of good versus evil, it's up to Mickey to overcome an array of villains. He first appears in cartoon form at the tip of Tom Sawyer Island and uses his imagination to make comets shoot across the sky while the river waters dance. Mickey materializes in a cone of light, and a shower of sparks seems to shoot from his fingers.

Spectacular technology makes Fantasmic! all the more fantastic. Mickey works his magic and a special film sequence appears, seemingly in midair above the river. This effect is achieved by projecting 70mm film onto three giant mist screens, each one 30

attempt to disrupt Mickey's fantasy. Fearsome creatures all have an opportunity, including an animated Maleficent, who morphs into the 45-foot-tall, fire-breathing dragon from *Sleeping Beauty*.

The villains turn Mickey's dreams into nightmares, and he must overcome them with his own powers of goodness, plus a little help from his friends. The *Columbia* sailing ship glides through the show with the swashbuckling cast of *Peter Pan* on board, and the *Mark Twain* riverboat brings along a host of favorite Disney characters.

Where to Watch: The best spots are in front of Pirates of the Caribbean (be sure you can see the water and a clear view of Tom Sawyer Island, and get there at least one hour early). If you decide to splurge, book "Premium Viewing" seats. They are set at the water's edge and come with tasty treats and beverages. The cost is $47 per adult, $37 per child. Call 714-781-4400 to reserve. The

feet tall by 50 feet wide. The screens are transparent, so that the live performers behind and in front of them appear to be interacting with the filmed images.

In one scene, Monstro the Whale from *Pinocchio* makes waves in the real water of the Rivers of America. In the "Pink Elephants on Parade" scene, the animated pachyderms from *Dumbo* interact with live performers in flexible, glow-in-the-dark elephant costumes. The illusions build toward a confrontation of good and evil, in which Disney villains

ticket office opens at 8 A.M. We recommend calling as soon as it opens, exactly one month before your desired reservation date. Late arrivals can usually find a decent place to watch below the Haunted Mansion, near the river's edge.

Note: Fantasmic! is shown twice nightly during the summer, and there can be a crush of people trying to leave after the show. The later show is always less crowded. Some of the effects are quite realistic and may be too intense for very young viewers.

Hot Tips

- Tuesday, Wednesday, and Thursday are the least crowded days to visit year-round. If you should come on a weekend, choose Sunday over Saturday.

- Measure your child's height before your visit so you'll know ahead of time which attractions he or she may be too short to ride. This can prevent intense disappointment later.

- Wear comfortable shoes. Blisters are the most common malady reported to First Aid.

- Main Street, U.S.A., often opens half an hour before the rest of the park. Take advantage of this to grab a quick snack, shop, or mingle with Disney characters.

- Check the daily entertainment schedule in your Disneyland guidemap and plan your day accordingly.

- Wait times posted at the attractions and on the Information Board at the north end of Main Street, U.S.A., are updated every hour.

- Break up your time in the park (unless you have only one day). Arrive early, see the major attractions until things get busy, return to your hotel for a swim or a nap, then go back to the park. Remember, you must have your hand stamped and your ticket to re-enter Disneyland.

- An attraction may reach its Fastpass limit before the end of the day, especially if the park is packed. Be sure to get yours early if you don't want to wait in the standby line.

- Try to have lunch before 11:30 A.M. or after 2 P.M., and dinner before 5 P.M. or after 8 P.M. to avoid lines (which tend to be shorter on the left side of the fast-food counters).

- For a change of pace foodwise, head to Downtown Disney or one of the three hotels on property. They have something for every budget and taste—from simple to sublime, sandwiches to sushi—as well as buffet meals with popular Disney characters (at the Disneyland resorts only).

- Avoid rides such as Star Tours, Splash Mountain, the Matterhorn Bobsleds, and the Mad Tea Party immediately after meals.

- On crowded days, you can make your way between the east and west sides of the park most quickly via the Big Thunder Trail.

- The lines are longest for the Disneyland Railroad at the Main Street station, but they tend to move quickly (lots of passengers disembark at this stop).

- Try to visit the major attractions—Space Mountain, Star Tours, the Indiana Jones Adventure, Big Thunder Mountain Railroad, Finding Nemo Submarine Voyage, Haunted Mansion, the Matterhorn Bobsleds, and Splash Mountain—early or during parades. The lines move faster then.

- During the busy afternoon hours, go to the smaller attractions, where the wait times are comparatively shorter; the *Mark Twain* riverboat is always a good choice. The afternoon is also prime time for shopping, enjoying outdoor musical performances, or taking in a show at the Golden Horseshoe Stage.

- Shops are a good place to escape the midday heat, but steer clear of them in late afternoon and at the end of the park's operating hours, when they tend to be crowded.

- For most rides, if you're in line even one minute before the park closes, you'll be allowed on. This is a great tactic for Splash Mountain and the Indiana Jones Adventure.

- Avoid the crowds by returning your stroller *before* the evening's fireworks presentation comes to an end.

Disney's California Adventure

Fame, fortune, and fun in the sun have lured adventurous spirits to California for centuries. But now visitors have a whole new way to enjoy the glories of the Golden State: through Disney's eyes. In February 2001, the company officially unveiled Disney's California Adventure theme park, the largest addition to the Disneyland Resort since Disneyland Park itself opened in 1955. It's been a work-in-progress ever since. To that end, a major, multi-year expansion was kicked off in 2008 with the addition of the interactive attraction, Toy Story Mania!

California Adventure sits snugly in the heart of the Disneyland Resort, sharing an entrance esplanade with Disneyland and neighboring Downtown Disney District and the three Disney hotels. But once you set foot inside the park, you're in a world all its own—a kaleidoscope view of California. Unlike Disneyland, where each land's theming is kept separate from the next, the lines here are blurred. Districts blend into each other, and no matter where you stand inside the park, you're sure to see (or hear whoops and hollers coming from) one of the park's towering icons—the Golden State's sierra-inspired Grizzly Peak mountain, or Paradise Pier's towering roller coaster, California Screamin'.

With a small vineyard, educational micro-factories, upscale restaurants, and scream-inducing thrill rides, the 55-acre theme park is clearly geared toward grown-ups. But there's bound to be something here for everyone to enjoy.

HOLLYWOOD PICTURES BACKLOT

1. Disney Animation
2. The Twilight Zone Tower of Terror
3. Hyperion Theater
4. Muppet*Vision 3D
5. Monsters, Inc.—Mike and Sulley to the Rescue!
6. Playhouse Disney—Live on Stage!

GOLDEN STATE

7. Bountiful Valley Farm
8. Golden Dreams
9. Golden Vine Winery
10. Grizzly River Run
11. It's Tough to be a Bug!
12. Mission Tortilla Factory
13. Redwood Creek Challenge Trail
14. Soarin' Over California
15. The Boudin Bakery

PARADISE PIER

16. California Screamin'
17. Golden Zephyr
18. Jumpin' Jellyfish
19. King Triton's Carousel
20. Maliboomer
21. Mulholland Madness
22. Orange Stinger
23. SS Rustworthy
24. Sun Wheel
25. Toy Story Mania!

Getting Oriented

Disney's California Adventure is smaller in area than Disneyland, its sister park next door. So guests should have no trouble covering all of the theme park on foot, as long as they wear comfortable walking shoes.

The entrance area—and much of the park—is expected to change a bit over the next few years. At press time, the esplanade directly outside the park faced a giant 3D picture postcard of California, where huge letters spelled the state's name and a stylized Golden Gate Bridge soared overhead, a conduit for monorails instead of automobiles.

In the hub of the park's Sunshine Plaza gleams a huge sun icon (also slated for big changes). A high-tech mirror system bounces rays from the real sun onto the reflective surfaces of the icon to create a welcome for park guests. It may also conjure up a romantic image of the sun setting over the Pacific Ocean, while a fountain at the base celebrated the dynamic energy of that body of water.

Four districts compose Disney's California Adventure park. East of the Sunshine Plaza lies the Hollywood Pictures Backlot, a mock studio backlot where guests can, among other things, learn about animation and take in a stage show based on Disney's *Aladdin*. Southwest of the Gateway Plaza is the Golden State, a district dedicated to the cultures, industries, and natural beauty that have shaped California, complete with a winery and micro-factories. Paradise Pier, the third California Adventure district, is located southwest of the Golden State and can be accessed through the Bay Area. Paradise Pier features nostalgic thrill rides with a modern twist, located around a lagoon. Finally, A Bug's Land is something of a mini-park within a park—designed for mini park guests!

PARKING

Guests park in the six-level Mickey & Friends parking structure on Disneyland Drive, which can be accessed from the I-5 freeway. There are also some ground lots that guests may be guided to park in if the parking structure is full or overly congested.

Parking Fees: Guests arriving in passenger vehicles pay about $11 to park. (The fee for vans and RVs is $13; for buses, $18.) You may leave the lot during the day and return later the same day at no extra fee. Just hold on to your parking stub as proof of earlier payment.

HOT TIP!
When you enter Disney's California Adventure through the Entry Plaza, east is to your left and west is to your right.

Lost Cars: Even if you take careful note of where you parked your car, you might have trouble remembering or recognizing the exact spot when you return hours later. Hundreds more vehicles will likely be parked around yours. If this happens, contact a cast member and tell him or her approximately when you arrived. With that little bit of information, parking lot personnel can usually figure out the car's general location, and someone will then comb the lanes for it on a scooter.

GETTING AROUND

You'll have to depend on your own two feet. There's no transportation within this easily traversed park. However, wheelchairs and Electric Convenience Vehicles are available.

Guests staying at Disney's Grand Californian hotel have their own private entry into Disney's California Adventure park (guests enter through the Golden State). All other visitors enter and exit the park through the main entrance, just across the esplanade from Disneyland's front gate. From here, trams transport guests to the Mickey & Friends tram station and the Timon parking lot. Since the area is pedestrian-friendly, guests may also opt to walk from the park along the esplanade to the hotel and the Downtown Disney part of the property.

Park Primer

BABY FACILITIES

Changing tables, baby-care products, and facilities for nursing can be found at the Baby Care Center by Cocina Cucamonga.

DISABILITY INFORMATION

Many park attractions and nearly all shops and restaurants are accessible to guests using wheelchairs. Services are also available for those with visual or hearing disabilities.

FIRST AID

Minor medical problems can be handled at the First Aid Center, located by the Pacific Wharf's Mission Tortilla Factory.

HOURS

Disney's California Adventure is generally open from 10 A.M. to 6 P.M. Monday through Thursday and 10 A.M. to 8 P.M. Friday, Saturday, and Sunday. For the exact times, visit *www.disneyland.com* or call 714-781-4565.

INFORMATION

Guest Relations, located on the east side of the Entry Plaza, is equipped with guidemaps and a helpful staff. Free guidemaps are also available at most park shops. The Information Kiosk is an important resource for attraction wait times and show schedules and is located in the Entry Plaza. Information is updated every hour.

PHOTO BY JILL SAFRO

LOST & FOUND

The theme park's Lost & Found department is located on the left side of the theme park's main entrance.

LOCKERS

Various-size lockers are located just inside the main entrance and at Golden Gateway near the Golden Gate Bridge. Rental fees range from $7 to $12 per day, depending on size.

LOST CHILDREN

Report lost children at Child Services near Mission Tortilla Factory in Golden State, or alert the closest employee to the problem.

MONEY MATTERS

There are several ATMs in the park. Currency exchange and Disney Dollar sales are handled at Guest Relations. Cash, credit cards, traveler's checks, Disney gift cards, and Disneyland Resort Hotel IDs are accepted for most purchases.

SAME-DAY RE-ENTRY

Be sure to have your hand stamped as you exit the park, and hold on to your ticket if you plan to return later the same day.

STROLLERS & WHEELCHAIRS

Strollers, wheelchairs, and Electric Convenience Vehicles (ECVs) can be rented near the Entry Plaza and in Condor Flats at Fly 'n' Buy. If you need a replacement, just present a receipt.

Ticket Prices

Although prices are always subject to change, the following will give you an idea of what you can expect to pay. Note that prices are likely to increase in 2009. For updates, call 714-781-4565, or visit *www.disneyland.com*.*

	Adults	Children**
One-Day Ticket (one park)	$66	$56
One-Day Ticket (hopper)	$91	$81
Two-Day Ticket (hopper)	$132	$112
Three-Day Ticket	$189	$159
Four-Day Ticket	$214	$184
Five-Day Ticket	$234	$204
Six-Day Ticket	$239	$209
Two-Park Deluxe Annual Passport		$259
Two-Park Premium Annual Passport		$379

*Discounts may be available through the Web site.
**3 through 9 years of age; children under 3 free

Hollywood Pictures Backlot

Lights! Camera! Action! The spotlight is on you in the glitzy Hollywood district of Disney's California Adventure, where the action unfolds all around you. Motion picture soundstages and backlot scenery provide the setting for the numerous movie-making antics and entertaining demonstrations that reveal the secrets behind a few tricks of the trade. No movies are actually filmed here, so you'll have to keep waiting for your big break. But you can think of this area as the "Hollywood that never was and always will be."

Pass through the studio gates and you enter into Disney's version of the legendary Hollywood Boulevard. And it all fits neatly into a two-block strip.

In contrast to starstruck Hollywood Boulevard, the Backlot peels away the facade and takes a backstage look at Hollywood without its makeup. Alongside soundstage buildings, behind-the-scenes support departments do their unseen, essential work: props are put into position (even the trees here are on wheels), klieg lights are set to shine on the scene, and the crew is busy making sure every performer is on his or her mark before the director yells "Action!"

BIRNBAUM'S BEST **MUPPET*VISION 3D:** FP One of the most entertaining shows at the Disneyland Resort, much of the appeal of this 3D movie is in the details. A funny song-and-dance pre-show, hosted by Gonzo and viewed on TV monitors, gives clues about what's to come. The theater (set inside a soundstage) looks just like the one from Jim Henson's classic television series *The Muppet Show* and comes complete with an orchestra of penguins. Even the two curmudgeonly fellows, Statler and Waldorf, are sitting in the balcony, bantering with each other and flinging barbs at the performers and the audience.

The production comes directly from Muppet Labs, presided over by Dr. Bunsen Honeydew and his long-suffering assistant, Beaker, and introduces a new character, Waldo, the "spirit of 3D." Among the highlights is Miss Piggy's solo, which Bean Bunny turns into quite a fiasco. Sam Eagle's patriotic grand finale leads to trouble as a veritable war breaks out, culminating with a cannon blast to the screen from the rear of the balcony, courtesy of everybody's favorite Swedish Chef.

The 3D effects, spectacular as they may be, are only part of the show: There are appearances by live Muppet characters, fireworks, and lots of funny details built into the walls of the huge theater. Including the pre-show, expect to spend about 25 minutes with Kermit and company. Shows run continuously.

MONSTERS, INC.—MIKE AND SULLEY TO THE RESCUE!:
A monster's-eye spin through Monstropolis, this colorful, slow-moving attraction was inspired by the hit film *Monsters, Inc.* It invites guests to follow affable monsters Mike and Sulley as they valiantly attempt to deliver Boo safely back to her room—all the while dodging trucks, helicopters, and the occasional yellow-suited member of the Child Detection Agency.

PLAYHOUSE DISNEY—LIVE ON STAGE!:
Put on your dancing shoes! Mickey Mouse and his pals will be disappointed if you don't join in the fun as they perform playful ditties from their Disney Channel show.

This show is presented at Playhouse Disney in the Animation Courtyard area of the theme park. Expect to see characters from *Mickey Mouse Playhouse*, *Handy Manny*, *Little Einsteins*, and *My Friends Tigger and Pooh*. Times Guides list performance times. This show is a big hit with the toddler set.

DISNEY ANIMATION: When you look around at all the attractions, themed hotels, and dozens of familiar animated faces that Disney has become famous for, it's almost impossible to remember it all started with a simple sketch of a mouse. This behind-the-scenes exploration invites guests to step into Disney's wonderful world of animation. Here visitors are given an insider's look at the process, the heritage, and, above all, the artistry of this world-renowned art form, along with a sneak preview of a few Disney animation feature works that are currently in progress.

Animation Courtyard: This central area makes visitors feel as if they are stepping into an animated film. Larger-than-life backgrounds from Disney film classics surround the area, as full-scale sketches of famous characters are projected onto the scene. Within moments, the sketches are transformed before guests' eyes into full-color animation. It's just one example of the Disney animation magic that awaits at the attractions inside.

Animation Academy: Inspired by the animation art in the courtyard, this attraction lets guests take a crack at drawing their favorite Disney characters. With step-by-step guidance provided by a Disney animator, you will use basic shapes and simple techniques to create your own souvenir sketch, suitable for framing. (Well, that's the goal, anyway!) Be sure to check out the *Toy Story* zoetrope as you exit.

Sorcerer's Workshop: Budding animators and artists particularly get a kick out of these three rooms. They are built around interactive exhibits featuring animation special effects. At Ursula's Grotto, for example, you can supply the voice of a favorite character from *The Little Mermaid*, and then see and hear the completed scene containing your own vocals. At Enchanted Books, you can take a personality survey (hosted by *Beauty and the Beast*'s Lumiere and Cogsworth) to determine which Disney character or villain you most resemble.

Turtle Talk with Crush: If ever there were an attraction that left guests smiling and asking, "How do they do that?!"—this is it. The concept is simple enough: a ten-minute, animated show featuring the surfer dude sea turtle from *Finding Nemo*. The amazing part? The cartoon critter actually interacts with the audience. In doing so, he imparts turtle-y wisdom, answers questions, and cracks more than a few jokes. You have to see it to believe it. To do that, you'll have to wait—the show is extremely popular with guests of all ages. It's like, totally awesome, dude.

DISNEY'S ALADDIN—A MUSICAL SPECTACULAR: Disney brings Broadway to its backyard with this 40-minute show, presented on the grand stage of the 2,000-seat Hyperion Theater. Inspired by the animated feature, this production tells the story of Aladdin, the magic lamp, and his trusty blue sidekick, Genie. The engaging staging even includes a magic carpet ride or two. Don't forget to look up!

You'll recognize all your favorite ditties from the classic Disney film, and be introduced to a new one, penned by renowned composer Alan Menken.

Note: The show is quite popular, and schedules vary. Performances are five days a week, usually Wednesday through Sunday. Check a park map for performance schedule, and plan to arrive at least 20 minutes before showtime.

BIRNBAUM'S **★BEST★** **TWILIGHT ZONE™ TOWER OF TERROR:** **FP** The Hollywood Tower Hotel houses a creepy-yet-thrilling ride. On the facade of the 199-foot-tall building hangs a sparking electric sign. As the legend goes, lightning struck the building on Halloween night in 1939. An entire guest wing disappeared, along with an elevator carrying five people.

The line for the popular ride runs through the hotel lobby, where dusty furniture, cobwebs, and old newspapers add to the eerie atmosphere. As guests enter the library, they see a dark TV set suddenly brought to life by a bolt of lightning. Rod Serling invites them to enter The Twilight Zone.

Guests are led toward the boiler room to enter the ride elevator. (This is your chance to change your mind about riding. Simply ask the attendant to direct you toward the "chicken exit.") Once you take a seat in the elevator, the doors close and the room begins its ascent. At the first stop, the doors open and guests have a view down a corridor. Among the many effects is a ghostly visit by the hotel guests who vanished. The doors close again and you continue your trip skyward.

At the next stop, you enter another dimension, a combination of sights and sounds reminiscent of *The Twilight Zone™* TV series. In fact, Disney Imagineers watched each of the 156 original *Twilight Zone* episodes at least twice for inspiration. This part of the ride is rather suspenseful, as you can't quite tell when you're going to take the plunge. What happens

PHOTO BY JILL SAFRO

next depends upon the whim of Disney Imagineers, who have programmed the ride so that the drop sequence can change. At press time, the elevator was taking an immediate plunge (of about eight stories) before shooting up to the 13th floor. At the top (about 157 feet up), passengers can look out at the park below. Once the doors shut, you plummet 13 stories. The drop lasts about two seconds, but it seems a whole lot longer.

Just when you think it's over, the elevator launches skyward, barely stopping before it plunges again. And again. From the time you are seated, the trip takes about five minutes.

Note: You must be at least 40 inches tall to ride. It is not recommended for pregnant women, those with a heart condition, or people with back and neck problems. Though thrilling (and rather scary), the drops are surprisingly smooth. Still, if you are susceptible to motion sickness, skip this one.

Did You Know?

The "Hyperion" name has a special Disney heritage. The Walt Disney Studios moved to 2719 Hyperion Street, Los Angeles, in 1926. It was there that Mickey Mouse was born. In 1940 Walt moved his studios to a bigger lot in Burbank, but he took some of the original Hyperion buildings with him.

FP = Fastpass attraction (see page 60)

Golden State

From pristine forests to fertile farmlands, the colorful valleys of Wine Country to the cultural hills of San Francisco, this district celebrates California's diverse geography, culture, and lifestyles. Whether it's through a bird's-eye view of the state or a bug's-eye view of the world, the Golden State's attractions offer guests a whole new perspective.

Condor Flats

Inspired by California's Vandenberg Air Force Base, home to some of aviation's most prominent pioneers, this airfield and its display area pay tribute to famous flyers and their aircraft. A huge aircraft hangar, the focus of this site, houses the Soarin' Over California attraction.

BIRNBAUM'S
★**BEST**★

SOARIN' OVER CALIFORNIA: 🄵🄿 It's no wonder California has an ongoing romance with aviation—how better to experience its breathtaking landscapes than by soaring through the skies above them. On this high-flying attraction, you're suspended up to 45 feet in the air, above a giant Omnimax projection dome that showcases some of the state's most glorious sights. With the wind in your hair and your legs

dangling in the breeze, the hang glider feels so convincingly real that you may even be tempted to pull up your feet for fear of tripping over a treetop as you dip down toward the ground. During the journey, flyers glide toward the

> ### HOT TIP!
> For a really soaring experience, try to sit in the first row—it flies the highest, while the third row stays closest to the ground.

Upper Yosemite Falls of Yosemite Valley, past an active naval aircraft carrier in San Diego Bay, by San Francisco's Golden Gate Bridge, and then down over the vast deserts of Death Valley and the lush wine country of Napa Valley, and up past skiers swooshing down the slopes in Lake Tahoe. In all, the airborne trip takes about 5 minutes and employs synchronized wind currents, scent machines, and a moving musical score set to a film that wraps 180 degrees around you, making this a thoroughly enveloping experience.

Note: You must be 42 inches tall and free of back problems, heart conditions, motion sickness, and other physical limitations to ride. If you're afraid of heights, skip this one.

Grizzly Peak Recreation Area

Just north of Condor Flats lies Grizzly Peak Recreation Area. Its centerpiece is the unmistakable grizzly bear–shaped mountain peak that juts 110 feet into the California Adventure skyline. The eight-acre mini-wilderness surrounding Grizzly Peak pays tribute to California's spectacular rural areas.

GRIZZLY RIVER RUN: Disney legend says that Grizzly Peak was once chock-full of gold—which made it a magnet for miners in search of riches, as is evidenced by the mining relics scattered about the mountain. But the gold rush has come and gone, and the peak has since been taken over by another enterprising group—the Grizzly Peak Rafting Company. They converted the area into a rafting expedition known as Grizzly River Run.

Each circular raft whisks six passengers on a drenching tour of Grizzly Peak. The trip begins with a 45-foot climb, and it's all gloriously downhill from there. Fast-moving currents send adventurers spinning and splashing along the river, bumping off boulders and rushing through an erupting geyser field. Because the raft is constantly spinning as it moves through the water, each rider's experience is slightly different, but one thing's for sure—everyone gets wet. During the expedition, rafters encounter two major drops. It's the 21-foot drop that earns Grizzly River the distinction of being the world's tallest, fastest raft ride.

HOT TIP!

Don't bring cameras or other valuables that must stay dry on Grizzly River Run. They will get drenched! Leave them with a non-riding member of your party or in a nearby (free) short-term locker.

Note: Passengers must be free of back problems, heart conditions, motion sickness, and other physical limitations to ride. Pregnant women, guests not meeting the 42-inch height requirement, and children under 3 will not be permitted to board.

REDWOOD CREEK CHALLENGE TRAIL: Lace up your sneakers and test your skills on this simple obstacle course set adjacent to the eastern slope of Grizzly Peak. The campsite features cable slides, rocks to scale, bouncy rope bridges, "floating" logs, and climbable cargo netting connecting treetops, to keep young mountaineers on their toes. Need a hand to assist you through the course? Just whistle for one of the workers outfitted in ranger gear. He or she will be happy to help.

The ranger's station has towers to climb (perfect for burning off excess energy) and an adjoining stage, the Ahwahnee Camp Fire Circle Story Theater (for when a rest is needed). Here, performers share animal folklore and tales of the land through storytelling and song. Keep an eye out for creature tracks; they lead to information on each type of species. There is also an amphitheater, which presents shows with a *Brother Bear* theme on select days.

Pacific Wharf

Inspired by Monterey, California's Cannery Row, this industrial waterfront salutes the diverse cultures, products, and industries that make California so international in nature. Guests can tour working micro-factories and watch local products, such as San Francisco sourdough bread and Mission tortillas, being prepared. There are also many tables scattered about, making this a good place to stop to enjoy a rest or a snack.

THE BOUDIN BAKERY: Soft sourdough bread is featured at this working bakery. While baking tips are shared in the walk-through corridor tour (courtesy of a short video), the famous Boudin-family recipe remains a well-kept secret.

MISSION TORTILLA FACTORY: Flour and corn tortillas are rolled flat and baked at Mission's display factory. Sample—at no charge—a warm tortilla once you're in the open kitchen, where chefs demonstrate simple ways to cook with the versatile wrap.

Golden Vine Winery

Northern California's fruitful Napa Valley provides inspiration for the Golden Vine Winery. Both an active micro-vineyard and a wine-tasting facility, the courtyard complex, nestled against the base of Grizzly Peak, is designed as a contemporary version of a classic Mission-style estate.

FP = Fastpass attraction (see page 60)

A Bug's Land

With the exception of It's Tough to be A Bug (which scares little ones silly), this colorful area was designed with the youngest of guests in mind.

BOUNTIFUL VALLEY FARM: The Farmers' Expo hosts its own farmers' market here each day; it resembles a cluster of rural roadside stands. Some of California's culinary staples are integrated into healthy snacks and meals.

While fruit smoothies and shaded picnic benches appeal to the grown-ups in the group, small children enjoy the area's interactive water course. Kids of all ages can splash through a simple maze made up of sprinklers and water gates that open and close when triggered. Budding horticulturalists are treated to an up-close view of gardens teeming with avocados, artichokes, citrus fruits, and other crops native to California, all grown and harvested on-site.

FLIK'S FUN FAIR: Guests of all ages are invited, but this area caters to the little ones. Who better to enjoy the experience of seeing the world from the vantage point of a bug?

Among the many diversions in this neck of the woods are a simulated hot-air balloon ride called Flik's Flyers, a mini railroad known as Heimlich's Chew Chew Train, and a drive-it-yourself bug-themed car ride called Tuck and Roll's Drive 'Em Buggies. Princess Dot's Puddle Park, a playground themed around a giant lawn sprinkler, is especially appealing to youngsters eager to make a big splash. Afterward they can spin themselves silly at Francis's Ladybug Boogie.

BIRNBAUM'S ★BEST★ IT'S TOUGH TO BE A BUG!: The underground Bug's Life Theater, by the entrance to the Bountiful Valley Farm, features an eight-minute, animated 3D movie augmented by some surprising "4D" effects. The stars of the show are the world's most abundant inhabitants—insects. They creep, crawl, and demonstrate why, someday, they just might inherit the earth. It's a bug's-eye view of the trials and tribulations of their multi-legged world.

As guests enter the dark auditorium, the orchestra can be heard warming up amid the chirps of crickets. When Flik, the emcee (and

star of *A Bug's Life*), makes his first appearance, he dubs audience members honorary bugs and instructs them to don their "bug eyes" (or 3D glasses). Then our oh-so-mild-mannered hero introduces some of his not-so-mild-mannered pals, including the black widow spider, a duo of dung beetles, and "the silent but deadly member of the bug world"—the stinkbug. Hopper, Flik's nemesis and the leader of the evil grasshopper pack, crashes the show and adds to the antics. What follows is a manic, often hilarious, not-to-be-missed revue.

Note: The combination of intense special effects and frequent darkness tends to frighten toddlers and young children. In addition, anyone leery of spiders, roaches, and their ilk is advised to skip the performance, or risk being seriously bugged.

HOT TIP!

Drivers, take note: In order to prove that you are 21 years old (the legal drinking age in California), you must present an official photo ID. So if your mug is not emblazoned on your license, be sure to bring it and a photo ID. Otherwise, you won't be allowed to imbibe—even though your driver's license is indeed the real McCoy.

Paradise Pier

Just south of the Bay Area, it's all about fun in the sun at Paradise Pier, a throwback to California seaside boardwalks of yesteryear. Like most classic amusement zones, the rides here offer simple thrills of speed and weight-lessness—but don't let the nostalgic look fool you: The technology is quite current.

At night, the district undergoes a dazzling transformation. Thousands of tiny lights illuminate the rides and building facades, creating a magical display—especially as you soar past them on one of the thrilling attractions.

BIRNBAUM'S **★BEST★** **CALIFORNIA SCREAMIN':** **FP** Like many classic boardwalks, the centerpiece of Paradise Pier is a gleaming roller coaster. A steel coaster, California Screamin' is designed to look (and sound) like an old-fashioned wooden roller coaster, but the thrills are as modern as they get. The ride starts at lagoon level, where the long car bursts up the track, as if cata-pulted up by a crashing wave. The car goes from zero to 55 mph in 4.7 seconds—before reaching the first hill. Several long drops are combined with an upside-down loop around the giant Mickey head that adorns the coaster, as well as a blasting sound track. The result is the longest and fastest roller coaster in the Disneyland Resort.

Along the way, vehicles travel through blue "scream" tubes that trap guests' yells as they test their vocal cords on the big drops, magni-fying the hoots and hollers, and adding to the excitement. Every time you approach a tube, you know you're in for a big thrill, so brace yourself and prepare to scream!

Daredevils should be sure to do this ride after the sun goes down, when the night sky is speckled with the pier's glowing lights, and the topsy-turvy twists and turns on the roller coaster will prove even more disorientingly thrilling.

Note: Passengers must be at least 48 inches tall and free of back problems, neck problems, heart conditions, motion sickness, pregnancy, and other physical limitations to ride.

SUN WHEEL: A modern loop-de-loop, this gleaming Ferris wheel, centered by a huge sun-burst, takes guests on a head-spinning trip. If you think this is a run-of-the-mill Ferris wheel, you're in for quite a surprise: While the wheel

---

Did You Know?

The origin of the roller coaster can be traced back to the 1400s in Russia, where thrill seekers took turns riding chairs down a series of icy wooden slides.

turns, most of its cabins rotate in and out along the interior edges of the wheel's giant frame—which creates a dizzying effect. At 150 feet, this is one of California Adventure's tallest attractions, and while it may wreak havoc on sensitive stomachs, thrill seekers rave over its ride within a ride.

Note: Passengers must be free of back problems, heart conditions, motion sickness, and other physical limitations to ride. Afraid of heights? Better skip this one! *This ride may not be open during your visit.*

HOT TIP!
A few Sun Wheel cars remain fixed on the edge as the wheel spins. Request to sit in one of these if you'd prefer to take a more tranquil trip.

ORANGE STINGER: This ride, set inside the giant swirl of a California orange peel, is sure to leave your brain buzzing. Riders take flight in swings resembling yellow-and-black-striped bumblebees. As the attraction's momentum picks up, buzzing sounds fill the air, and the bees swarm into a frenzy inside the peel.

Note: Riders must meet the Orange Stinger's height requirement of 48 inches, plus be free of back problems, heart conditions, motion sickness, and other physical limitations to follow this flight of the bumblebee. *This ride may not be open during your visit.*

MULHOLLAND MADNESS: **FP** No license? No problem. This compact (though jarring)

coaster, inspired by the famous road that winds its way from Hollywood to the Malibu coast, invites "drivers" of all ages to jump into a vehicle and experience the hectic and harrowing nature of California's congested freeways. Small police cars, red fire engines, and old vans follow a winding freeway map while careening over a maze of roundabout roadways and interchanges. Unlike the real thing, riders of this attraction won't be stuck in the infamous Southern California traffic—unless, of course, you count the line for the ride.

Note: Although it's small as roller coasters go, the ride's sudden stops and herky-jerky motion during turns may prove too scary for riders not used to more strenuous coasters.

Riders must be at least 42 inches tall and free of back problems, neck problems, heart conditions, motion sickness, and any other physical limitations to take this jolting ride. *This attraction may not be operating during your visit.*

JUMPIN' JELLYFISH: A dense kelp bed tops this sea-themed attraction, from which riders sitting in brightly colored jellyfish seats are lifted straight up in the air. When you reach the top, hang on to your tentacles! A parachute unfolds, and fish and friends float safely

PHOTO BY: JILL SAFRO

back down to the ground. While the trip is a gentle one with special appeal for younger riders, it might take a few minutes for guests with the most sensitive of stomachs to get their land legs back.

Note: Guests must be at least 40 inches tall and be free of back problems, heart conditions, motion sickness, and other physical limitations to ride.

SS RUSTWORTHY: A cleverly themed McDonald's playground, the SS *Rustworthy* is a nice place for young children to cool down and burn off some excess energy. Don't forget to pack kids' bathing suits or a change of clothes (and a supply of waterproof diapers for toddlers), and remember to reapply kids' sunscreen after they're finished romping around the soggy vessel.

MALIBOOMER: Along the boardwalks of yesteryear, strollers were sure to hear the resounding ring of the high bell on a slam machine, followed by uproarious cheers for the sledgehammer-wielding contestant, who had just won the game of strength. This ride represents Disney's twist on that old game, only this updated version is more a test of endurance than strength. Here, guests challenge their nerves as they become the high-flying projectiles on this extra large, ultramodern slam machine.

Riders are strapped into the vehicle, enveloped by a plastic shield, where they wait for the gong to sound. That's the cue to launch them skyward toward the target, 180 feet into the air, in two seconds. A string of bells and flashing lights erupt when the goal is hit, sending the vehicle dropping to the ground.

Note: Guests must be at least 52 inches tall and be free of back problems, heart conditions, claustrophobia, motion sickness, and other physical limitations to ride.

KING TRITON'S CAROUSEL: Take a spin under the sea on this merry-go-round inspired by *The Little Mermaid* and presided over by Ariel's father, King Triton. The deep-sea theme is carried out in aquatic detail right down to the ride vehicles themselves. The only horses you'll find here are golden sea horses. They're joined by dolphins, sea otters, seals, and fish, which rise up and down to classic organ tunes as the elegant carousel revolves. Be sure to notice all of the fish and marine mammals as they float by—each one was hand-carved, and no two creatures are exactly alike.

GOLDEN ZEPHYR: Disney Imagineers took the rocket ride to new heights with the launch of Astro Orbitor in Disneyland. But long before those space-age ships took off, riders were taking flights in rocket-shaped swings on boardwalks and amusement piers across America. Disney pays homage to those old-fashioned attractions with rocket ships that take guests for a spin beneath the Golden Zephyr tower. As speed picks up, the rockets lift into the air and fly over the lagoon several times before touching down for a landing.

Note: Passengers must be free of back problems, neck problems, heart conditions, motion sickness, and other physical limitations to ride. This attraction doesn't run when it's windy.

HOT TIP!
Even the hardiest stomachs may start to suffer if the thrilling Paradise Pier rides are tackled back to back. Spend time at the Midway when you need to take a short break.

GAMES OF THE BOARDWALK: The games of skill and chance that make up Paradise Pier's Midway are themed to Southern California locales and sea creatures. Guests can try their hand at amusements like Reboundo Beach (a basketball toss) and Dolphin Derby (a wooden ball–propelled porpoise race).

Note: The games here are pay-per-play (usually about $2), but winners may be rewarded with a prize.

BIRNBAUM'S BEST **TOY STORY MANIA!:** This dazzling newcomer (it opened in 2008) is an energetic, interactive toybox tour with a twist: Guests wear 3D glasses as they take aim at animated targets with spring-action shooters. The adventure is about as high-tech as they come, yet rooted in classic Midway games of skill. As points are scored, expect effusive encouragement from a colorful cast of cheerleaders—*Toy Story*'s Woody, Buzz, Hamm, Bo Peep, and, of course, the Little Green Men.

Fans of Disneyland's Buzz Lightyear's Space Ranger Spin will no doubt delight in this adventure, which takes the experience of the interactive attraction into a whole new dimension. As far as skill level goes, there's something for everyone—from beginners to seasoned gamers alike. (Most folks up their score with a little practice.)

Note that the experience can be a teeny bit disorienting. Those especially sensitive to motion might consider opting out of this one.

Shopping

While Mickey Mouse and his cartoon cohorts adorn much of the merchandise sold at Disneyland, the wares here are somewhat less recognizably Disney. When characters do crop up on merchandise, they may appear in a more subtle form. That said, a Disney theme park would not be complete without at least a few shelves of plush toys.

Entry Plaza

ENGINE-EARS TOYS: Located in an oversize model train, this store sells innovative interactive toys, mini train sets and related railroad items, small versions of theme park rides, plush toys, and character merchandise, and has a create-your-own-Mr. Potato Head area. This store is a package pick-up location (if you purchase items elsewhere in the park, you may have them sent here for pick-up).

PHOTO BY JILL SAFRO

GREETINGS FROM CALIFORNIA: The counterpart to the sprawling Emporium in Disneyland, this well-stocked shop is the place to head for nearly everything under the sun at Disney's California Adventure—souvenirs, books, toys, clothing, and Disney character plush toys. Merchandise themed to all the major attractions in the park can be found here, along with a selection of items specific to each district. Here's the place to view and purchase any photos taken by Disney's PhotoPass photographers (for details, see page 12).

HOT TIP!

Looking for more traditional (i.e., character-adorned) Disney souvenirs? Greetings from California and Engine-Ears Toys are your best bets.

Hollywood Pictures Backlot

GONE HOLLYWOOD: "Kitsch" is the key word in this larger-than-life boutique, which parodies the shopping styles of Hollywood's rich and famous. Here you will find kids' apparel, sleepover kits, costumes, and over-the-top cosmetics and accessories.

OFF THE PAGE: The magic of Disney animation leaps off the page at this special shop that showcases collectible Disneyana pieces. Cels, limited-edition prints, and figurines are sold here, as well as attraction-inspired items. A selection of books about Disney history, art, and animation is also available.

RIZZO'S PROP & PAWN SHOP: The wares at this wacky gift shop reflect the Muppets' irreverent sense of humor. Clothes, toys, and souvenirs featuring Kermit, Miss Piggy, Gonzo, Fozzie, and other familiar Muppet faces are for sale here. The stand is worth a browse for the clever Prop Shop theming, which feels like an extension of the nearby Muppet*Vision 3-D attraction.

Golden State

FLY 'N' BUY: When you see the large selection here, you know this is no fly-by-night operation. The aviation-inspired merchandise includes model airplanes, pilot patches, decals, and other accessories. To enhance the wardrobe of aspiring pilots, there are also authentic flight jackets, T-shirts, hats, ties, designer sunglasses, and watches. Merchandise from Soarin' Over California—postcards, music, videos, books, and T-shirts—is showcased here as well.

PT FLEA MARKET: Named after the infamous circus owner from *A Bug's Life*, this retail outlet is the place to pick up pins.

RUSHIN' RIVER OUTFITTERS: This outpost is the perfect place to gear up for an adventure in the wilderness. Expect to find hiking wear, gear, and supplies—items such as backpacks, sport bottles, polar fleece pullovers,

HOT TIP!

Still haven't quenched your thirst for shopping? Head to the World of Disney in nearby Downtown Disney. It's teeming with character merchandise and Disney souvenirs. (This is also one of the many spots to offer a discount to Premium Annual Passholders.)

multi-pocket jackets, and compass watches. California wildlife is represented in animal wood carvings, patches, plush hats, and jackets. And don't overlook the great Grizzly Bear icon of Disney's California Adventure, represented in an assortment of goods themed to the great outdoors.

Paradise Pier

DINOSAUR JACK'S SUNGLASS SHACK: The California look is not complete without a pair of shades. Head here for the ultimate selection in eyewear—sun specs in both classic and wacky styles.

PHOTO BY JILL SAFRO

MAN, HAT 'N' BEACH: Beach towels, swimwear, flip-flops, surfboards, and headgear line the shelves and vie for space with beach-themed souvenirs, such as key chains, magnets, and decals at this lakeside shop.

POINT MUGU: Fashion accessories are the stock-in-trade at this shop. Point Mugu has watches, earrings, necklaces, bracelets, and a large selection of hair accessories (barrettes, combs, headbands, and hair twisters), along with sunglasses, purses, and bags. To add sparkle, there's also a selection of lip gloss,

glitter, nail polish, and tattoos (the temporary kind, of course).

SIDESHOW SHIRTS: The spotlight here is on shirts of all sorts—tanks, tees, and sweat-shirts representing Paradise Pier attractions, as well as other surf-inspired gear. To complete the look, hats with similar logos are also available.

SOUVENIR 66: The well-traveled road, Route 66, provides the inspiration for this roadside souvenir shop. The mementos here come in the form of Paradise Pier–themed key chains, magnets, pins, iron-on patches, and postcards. Many items, such as mugs, beaded necklaces, and T-shirts, can be personalized.

TREASURES IN PARADISE: Here you'll find a vast assortment of Paradise Pier–themed merchandise, such as plush sea creatures and candy containers inspired by King Triton's Carousel. There's also California Screamin' memorabilia—toys, earrings, necklaces, wristwatches, and the like.

Pin Trading

It's the latest collectibles craze to sweep through Disney's land—pin trading. These small enamel pins (there are hundreds of different styles) can be purchased all over the property, but buying them is only half the fun. The real joy comes when you encounter another pin trader with a worthy swap. To get a head start, bring pins from home (Disney Stores carry pins, too). Once on-property, keep an eye out for cast members sporting a good selection of pins—they tend to be agreeable to almost any trade. And when negotiating with a cast member, always remember these rules: (1) only Disney pins may be traded, and (2) every trade must be an even pin-for-pin exchange.

Entertainment

PIXAR PLAY PARADE: This playful processional features a panoply of Pixar pals. Leading the way is Roz from *Monsters, Inc.* Right behind her see Heimlich and his buddies from *A Bug's Life*, followed by the incredible Parr family, Crush and Squirt (of *Finding Nemo* fame), Remy from *Ratatouille*, and many more. The parade is presented daily. Check a Times Guide for schedule.

BIRNBAUM'S ★BEST★ DISNEY'S ELECTRICAL PARADE: A sequel of sorts to the Main Street Electrical Parade (the classic processional first performed at Disneyland Park in 1972) this updated version made its California Adventure debut in the summer of 2001. It features 26 floats aglow with more than half a million twinkling lights, as well as a cast of 100 performers and a score of electronically synthesized Disney favorites. Performed select nights; check a Times Guide for times and grab a spot along the route at least 20 minutes before it starts. This whimsical parade is a hit with guests of all ages. *Note that the Electrical Parade may not be presented during your visit.*

"THE MAGIC OF BROTHER BEAR" TOTEM CEREMONY: Presented at the Redwood Creek Challenge Trail, this sweet and simple show invites guests to join Koda and Kenai for an inspirational totem ceremony. Presented on select days. Check a Times Guide for schedule.

HIGH SCHOOL MUSICAL SHOW: Are you ready to get'cha head in the game? Dance on over to Sunshine Plaza or the area by Golden Dreams Theater for a zippy, interactive *High School Musical*–inspired song-and-dance party. It's presented on select days. Check a Times Guide for specifics.

DRAWN TO THE MAGIC: If you enjoy classic Disney tunes, don't miss this lively little musical show. In it, artists share their love of animation, bringing Disney characters to life before your eyes. It's presented on select days on the Hollywood Pictures Backlot stage. Check a Times Guide for schedule.

Hot Tips

- Disney characters (including Mickey Mouse) make scheduled appearances throughout the day. Check a park Times Guide for specifics.

- Take advantage of Disney's free, time-saving Fastpass system whenever possible.

- Check the Information Boards often to get an idea of showtimes and crowds.

- It's sometimes possible to get a free sample at Mission Tortilla Factory and Boudin Bakery.

- Golden Vine Winery offers wine tastings (for a fee).

- The line for Soarin' Over California tends to dwindle a bit by midday. Ride it then if you choose to forgo the Fastpass option (the experience is enjoyable any time of day).

- Shops in the Entry Plaza stay open a half hour after the park closes.

- On a steamy day, head to Grizzly River Run, the SS *Rustworthy*, or Princess Dot's Puddle Park in A Bug's Land. These splashy spots provide much-needed heat relief.

- California Screamin' can wreak havoc with a digital camera. Store yours in a locker or leave it in the care of a non-riding member of your party.

- Ready for a break from the park? Head to neighboring Downtown Disney District for a shopping spree or to grab a bite to eat. There are several (relatively) cost-efficient snacking spots to choose from (i.e., Wetzel's Pretzels, Häagen-Dazs, Napolini, Tortilla Jo's, Jamba Juice, and La Brea Bakery).

- Some entertainment may take you by surprise—be on the lookout for comedians and other performers in Hollywood Backlot.

- Don't risk water-logging your valuables while riding Grizzly River Rapids. Take advantage of the complimentary lockers (located near the ride's exit). Each locker is free for up to one hour.

Good Meals, Great Times

GOOD MEALS, GREAT TIMES

Dining at the Disneyland Resort is definitely an adventure—and not just in Adventureland. There's more to any meal in a theme park, Downtown Disney, or Disneyland Resort hotel than just food. Disney friends such as Goofy, Tigger, Pooh, Minnie, Chip and Dale, or Donald Duck might drop by your table to say hello. A colorful parade or a romantic paddle wheeler could drift by. Or you might find yourself surrounded by twinkling stars and fireflies (in the middle of the day!) as you savor Cajun cooking in a bayou setting.

In this chapter, the Disneyland Resort restaurant section is divided by location (Disneyland Park, Disney's California Adventure, the three Disney hotels, and Downtown Disney District), within the theme parks arranged by area, and then by category—table service or fast-food and snack facilities, including food courts; individual eateries are alphabetized within each category.

If you're hankering for something to do after dinner, or you just need to take a break from the theme parks, you'll find plenty of suggestions at the end of the chapter. Downtown Disney, the property's dining and entertainment district, is party central. For a more relaxed atmosphere, select a lounge at one of the Disneyland Resort hotels. If it's a particular concert or dinner show in Orange County that interests you, spend the evening at that locale or venue.

Dining
In Disneyland Park

Restaurant Primer

Eateries in this chapter have been designated inexpensive (lunch or dinner under $15), moderate ($15 to $29), expensive ($30 to $50), and very expensive ($51 and up). Prices are for an entrée, a soft drink, and either soup, salad, or dessert for one person, excluding tax and tip.

The letters at the end of each entry refer to the meals offered: breakfast (B), lunch (L), dinner (D), and snacks (S). An asterisk (*) after a letter means that the meal is served only during the park's busy seasons.

Cash, credit cards, traveler's checks, or personal checks with proper ID can be used as payment at all of the following full-service restaurants and fast-food spots. Disneyland Resort hotel guests can charge meals from most theme park eateries to their rooms. Only cash is accepted at snack carts.

While only a few theme park restaurants (i.e., Blue Bayou and Café Orleans in Disneyland; Ariel's Grotto and the Vineyard Room, in California Adventure) take reservations, you can book a table at most dining spots in Downtown Disney and at the Disney hotels. Unless otherwise noted, make arrangements by calling 714-781-3463.

The most popular food in Disneyland is the hamburger, followed closely by ice cream and *churros* (sticks of deep-fried dough rolled in cinnamon and sugar). But health-conscious eaters will also find salads, grilled chicken, and vegetable stew, plus fresh fruit and juices. Disneyland's table-service restaurants, the

HOT TIP!

For a jolt of java, head to the Blue Ribbon Bakery on Main Street, Bengal Barbecue in Adventureland, or Royal Street Veranda in New Orleans Square. Their iced and hot specialty coffees are sure to please.

Blue Bayou, Café Orleans, and the Carnation Cafe, provide full-course meals and lighter fare, plus a welcome break from long lines and the California sun.

Main Street, U.S.A.

Table Service

CARNATION CAFE: On the west side of Main Street, near Town Square, this outdoor cafe is exceptionally pleasant, especially in springtime, when its planters are bursting with seasonal flowers. Stroll through a gazebo to enter the courtyard dining area, filled with umbrella-shaded tables and surrounded by a cast-iron fence; from your table you'll get glimpses of any passing parade. Breakfast choices include Mickey Mouse waffles, cinnamon-roll french toast, sticky buns, "croissantwiches" (egg, cheese, and ham grilled in a croissant), cereal, or continental breakfast, along with coffee or tea and fresh-squeezed orange juice.

For lunch and dinner, sandwich plates are the big draw, with fruit and a variety of salads to choose from. The sandwiches include a yummy smoked chicken club. A meatloaf stack, pot pies, soup, and kids' specials are also on the menu, along with dessert items such as banana splits, fruit pies, and specialty coffees. This cafe is one of three restaurants at Disneyland that offer table service for lunch and dinner (Blue Bayou and Cafe Orleans in New Orleans Square are the others).
B L D **S-$$**

Fast Food & Snacks

BLUE RIBBON BAKERY: Enticing aromas emanate from the espresso machines; fresh cinnamon rolls, muffins, scones, chocolate croissants, giant sticky buns, mini-Bundt cakes, biscotti, jumbo cookies, and demi-baguettes beckon from the display counter; and a chef adds finishing touches to freshly baked cakes and pastries in an open preparation area. Among the less caloric choices: yogurt; vegetables, tuna fish, peppered turkey, or smoked-ham sandwiches in bread pouches;

PHOTO BY JILL SAFRO

and hot chocolate, soft drinks, orange juice, lemonade, fresh-brewed coffee, cappuccino, cafe latte, and cafe mocha (the coffees are served iced or hot). It's hosted by Nestlé Toll House. **B L D** $

GIBSON GIRL ICE CREAM PARLOR: Next door to the Blue Ribbon Bakery, this perennially popular place, with a polished-wood soda fountain, marble countertop, and black-and-white-checkered floor, serves up a delightful array of scoops and toppings in cups, sugar cones, or handmade waffle cones, plain or

dipped in chocolate. Don't be daunted by the long line; it moves fast. **S** $

LITTLE RED WAGON: Between the Main Street Photo Supply Co. and the Plaza Inn, it's a throwback to the delivery trucks of the early 1900s, with ornate beveled and gilded glass panels. Step right up and get your hand-dipped corn dogs, the specialty of the wagon. Lemonade and soft drinks are also served. **L D S** $

MAIN STREET CONE SHOP: Located between Disney Clothiers Ltd. and Market House, behind the fruit cart, this busy window dispenses single or double cones with vanilla, strawberry, chocolate, mocha almond fudge, chocolate chip, and chocolate mint ice cream, and orange sherbet. Two-scoop sundaes are smothered in hot fudge or caramel and topped

Where to Dine with the Characters

Character meals take place at Disneyland's Plaza Inn (breakfast with Minnie and friends), Ariel's Grotto in Disney's California Adventure (Ariel's princess celebration), Paradise Pier Hotel (breakfast with Lilo and Stitch), Storytellers Cafe (breakfast with Chip and Dale) in the Grand Californian Hotel, and Goofy's Kitchen in the Disneyland Hotel (lunch and dinner with Goofy and friends).

with whipped cream and a cherry. Mickey Mouse Ice Cream Bars, apple slices covered with caramel, and soft drinks are also available. Tables with umbrellas provide a pleasant resting spot. **S** **$**

MAIN STREET FRUIT CART: Parked between Disney Clothiers Ltd. and Market House, this old-fashioned cart is stocked with fresh fruit and chilled juices, bottled water, and soft drinks. It's the perfect pit stop for a healthy snack. **S** **$**

MARKET HOUSE: This quaint Victorian-style market offers a generous selection of cookies in tins, tangy dill pickles plucked right from a barrel, dried fruit, and various candies. Hot coffee and ice-cold apple cider are also available. The market is hosted by Hills Bros. **S** **$**

PLAZA INN: On the east side of Central Plaza, this fast-food restaurant is the one Walt Disney was most proud of, and with good reason. Tufted velvet upholstery, gleaming mirrors, and a fine, ornate floral carpet elevate this cafeteria well above similar eateries. Two ceilings are stained glass, framed by elaborate painted moldings. Sconces of Parisian bronze and Baccarat crystal are mounted on the walls, and two dozen basket chandeliers hang from the ceiling.

The setting, including front-porch and terrace dining (with heat lamps at night), creates a lovely backdrop for the food—roast chicken; choice of pasta with marinara, Bolognese, or Alfredo pesto sauce with chicken; pot roast or turkey; Cobb salad; and specialty desserts.

An extremely popular character breakfast is held here daily, from park opening until 11 A.M. Minnie Mouse and her Disney character pals make the rounds, signing autographs and posing for pictures with guests. A fixed-price buffet features made-to-order omelets, scrambled eggs, French toast, Mickey waffles, cheese blintzes, sausage, bacon, fresh fruit, pastries, and more. **B L D S** **$-$$**

REFRESHMENT CORNER: Better known as Coke Corner, this lively eatery at the northern end of Main Street, opposite Main Street Photo Supply Co., is presided over by a talented ragtime pianist who tickles the ivories periodically throughout the day while visitors nibble hot dogs, chili cheese dogs, or chili in a bread bowl. Mickey Mouse pretzels (cheese optional), potato chips, soft drinks, lemonade, and coffee are sold, too. **L D S** **$**

PHOTO BY JILL SAFRO

Adventureland
Fast Food & Snacks

BENGAL BARBECUE: Opposite the entrance to the Jungle Cruise, this is a great place to listen to the rhythms of Alturas while munching on a skewered snack of bacon-wrapped asparagus (a local favorite), or chicken, beef, or veggies. Other menu items include fresh fruit with yogurt topping, Mickey Mouse pretzels, leopard tails (bread sticks), and cinnamon snake twists (pastries). A variety of specialty coffees is also available. **L D S** **$**

TIKI JUICE BAR: Located at the entrance to Walt Disney's Enchanted Tiki Room, this thatched-roof kiosk sells fresh Hawaiian pineapple spears and pineapple juice, but the biggest draw here is the Dole Whip soft-serve—an extremely refreshing pineapple sorbet (it's nondairy). Coffee is also offered. It's presented by Dole Pineapple. **S** **$**

Critter Country
Fast Food & Snacks

CRITTER COUNTRY FRUIT CART: This peddler's cart is filled with healthy selections, including fresh fruit, muffins, dill pickles, chilled bottled water, and soft drinks. It's perfect if you need some fortification after taking the big Splash Mountain plunge. **S** **$**

HARBOUR GALLEY: If you're looking for McDonald's french fries and soft drinks, stop here. If not, keep moving. **S** **$**

B breakfast **L** unch **D** dinner **S** snacks   **$** under $15   **$$** $15–$29   **$$$** $30–$50   **$$$$** $51 and up

New Orleans Square

Table Service

BLUE BAYOU: The lure of this popular dining spot is as much the atmosphere as it is the menu. Occupying a terrace alongside the bayou in the Pirates of the Caribbean attraction, the restaurant appears perpetually moonlit. Fireflies twinkle above bayou grasses, and stars shine through Spanish moss draped languidly over the big, old live oaks. Off in the distance, an old settler rocks away on the porch of a tumbledown shack.

This enchanting Disneyland eatery, located on Royal Street, is one of just three that accept reservations. We advise you to make them as far in advance as possible (up to 60 days), as the restaurant is extremely popular.

For lunch, choose from items like New Orleans–style chowder, Creole gumbo, colorful Mardi Gras salad, jambalaya, and the decadent Monte Cristo sandwiches. Shrimp remoulade, calamari rings with Creole sauce, broiled portobello mushroom with couscous, molasses-brined bayou pork chop, crab cakes, and five-pepper prime rib are served at lunch and dinner.

The dinner menu has featured Cajun spiced salmon, Alaskan king crab legs, and filet mignon. Be sure to save room for pecan pie or crème brûlée. Kids' selections include kid-cut prime rib, citrus chicken drummets, Mickey's cheesy macaroni, and a peanut butter and jelly Monte Cristo sandwich, served with a beverage and dessert.

Note that menu items are subject to change. The busiest periods are from about noon to around 2 P.M. and again from about 5 P.M. until 9 P.M. Reservations are suggested.

`L D` `$$-$$$`

CAFE ORLEANS: A Disneyland classic, this spot recently morphed into a table-service eatery. Guests may dine inside or outside on a terrace overlooking a gristmill on Tom Sawyer Island, and the *Columbia* and the *Mark Twain* plying the Rivers of America.

`B L D S` `$$-$$$`

Fast Food & Snacks

FRENCH MARKET: Beside the old-time train depot in New Orleans Square, this eatery is a destination in its own right.

On a pleasant day, nothing beats sitting on the open-air terrace, munching on fried

HOT TIP!

A gratuity is automatically added to the bill at some Disney restaurants. Examine the bill and tip accordingly.

chicken, beef stew, fettuccine, clam chowder served in a bowl made from a scooped-out loaf of bread, pasta salad, or jambalaya, the house specialty. Cakes are the featured desserts. Children's portions of fried chicken and

Happy Birthday, Disney Style

For starters, it's always a good idea to inform cast members when you are celebrating a special occasion, no matter where you are at the Disneyland Resort. But it also helps to plan ahead. Goofy's Kitchen, at the Disneyland Hotel, hosts birthday parties with characters on hand to help celebrate the occasion. Cost is $5 per birthday "goodie bag," plus the price of the meal.

If you prefer a character-filled party at Disneyland, arrange "My Disneyland Birthday Party" at the Plaza Inn. Mickey and Minnie make a special appearance, as does the Plaza's own wacky baker/host, Pat E. Cake. In addition to cake, everyone in attendance gets a party hat and souvenir sipper cup. Cost is $10 per person. Park admission is required. Reserve at least 5 days ahead.

The Paradise Pier Hotels' PCH Grille has birthday celebrations, too. Cost is $5 per person (plus the meal) and includes party favors.

For more information or to make reservations, call 714-781-3463.

Finally, guests (of all ages) may enjoy a "bucketful of birthday magic" by purchasing a special Disney-themed bucket. Topped with a tiny birthday cake, buckets are filled with birthday treats. They cost about $20 (plus tax) and are available at many Disneyland eateries that offer table service.

fettuccine are available. Music is played onstage periodically throughout the evening; the Royal Street Bachelors hold forth with such spirit that you could listen for hours. It's hosted by Stouffer's. `L D S` `$-$$`

MINT JULEP BAR: Beside the New Orleans Square train station, this window-service bar serves fritters (doughy concoctions), croissants, bagels and cream cheese, biscotti, cookies, ice cream, hot chocolate, coffee, cappuccino, and espresso.

The (alcohol-free) mint juleps taste a bit like lemonade spiked with mint syrup (definitely an acquired taste); happily, real lemonade is also on tap. A variety of sweets and frozen novelties, including Mickey's ice cream sandwiches, round out the selections. Head to one of the tables on the French Market's terrace. `B S` `$`

ROYAL STREET VERANDA: Situated opposite Café Orléans, this little snack stand has bread bowls overflowing with creamy clam chowder, vegetable or steak gumbo (each with a bit of a spicy kick); fritters that come with a fruit dipping sauce; and a variety of beverages. Check out the wrought-iron balustrade above the Royal Street Veranda's small patio. The initials at the center are those of Roy and Walt Disney (this bal-

HOT TIP!
If you plan to celebrate a special event while at the Disneyland Resort (anniversary, honeymoon, engagement, etc.) tell them ahead of time! They can help you make the occasion even more special. Call Disney Dining at 714-781-3463 for more information and to make reservations.

cony belonged to an apartment that was being constructed for Walt before he died). `L D S` `$`

Frontierland
Fast Food & Snacks

CONESTOGA FRIES: The aroma coming from this little chuck wagon is awfully familiar. Yup, McDonald's fries. `S` `$`

RANCHO DEL ZOCALO: Situated by the entrance to Big Thunder Mountain Railroad, this Frontierland eatery features south-of-the-border specialties. Popular Mexican dishes, including tacos and burritos, along with selections such as fire-grilled chicken, tostada salad, and chicken Caesar salad are sure to hit the spot. The food is a cut above the usual theme park fare. `L D S` `$`

PHOTO BY JILL SAFRO

GOOD MEALS, GREAT TIMES

B breakfast **L** lunch **D** dinner **S** snacks   **$** *under $15* **$$** *$15–$29* **$$$** *$30–$50* **$$$$** *$51 and up*

RIVER BELLE TERRACE: The terrace, between the Golden Horseshoe Saloon and the Pirates of the Caribbean, offers one of the best views of the Rivers of America and of the passing throng, and the food is wholesome and hearty. Walt Disney himself used to have breakfast here most Sunday mornings. The menu features scrambled eggs, country-style potatoes, a fruit plate, and cinnamon rolls. Of the breakfast fare, the popularity prize goes to the Mickey Mouse pancakes—a large flapjack for the face, two small pancakes for the ears, a curve of pineapple for the mouth, a cherry for the nose, and berries for the eyes.

For lunch or dinner, the restaurant offers "signature sandwiches" (River Belle's Prime Rib, Mississippi Turkey Breast, Tennessee BBQ Pork, and Vegetable Po' Boy), as well as entrées such as Plantation Prime Rib, Rosemary Turkey Breast, and Aunt Polly's Harvest Medley. Kid's meals (turkey, prime rib, and PB&J sandwiches) come with grapes, sliced apples, and soft drink. With its lovely interior, it's almost as pleasant to dine inside as it is to eat outside. **B L D** **$-$$**

STAGE DOOR CAFE: This small fast-food stand adjoins the Golden Horseshoe Stage and serves french fries, fish sticks, chicken strips, and beverages. A children's meal is available. Grab a seat at a cafe table outside. **L D S** **$**

Sweet Treats

The biggest treat in the park is the "Premium Viewing" package for Fantasmic! Guests enjoy unlimited servings of pastries, fruit, and coffee, tea, and other beverages, plus they see Fantasmic! from the best possible vantage point at the water's edge. At about $47 per adult (kids pay $37), this is a super splurge. The 75 seats sell out quickly, so call 714-781-4000 up to 30 days in advance or sprint to the Guest Relations window at the entrance to the park (it's to the right of the turnstiles) and make your reservation first thing. Check in time is 7 P.M. Seating is first-come, first-served.

Or make a beeline for Main Street, U.S.A., and the Blue Ribbon Bakery, the Gibson Girl Ice Cream Parlor, and the Candy Palace, which has tasty saltwater taffy. And by all means, sample a *churro* (fried dough rolled in cinnamon and sugar) from a food cart—it's quite popular.

Fantasyland
Fast Food & Snacks

ENCHANTED COTTAGE SWEETS 'N' TREATS: Located within the Fantasyland Theatre, this spot is open only during the theater's operating hours, dispensing cheese or pepperoni pizza, hot dogs, potato chips, pretzels, nachos, ice cream and other snack items. **L S** **$**

FANTASIA GARDENS: Next door to the Matterhorn, this cluster of carts can supply a quick post-ride pick-me-up in the form of turkey legs, and a choice of soft drinks. **S** **$**

VILLAGE HAUS: Near Pinocchio's Daring Journey, this house with its gables, pointy roof, and wavy-glass windows could easily have been relocated to Fantasyland from an alpine village. Inside, murals recount the story of Pinocchio. The menu features personal pizzas,

burgers and fries, fruit salad, cookies, and soft drinks. A children's meal is available. **L D S** **$**

Mickey's Toontown
Fast Food & Snacks

CLARABELLE'S: On Toon Squ[...]
Pluto's Dog House, Cl[...]
"udderly" tast[...]
Mous[...]

[...]
i[...]
w[...]
dri[...]
the [...]

GOOF[...]
parked[...]
large fr[...]

118

The Blue moon glow a[...] the French Ma[...] Bachelors perform[...]

The Plaza Inn, for it[...] front-porch seating.

Main[...]

Di[...] orab[...] out the[...]

B breakfast **L** lunch **D** dinner

PLUTO'S DOG HOUSE: Nestled between Clarabelle's and Daisy's Diner, head here for Pluto's Hot Dog Combo, a hot dog served with chips and a large soft drink. Extras include cookies, Pluto's crispie treats, and soft drinks. The kids' meal comes with a small hot dog or mac and cheese, chips, and a small soft drink. `L` `D` `S` `$`

Tomorrowland
Fast Food & Snacks

TOMORROWLAND TERRACE: Near the Premiere Shop, this is one of the largest dining facilities in all of Disneyland. Breakfast choices include scrambled eggs with bacon (or egg substitute with turkey sausage), potatoes, muffin, and beverage; a fruit plate with yogurt dressing, muffin, and beverage; or French toast sticks with powdered sugar, syrup, and fresh fruit.

At lunch and dinner, guests bear trays piled high with fried chicken, corn-on-the-cob, a biscuit, and wedge-cut fries; oversize deli sandwiches; smoked chicken and pepper jack cheese in a wrap with avocado, lettuce, and tomato; Caesar salad with optional grilled chicken; or charbroiled burgers. At full capacity, the eatery can—and often does—handle about 3,000 people an hour. `B` `L` `D` `$`

MOONLINER: Near the entrance to Redd Rockett's Pizza Port, this refreshment stand set in the base of the Moonliner rocket "launches" bottled beverages right into the server's hands (on request). `S` `$`

REDD ROCKETT'S PIZZA PORT: Situated directly across from Innoventions, this food court overlooks the Moonliner and Cosmic Waves. Three food stations serve fresh pasta, pizza, and large salads, all prepared in an open display kitchen.

Menu choices include pizzas (cheese, pepperoni, and a daily special, all sold by the slice or pie), Celestial Caesar Salad, the Planetary Pizza Salad, Mars-inara (spaghetti with tomato sauce), Terra Nova Tomato Basil Pasta, and Count-Down Chicken Fusilli. A beverage counter and cooler supply drinks. The pasta dishes here, though rather basic, are large enough to share. `L` `D` `S` `$-$$`

A+ for Atmosphere

...sney's talent for creating a unique and memor...le setting extends to the eateries through-...e park. For atmosphere, we pick:

New Orleans Square
... Bayou restaurant, for its perpetual ...nd grown-up atmosphere, and ...rket when the Royal Street ...m.

...Street, U.S.A.
...s antiques, charm, and

Critter Country
Hungry Bear restaurant, for a wooded setting that lets you feel in the heart of things, yet curiously removed.

Frontierland
River Belle Terrace, for its pleasant Rivers of America views.

(sidebar, vertical) **GOOD MEALS, GREAT TIMES**

In Disney's California Adventure

PHOTO BY JILL SAFRO

With a winery and an elegant bayside eatery, the tastes at Disney's California Adventure are clearly grown-up. But several fast-food spots and snack stands supply theme park fare with an entertaining flair—retro Hollywood decor or a laid-back surfer setting. Just remember: It's best not to gorge just before riding any of the attractions along Paradise Pier.

Both of the full-service eateries here—Ariel's Grotto and the Vineyard Room—accept reservations. Call 714-781-3463 to book a table.

morning with freshly baked muffins, croissants, and pastries—each, along with a fresh-brewed cup of coffee, is a sweet way to start the day. Brownies, large cookies, and slices of cake round out the tasty options. Refreshing iced specialty coffees and steaming hot brews (including espresso drinks) make the perfect pairing with your pastry of choice. **S** **S**

BUR-R-R BANK ICE CREAM: Cones, shakes, and sundaes are the chilly treats served here. A chocolate-dipped, candy-coated waffle cone piled high with ice cream is a favorite. Expect the line to be longest at midday, when the energy-sapping sun is at its peak. **S** **S**

Hollywood Pictures Backlot

Fast Food & Snacks

AWARD WIENERS: Hot and heaping cheese and chili dogs—with the occasional autograph request or two—are the specialties here. Sausages round out the menu. **S** **S**

Entry Plaza

Fast Food & Snacks

BAKER'S FIELD BAKERY: Follow the enticing aroma that wafts out over California Adventure's entrance area, and you'll end up at this bustling bakery. Shelves are filled each

SCHMOOZIES: Yogurt-and-fruit smoothies are the specialty. For some, these chilly drinks are a meal unto themselves. Lattes, cappuccinos, and other coffees are also available. **S $**

Golden State

Table Service

THE VINEYARD ROOM: This second-story restaurant, divided between an indoor dining area and a covered balcony at this mission-style villa, offers some of the finest (and most expensive) American cuisine on Disneyland property. An à la carte meal (there is one fixed price option, too) is matched by some of the winery's best pressed wines (grape juice is served to teetotalers and guests under 21). It's possible to order from a menu, too. Chefs prepare a selection of appetizers and entrées in serving skillets; the menu constantly evolves to incorporate the season's freshest ingredients. A limited à la carte menu is available on the balcony. Reservations are suggested. **L D $$$-$$$$**

WINE COUNTRY TRATTORIA: Located on the lower level of the mission house at the Golden Vine Winery, this family-friendly spot offers creative Italian cuisine (including vegetarian options). Specialties include lasagna, baked pastas, grilled sandwiches, and soups. California wines are available by the glass or the bottle (of course!). There is a children's menu for the little ones. Dine at one of the shaded tables beside the vineyard. Reservations are recommended. **L D S $-$$**

Fast Food & Snack

COCINA CUCAMONGA MEXICAN GRILL: Tasty corn and flour tortillas are the house specialties and serve as the foundation for most menu items. This cocina cooks steak, pork, and grilled chicken or fish tacos. A creamy, sweet rice pudding makes the perfect finale to the meal. Plan to tour the adjoining tortilla factory before dining at this fast-food spot; the educational trip will make the meal all the more enjoyable. You may even snag a free sample. **L D $-$$**

TASTE PILOTS' GRILL: The juicy patties grilled at this Condor Flats establishment just may leave flame-broiled burger lovers on cloud nine. (These vittles are best enjoyed *after* taking a high-flying voyage at Soarin' Over California next door.) Hot stuff is the name of the game here, so expect items such as ribs, chicken wings, and onion rings to round out the menu. **B L D S $**

PACIFIC WHARF CAFE: At this extension of Boudin's display bakery, guests here have the opportunity to sample some of the country's finest sourdough bread (from a secret family recipe dating back to 1850). Hearty soups and

B breakfast **L** lunch **D** dinner **S** snacks | **$** under $15 **$$** $15–$29 **$$$** $30–$50 **$$$$** $51 and up

salads are served up in thick bread bowls for lunch and dinner. Croissants and muffins are offered in the morning hours. `B L D S` $-$$

RITA'S BAJA BLENDERS: This colorful kiosk next to Cocina Cucamonga serves up slushy fruit drinks and cocktails in your choice of lemon-lime, strawberry, peach, banana, and other flavors. `S` $

Paradise Pier

Table Service

ARIEL'S GROTTO: This character-laden dining spot offers enchanting views of Paradise Pier's amusements and the water below (dinner is especially festive, when the boardwalk is aglow with twinkling lights). What's more, Disney princesses arrive to mingle with diners throughout the day. Guests pay one price and select one item for each course. Fish, salads, and pastas fill the menu. Reservations are suggested. `B L D` $$$

Fast Food & Snacks

BURGER INVASION: An "out of this world" burger stand, it's memorable more for the cheeseburger spaceship that hovers above it than for the food it serves. `L D S` $

CATCH A FLAVE: A selection of refreshing soft-serve flavors helps guests cool off after a long day of fun in the sun. `S` $

CORN DOG CASTLE: Hot dogs, links, and cheese, fried to a golden brown and served on a stick, reign supreme. `L D S` $

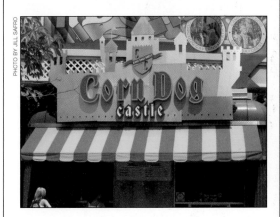

PHOTO BY JILL SAFRO

PIZZA OOM MOW MOW: Surf's up, dude! California's Venice Beach was the inspiration for this pizza place's decor. Surfing memorabilia provide the backdrop for the cheesy entrées of choice—available plain or with a combination of toppings. `L D S` $

In the Disneyland Resort Hotels

Disneyland Hotel

The diverse dining possibilities here range from grand to Goofy. For reservations or information, call 714-781-3463.

CAPTAIN'S GALLEY: Specialty coffees, muffins, bagels, cereal, fruit, kids' meals, and boxed lunches (salads and sandwiches) are sold in this tucked-away shop. Perfect for a poolside meal or a healthy snack. Alcohol, including bottles of California wine, is available. Open June through September. **B L S** **$**

THE COFFEE HOUSE: Order bagels, muffins, pastries, fruit, yogurt, cookies, and coffee in this small shop. Sandwiches and salads are available at lunchtime. Outside seating only. Expect long lines in the morning. **B S** **$**

CROC'S BITS 'N' BITES: Part of the Never Land pool area, it's perfect for a quick burger, grilled chicken sandwich, or ice cream. There's outdoor seating nearby. **S** **$**

PHOTO BY KEITH GROSHANS

GOOFY'S KITCHEN: This whimsical dining room features popular meals and personal encounters with Goofy and other Disney characters. Service here is buffet style, so fill your plate as high and as often as you please. Just be sure to clean your plate!

Highlights at breakfast include Mickey Mouse–shaped waffles and made-to-order omelets. Lunch and dinner offer carved ham, prime rib, pasta, chicken dishes, macaroni and cheese, pizzas (including peanut-butter-and-jelly pizza, a favorite with youngsters and Birnbaum editors alike), salads, breads, fruit, and desserts. Don't forget your camera—characters provide prime photo opportunities. Reservations are suggested (same-day reservations are not accepted, but you can put your name on the standby list). **B L D** **$$-$$$**

HOT TIP!

Expect a long line at The Coffee House in the morning and head to Captain's Galley or La Brea Bakery for a quick breakfast or cup of coffee.

STEAKHOUSE 55: An upscale dining establishment, Steakhouse 55 is decorated with oak paneling and etched glass, and has a nostalgic Hollywood motif featuring pictures of the matinee idols of yesteryear. But the real stars here are the steaks, all cooked to perfection. The menu also boasts pork, lamb, and seafood selections. The specialty of the house is a bone-in rib-eye with a Steakhouse 55 rub that was created especially for this restaurant. The wine list touts fine California vintages. Reservations are suggested. Menu selections are subject to change. **B D** **$$$$**

HOOK'S POINTE & WINE CELLAR: This sophisticated, contemporary dining room overlooks the Never Land pool. Specialties include grilled salmon, seared ahi tuna, Kansas City-style pork chop, and sausage fettuccini. Unique appetizers (including Hook's signature chowder) and desserts round out the menu, along with children's selections. Reservations are suggested. **L D** **$$$**

B breakfast **L** lunch **D** dinner **S** snacks   **$** *under $15* **$$** *$15–$29* **$$$** *$30–$50* **$$$$** *$51 and up*

GOOD MEALS, GREAT TIMES

Disney's Paradise Pier Hotel

It has all the bases covered—from sushi to wood-fired pizza. And wait till you see what Lilo and Stitch have cooked up for breakfast! For reservations, call 714-781-3463.

HOT TIP!
For Japanese dining in the most traditional setting, ask to sit in the Tatami Room at Yamabuki.

DISNEY'S PCH GRILL: Besides hosting a character breakfast with Lilo and Stitch that offers both table service and a buffet, Disney's PCH Grill—the initials stand for Pacific Coast Highway—reflects classic California tastes. The focal point is the open kitchen, which features a large pizza oven. The decor incorporates primary colors and Mickey silhouettes, while the menu, designed like a road map, features tasty American dishes. For lunch or dinner, consider sampling the burgers, sandwiches, or wood-fired specialty pizzas. Kids can "design" their own pizzas. Reservations are suggested. **B L D $$**

YAMABUKI: This restaurant is named after a flower known as the Japanese rose. Authentic traditional and contemporary Japanese dishes are described clearly and concisely on the menu. Japanese beers and sake are served, along with wine and other beverages. In addition to sushi, sashimi, edamame, salads, and miso soup, the menu includes citrus-marinated black cod, grilled *petit* filet mignon with sautéed Japanese ratatouille, shrimp tempura, chicken teriyaki, lemon sake–poached Alaskan halibut, as well as a daily grilled fish special. The children's menu (for ages 3 to 9) includes shrimp, beef, and chicken "bento" boxes and udon noodle soup. The sushi bar offers a fine selection of fresh fish and it rarely has a wait. Reservations are suggested for the dining room. **L* D $$$** (*Lunch weekdays only)

Disney's Grand Californian Hotel & Spa

The restaurants here offer a taste of (and a twist on) California cuisine. For reservations, call 714-781-3463.

NAPA ROSE: This popular, nationally recognized, award-winning restaurant features a creative menu of market-fresh, wine country–inspired dishes flavored by fruits of the sea and vine (the eatery is named after California's most famous valley of vineyards). A striking 20-foot stained-glass window offers sweeping views of Disney's California Adventure, while the open kitchen gives insight into California cooking. The offerings evolve as new items are introduced each season. Selections have

included cashew–crusted red ocean trout, Colorado lamb, roasted breast of pheasant, and braised short rib of Angus beef. A tasting menu (with items selected by the chef) is also an option. The dessert tray offers a trio of citrus temptations: Key lime custard, orange napoleon, and a lemon cream nut tart. The California wine list is one of the most extensive on-property. Reservations are suggested. **D $$$-$$$$**

HEARTHSTONE LOUNGE: Though primarily a drinking spot, this lounge offers appetizers and is open in the morning for early risers in search of coffee and the day's paper. Continental breakfast items are also available. **B S $**

STORYTELLERS CAFE: It's hard to imagine a time before computers and television (especially for the youngest members of the group), when children were exposed to new cultures and histories only through the stories of others. This restaurant salutes tales set in California, like "The Celebrated Jumping Frog of Calaveras County" and "Island of the Blue Dolphin," through murals that act as backdrops to the chefs at work in the exhibition kitchen. In the morning, the stage is set for a

festive, character-hosted buffet. Chip, Dale, and other Disney characters entertain guests, while the buffet offers a bounty of breakfast options, from pancakes and waffles to eggs, sausage, and a selection of fresh fruit. Lunch and dinner offer such pleasers as wood-fired pizzas, homemade pastas, and burgers, plus salads, grilled fish, and spit-roasted chicken. Reservations are suggested. **B L D $$-$$$**

WHITE WATER SNACKS: The splish-splash of the waterfall and kids soaring down the slide at the Redwood pool set the mood for this ultra-casual dining spot. Open for breakfast, lunch, and dinner (though hours vary), the snack bar serves coffee, muffins, bagels, sweet rolls, and breakfast burritos in the morning. Large salads, deli sandwiches, burgers, hot dogs, and grilled chicken are lunch and dinner options. **B L D S $**

CATAL RESTAURANT & UVA BAR: A sun-kissed balcony, outdoor tapas bar, and villa-style dining room set the Mediterranean mood at this casual but classy restaurant. The menu focuses on grilled seafood, chicken, and vegetables, infused with olive oil and citrus accents. With pastas and salads available, vegetarians have much to choose from here. The courtyard bar serves appetizers and cocktails. Reservations are suggested; 714-774-4442. **B L D** **$$$**

COMPASS BOOKS & CAFE: Once they've bought (or browsed) a best seller, bookworms may treat themselves to a coffee break, courtesy of this bookshop's cafe. In addition to beverages (coffees, teas, and smoothies), light fare and pastries are available. **S** **$**

ESPN ZONE: This spot serves up baskets of ballpark fare, plus items like grilled chops and New York strip steaks. If you want to get close to the action, you'll want a table (and be prepared to place an order). Hard-core fans may want to ask about the leather easy chairs complete with sound systems and serving tables. If there's a big game on the schedule, plan to arrive at least an hour early. **L D S** **$$**

HAAGEN-DAZS: The dessert specialist has ice cream, frozen yogurt, sorbet, and gelato—as well as baked goods and coffee. **S** **$**

HOUSE OF BLUES: Diners with a craving for Southern cookin' will find bliss at this Delta dive (all part of the theme). With a menu set deep in the South, the eatery offers items such as Memphis-style ribs, voodoo shrimp, jambalaya, and tasty thin-crust pizzas. On Sundays, guests sing hallelujah for the all-you-can-eat Southern-style Gospel Brunch (gospel touring groups provide the stirring entertainment). Reservations are suggested; 714-778-2583 or 714-781-3463. **B L D** **$$$**

JAMBA JUICE: In the mood for a tropical smoothie? Perhaps one with protein or a berry blast? They've got that and more. **S** **$**

LA BREA BAKERY: The offerings at this casual Downtown Disney spot—breakfast treats, grilled panini sandwiches, and crostini (small, open-face sandwiches)—are built on

their legend... blends up hea... plus coffees. W... brewed beers are...

NAPLES RISTORAN... indoors or alfresco at t... trattoria. A large outdoor... perfect views of the Disney... peaceful and romantic settin... or dinner. Pizzas are served in indivi... portions or *al metro* (one meter long and perfect for a hungry family to share). The menu also includes *piccoli piatti* (small salads served tapas style), pasta dishes, and seafood entrées. Seating is on a first-come, first-served basis. **L D** **$$$**

NAPOLINI: Adjacent to the popular Naples Ristorante e Pizzeria, this quick-serve spot also offers Italian fare, but on the lighter side than that served by its neighbor. **L D** **$$**

RAINFOREST CAFE: Greenery, misty waterfalls, tropical storms, mechanical animals, and several real-life creatures create a sometimes hectic, always colorful atmosphere in this spot. The menu features sizable environmentally themed appetizers and entrées, including pastas, burgers, and sandwiches. Reservations, which are available up to one year in advance, are recommended; call 714-772-0413 at least two weeks ahead. **B L D S** **$$-$$$**

RALPH BRENNAN'S JAZZ KITCHEN: Sample some home-style New Orleans specialties at this comfy cafe while listening to jazz. Gumbo, jambalaya, chicken, and fresh pasta dishes are house favorites. Reservations are suggested; 714-781-3463. **L D S** **$$-$$$**

TORTILLA JO'S: A colorful Mexican restaurant and open-air cantina, this spot offers a mix of culinary traditions including taquitos, quesadillas, hand-made tortillas, made-to-order (scrumptious) guacamole, and lime-marinated ceviches. Reservations are suggested; 714-781-3463. **L D S** **$$-$$$**

WETZEL'S PRETZELS: Whether you prefer pretzels salty or sweet, Wetzel's can satisfy. Ambitious snackers enjoy the Sinful Cinnamon and the Cheese Meltdown. **S** **$**

Restaurant Roundup

There are more dining choices than ever before at the Disneyland Resort. We've picked our favorites, based on food quality, restaurant atmosphere, and overall value. Use these Birnbaum's Bests to help you decide where to grab a quick bite or have a hearty meal.

BEST RESTAURANTS FOR FAMILIES

TABLE SERVICE

Goofy's Kitchen ....Disneyland Hotel (p. 122)
Blue Bayou ....Disneyland Park (p. 115)
Storytellers Cafe ....Grand Californian Hotel (p. 124)
Rainforest Cafe ....Downtown Disney (p. 125)

FAST FOOD

Royal Street Veranda ....Disneyland Park (p. 116)
Rancho del Zocalo ....Disneyland Park (p. 116)
Refreshment Corner ....Disneyland Park (p. 114)
Pacific Wharf Cafe ....California Adventure (p. 120)
Award Wieners ....California Adventure (p. 119)

BEST PIZZA

Naples Ristorante e Pizzeria
Downtown Disney (p. 125)

BEST SUSHI

Yamabuki
Paradise Pier Hotel (p. 123)

BEST QUICK SERVICE

Rancho del Zocalo
Disneyland Park (p. 116)

BEST CHARACTER MEAL

Goofy's Kitchen ....Disneyland Hotel (p. 122)

RUNNERS-UP

Ariel's Grotto.....................California Adventure (p. 121)
Plaza Inn ....Disneyland (p. 114)
Storytellers Cafe ....Grand Californian Hotel (p. 124)

BEST RESTAURANTS FOR ADULTS

Catal Restaurant and Uva Bar........................Downtown Disney (p. 125)
Napa Rose..Grand Californian Hotel (p. 123)

RUNNERS-UP

Hook's Pointe & Wine Cellar ....Disneyland Hotel (p. 122)
Ralph Brennan's Jazz Kitchen ....Downtown Disney (p. 125)
Steakhouse 55 ....Disneyland Hotel (p. 122)

BEST SNACKS

Blue Ribbon Bakery...........................Disneyland Park (p. 112)
Bur-r-r Bank Ice Cream ....California Adventure (p. 119)

GOOD MEALS, GREAT TIMES

126

Entertainment
Disney Hotels

There's more to Disney than thrill rides and characters. Whether you're looking for a break from the parks or a place to party the night away, the following options are sure to please. There's plenty to do at Disney's three hotels and in Downtown Disney. We've also included some Anaheim-area options for those interested in venturing beyond Disney borders.

Note: For additional information on evening theme park happenings, refer to the *Disneyland Park* and *Disney's California Adventure* chapters of this book.

Lounges

DISNEYLAND HOTEL: The cozy **Wine Cellar** is located on the lower level of Hook's Pointe & Wine Cellar (pictured below) and serves California wines by the bottle, glass, or taste. The **Lounge at Steakhouse 55**, with its leaded-glass door, brass rails, and striking watercolor of the Anaheim orange groves circa 1962, provides an intimate meeting place.

An open-air lounge, offering a menu long enough that the place could almost be called a restaurant (burgers, sandwiches, and such are served), the **Lost Bar** is this hotel's most happening hot spot, especially when the resident musicians are performing. Outdoor tables are kept toasty warm by the heat lamps that are lit each evening. The Lost Bar tends to stay open as late as, or later than, other Disneyland lounges.

DISNEY'S GRAND CALIFORNIAN HOTEL: The lounge adjoining the elegant Napa Rose restaurant offers an extensive selection of wines by the glass and a soothing atmosphere.

At the handsome **Hearthstone Lounge**, you can sip a cocktail or after-dinner cordial opposite a roaring fireplace. If so inclined, you may enjoy your beverage on a comfy couch in the majestic lobby, where live piano music is always a possibility.

DISNEY'S PARADISE PIER HOTEL: The small lobby **Coffee Bar & Lounge** has perhaps the only cappuccino maker and "Henri Rousseau" print with Mickey ears in existence. It serves lunch and has a "grab and go" section.

The small, inviting lounge inside the Yamabuki restaurant is a quiet retreat and the perfect place to join friends for a nightcap.

Live Entertainment

DISNEYLAND HOTEL: Hear music on select nights and watch sporting events on others at The Lost Bar.

DISNEY'S GRAND CALIFORNIAN HOTEL: As a tribute to the early 1900s storytelling tradition, entertainers tell tall tales in the hotel's main lobby throughout the day. A piano player adds to the ambience.

Fun & Games

DISNEYLAND HOTEL: Kids can steer small, remote-control Jungle Cruise Boats by the hotel's lagoon. The beach's volleyball court is a hit, especially in the afternoon; the Game Arcade in the shopping enclave scores high points on evenings when the parks close early.

DISNEY'S PARADISE PIER HOTEL: Youngsters have a blast at this hotel's arcade, located off the main lobby.

GOOD MEALS, GREAT TIMES

127

Downtown Disney

Easily accessed by foot (from the Disneyland Resort hotels or theme parks) or monorail (from Disneyland Park's Tomorrowland), this entertainment district offers escape from the hustle and bustle during the day, and a place to mix and mingle in the evening hours. Many Downtown Disney venues serve double (or triple) duty—as dining and dancing (and sometimes shopping) spots.

Shops open early and don't close until late in the evening. Club performers generally hit the stage post-dinner and wrap past midnight.

Clubs & Concerts

HOUSE OF BLUES: Don't let the name of this jumping joint fool you—the lineup features a rousing mix of rock, R & B, hip-hop, reggae, and Latin music, along with a touch of the blues. Big-name bands and local acts are slotted to perform throughout the week. Call 714-778-2583 to learn the House's schedule during your visit. Ticket prices range from about $5 to $30, depending on the performer. Call TicketMaster or visit *www.ticketmaster.com* to purchase tickets in advance, or stop by the club's box office the day of the performance.

RALPH BRENNAN'S JAZZ KITCHEN: The sounds of jazz set the tone for the relaxed atmosphere at this restaurant's lounge. Bands and singers entertain on select days of the week. A smooth sound track provides music when the stage is dark. Special tickets may be required for certain performances. Call 714-776-5200 to inquire about ticket reservations.

Lounges

CATAL RESTAURANT AND UVA BAR: Designed to resemble the Art Nouveau–style of a Paris metro station, this large wine-and-tapas bar tempts guests with the fruits of the vine and sea. Guests can drink under the stars at the outdoor bar or mingle indoors, and can select from the extensive wine list.

ESPN ZONE: Stop by the bar area of the Zone's Studio Grill for a tall one before heading upstairs to play arcade games at the Sports Arena. With large-screen TVs blaring from each section of the room, expect the joint to be jumping on big-game nights.

MAGIC MUSHROOM BAR: Part of the lush Rainforest Cafe, this circular drinking hole is capped by a giant mushroom and serves up aptly named blended beverages, such as the Margarilla and the Tropical Toucan (nonalcoholic versions are also available). Don't be surprised if a tot takes over a neighboring stool—this establishment is a big family spot.

Shopping

ANNE GEDDES: This vivid emporium showcases photos, clothing (the baby bunny suit is beyond precious), and gift items from the photographer for whom it is named.

BASIN: Indulge in the lavish bath and body products available at this inviting boutique.

BUILD-A-BEAR WORKSHOP: Create your own stuffed animal, as you "choose, stuff, stitch, fluff, name, and dress" your way through a series of bear-making stations. It's a "beary" special experience.

CLUB LIBBY LU: "It's a girl thing!" is the motto of this club for kids. Makeovers, parties, and assorted "fun stuff" mean fun and entertainment for the young and feminine.

COMPASS BOOKS AND CAFE: This branch of the West's oldest (since 1851) independent bookstore is heavy on the travel tomes, and also features a coffee bar and outdoor newsstand.

DEPARTMENT 56: 'Tis always the season to be jolly at this shop featuring miniature houses and other holiday collectibles.

DISNEY PIN TRADERS: Do we really need to tell you what this spot specializes in? Didn't think so.

DISNEY VAULT 28: A chic boutique, this spot showcases trendy items designed by local artists and cutting-edge merchandise inspired by Disney characters and films.

FOSSIL: Got the time? They do! Stop here for watches galore, plus fashionable leather goods, T-shirts, hats, and jewelry.

HOUSE OF BLUES COMPANY STORE: A slew of spicy sauces lets you take a bit of this House back to your house. Home accessories and House of Blues logo merchandise round out the options here.

ILLUMINATIONS: Light up your life with an assortment of handcrafted candles, aromatherapy products, and accessories.

ISLAND CHARTERS: Ahoy! This shop offers one-of-a-kind nautical and aviation gifts for seafarers and landlubbers alike.

LEGO IMAGINATION CENTER: Four hundred of the world's most famous building brick sets and products are for sale, along with Lego shirts, hats, and other apparel.

MARCELINE'S CONFECTIONERY: Named for Walt Disney's childhood hometown, this sweetshop offers classic and contemporary candies and other treats.

QUICKSILVER: Surfer wear and accessories help guests dress the part of beachcomber.

RAINFOREST SHOP: Adjacent to the Rainforest Cafe, this shop sells lush animals, environmentally themed toys, Rainforest Cafe logo items, and snacks.

SEPHORA: A black-and-white motif provides a perfect backdrop for the colorful palette of products in this cosmetics mecca. Sephora's own line of makeup and bath products is complemented by a selection of popular beauty products and perfumes. It's possible to create personalized gift baskets, too.

SOMETHING SILVER: Perfect for celebrating a 25th anniversary, or just creating a look, the jewelry here is simple and stylish. Note that there are many lovely non-silver selections to choose from, too.

SPORTSCENTER STUDIO STORE: Sports fans will cheer over the ESPN, SportsCenter, and Monday Night Football–branded apparel and other merchandise at this shop within the ESPN Zone.

STARABILIAS: Shoppers can walk down memory lane at this spot, which showcases TV, movie, music, and political memorabilia.

SUNGLASS ICON: Cool, custom-fit shades are the stock-in-trade at this shop. All the big name designers are represented.

WORLD OF DISNEY: Shelves are stacked sky-high at this souvenir shopper's dream come true. Each overflowing room features a different theme and type of merchandise: the Lion King room is well suited to adult apparel, while Disney Villains add dastardly decor to the watch and accessories department. With an entire room dedicated to plush toys, and rooms for dolls, figurines, toys, videos, clothing, and collectibles, everyone is bound to find something here. Expect the place to be packed most evenings and on weekends.

Fun & Games

AMC MOVIE THEATRES: Moviegoers enjoy wall-to-wall movie screens and comfy stadium seating at each of the 12 cinemas located inside this megaplex. Current releases are shown throughout the day, with special matinee and late-night screenings. The first showing of the day usually comes at a discount.

ESPN ZONE: This sports shrine offers dining options and a lounge area, plus two distinct fun zones. In the Screening Room, sports fans can cheer their teams to victory, as games from around the world are televised on one central 16-foot screen and a dozen 36-inch monitors.

The Sports Arena challenges guests with sports-themed games that put your skills, strength, and smarts to the test. Game cards (necessary to play the arena's games) can be purchased in $5 increments.

Beyond the Disneyland Resort

Clubs & Concerts

CERRITOS CENTER FOR THE PERFORMING ARTS: This theater presents popular artists, musicians, dance companies, and Broadway shows. Performers have included the Alvin Ailey American Dance Theater, Trisha Yearwood, and Bernadette Peters. 12700 Center Court Dr.; Cerritos; 562-916-8501 or 800-300-4345; *www.cerritoscenter.com*.

HONDA CENTER: Besides being the home of the 2007 Stanley Cup–champion Anaheim Ducks, the Center hosts sporting events, ice shows, and concerts, from rap to country. Alcohol and open-flame barbecues are not allowed in the parking lot. 2695 E. Katella Ave.; Anaheim; *www.hondacenter.com*; 714-704-2500.

HYATT REGENCY NEWPORT BEACH SUMMER JAZZ SERIES: On Friday nights from June through October, jazz artists perform in the hotel's amphitheater. Tickets cost $45 to $90. 1107 Jamboree Rd.; Newport Beach; 949-729-6400; *www.summerjazzseries.com*.

IMPROV COMEDY CLUBS: Two sister comedy venues present shows three to six nights a week; call or visit *www.improv.com* for current schedules and headliners. 4555 Mills Circle; Ontario; 909-484-5411; and 71 Fortune Dr. #841; Irvine; 949-854-5455.

ORANGE COUNTY PERFORMING ARTS CENTER: This complex of theaters presents a variety of performing artists including orchestras, opera and dance companies, and Broadway tours in the larger concert hall in addition to chamber music, cabaret, and jazz concerts in the more intimate spaces. Concessions and a fine-dining restaurant are on-site. 600 Town Center Dr.; Costa Mesa; 714-556-2787; *www.ocpac.org*.

Dinner Theater

MEDIEVAL TIMES: Guests feast on several courses served by wenches and knaves while knights on horseback twist and joust. 7662 Beach Blvd.; Buena Park; 888-935-6878 or 714-521-4740; *www.medievaltimes.com*.

PLAZA GARIBALDI: It's a Mexican fiesta with mariachis, singers, dancers, traditional food, margaritas, and more. 500 N. Brookhurst; Anaheim; 714-758-9014; *www.plazagaribaldi.com*.

Lounges

In Anaheim, **JT Schmid's Restaurant & Brewery**, across the road from the Honda Center, has home-brewed ales, with gleaming vats on view; 2610 E. Katella Ave..; 714-634-9200; *www.jtschmids.com*. In nearby Orange, the **Alcatraz Brewing Co.** is ensconced in the lively Block at Orange; 20 City Blvd. West; Orange; www.*alcatrazbrewing.com*; 714-939-8686. On the coast, the **Huntington Beach Beer Company** mixes brews with ocean-view seating; 201 Main St. East; Huntington Beach; 714-960-5343; *www.hbbeerco.com*.

The **National Sports Grill** has sports memorabilia, 4 big-screen TVs, 80 TVs, and 11 pool tables; 450 N. State College Blvd.; Orange; 714-935-0300; *www.nationalsportsgrill.com*.

Fun & Games

THE BLOCK AT ORANGE: This outdoor entertainment complex, a mere three miles from Disneyland, has a 30-screen **AMC Theatres**, **Dave & Buster's**, and **The Powerhouse**, a state-of-the-art arcade. Valet parking available. 20 City Blvd. West; Orange; 714-769-4001; *www.theblockatorange.com*.

Sports

Southern California's appealing combination of warm, sunny weather and invigorating ocean breezes has created a population of outdoors and exercise enthusiasts. Well-toned athletes flex their muscles on golf courses and tennis courts; atop surfboards, bicycles, and in-line skates; on hiking and jogging trails; or 15 feet underwater, mingling with schools of fish.

In Orange County alone, there are more than 35,000 acres of parkland and several hundred miles of bike trails. Hiking paths and fishing streams crisscross 460,000 acres of mountain terrain in Cleveland National Forest. Just 15 miles south of Anaheim, prime Pacific Ocean beaches, perfect for basking in the sun or catching the ultimate wave, await the wayfarer. In fact, 42 miles of glistening sand and sleepy seaside communities lie within an hour's drive of Anaheim.

Those who delight in spying on Mother Nature can catch glimpses of California's gray whales as they migrate to Mexico for the winter, or ospreys, blue herons, and swallows returning to the area in the spring. A team of Orange County's most entertaining creatures, hockey-playing Ducks, can be spotted from September through April (and later, if they make another run for the Stanley Cup). Even Angels have been sighted, gracing the bases at Angel Stadium, April through September (and possibly October!).

To be sure, the sporting life in Orange County is bountiful.

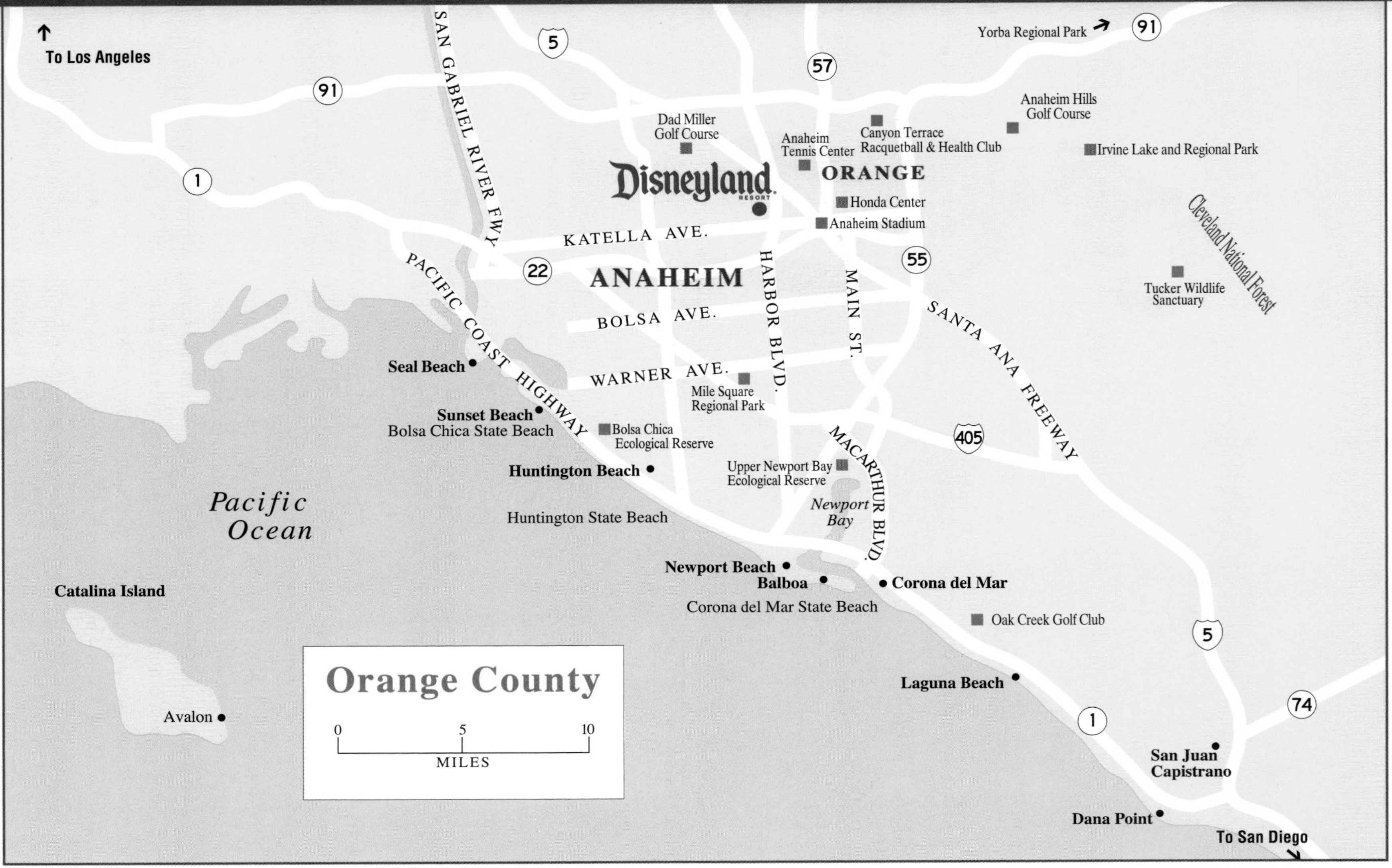

Orange County

To Los Angeles

91

5

SAN GABRIEL RIVER FWY.

1

Yorba Regional Park

91

57

5

Irvine Lake and Regional Park

Anaheim Hills
Golf Course

Cleveland National Forest

Tucker Wildlife
Sanctuary

Canyon Terrace Racquetball & Health Club

ORANGE

Honda Center

Anaheim
Tennis Center

Anaheim Stadium

Dad Miller
Golf Course

Disneyland RESORT

KATELLA AVE.

ANAHEIM

22

HARBOR BLVD.

BOLSA AVE.

MAIN ST.

55

SANTA ANA FREEWAY

405

WARNER AVE.

Mile Square
Regional Park

Bolsa Chica
Ecological Reserve

PACIFIC COAST HIGHWAY

Seal Beach •

Sunset Beach •
Bolsa Chica State Beach

Huntington Beach •
Huntington State Beach

Upper Newport Bay
Ecological Reserve

*Newport
Bay*

MACARTHUR BLVD.

Corona del Mar •

Newport Beach •
Balboa •

Corona del Mar State Beach

Oak Creek Golf Club

Laguna Beach •

1

5

74

**San Juan
Capistrano** •

Dana Point •

To San Diego

*Pacific
Ocean*

Catalina Island

Avalon •

0	5	10

MILES

Eye on the Ball

Golf

ANAHEIM HILLS GOLF COURSE: This challenging championship course is a hilly, par-71, 6,245-yard layout nestled in the valleys and slopes of the scenic Anaheim Hills. Greens fees are $45 Monday through Thursday, $54 on Friday, and $60 on weekends and holidays, cart included. Guests ages 55 and older can play Monday through Thursday for $31, and Fridays for $36. Clubs can be rented for $15. Reservations are recommended (call seven days ahead for both weekend and weekday play). 6501 Nohl Ranch Rd.; Anaheim; 714-998-3041; *www.playanaheimgolf.com.*

DAD MILLER GOLF COURSE: "Dad" Miller made a hole in one on this course (on the 116-yard 11th hole) when he was 93 years old, and it's still a favorite with older guests, who appreciate the flat, walkable terrain and park-like setting. But if you're a tad on the younger side, don't let that keep you from playing here. This par-71, 6,025-yard golf course is one of the busiest in California—partly because of its

HOT TIP!

To get the scoop on these and other Orange County area golf courses, tournaments, and golf vacation packages, visit *www.playocgolf.com.*

convenient location in the northwest corner of the city, but also because it's just right for the strictly recreational golfer. The cost to play here is $25 Monday through Thursday, $33 on Friday, $37 on Saturday, Sunday and holidays. Guests 62 and older can play standby for only $14 Monday through Friday. Golf carts cost $24 for 18 holes, $15 for nine holes.

Reservations are suggested, and may be made up to a week in advance. 430 N. Gilbert St.; Anaheim; 714-765-3481 (pro shop and reservations); *www.playanaheimgolf.com.*

Tennis & Racquetball

ANAHEIM TENNIS CENTER: This public facility has all the perks of a private tennis club—an inviting clubhouse, a well-stocked pro shop, computerized practice machines, lockers, and showers. The accommodating staff will even try to pair you with a suitable partner, if you make a request in advance.

There are 12 fast, hard-surface courts, all lighted for night play. Singles and doubles rates range from $4.50 to $8 per person per hour, depending on time of day. Use of ball machines is about $20 per hour; they are separated from the courts, but this area is still a good place to practice forehand and backhand strokes.

Playing hours begin at 8 A.M. and end at 10 P.M. Monday through Friday, and 5 P.M. weekends and holidays. Racquets rent for $3 for those who are taking lessons. Locker and shower facilities are free (you must supply towels). A half-hour private lesson with the resident pro costs $30; call for rates for semiprivate and group lessons.

Reservations (bookable up to three days in advance for

nonmembers) are suggested, especially for court times after 5 P.M. It's approximately three miles from Disneyland. 975 S. State College Blvd.; Anaheim; 714-991-9090; *www.anaheimtenniscenter.com*.

CANYON TERRACE RACQUETBALL AND HEALTH CLUB: A real find for visitors, this facility has five air-conditioned racquetball courts and low court fees—$8 per person on weekends or before 3:30 P.M. Monday through Friday. After 3:30 P.M. it is $9 for one or two players and $8 for three or four players. The club rents racquets for $2 to $4 and offers its full-size weight room to nonmembers for $7. Towels may also be rented for a small fee. There is a pro shop, too. Hours are 5:30 A.M. to 10 P.M. Monday through Thursday, 5:30 A.M. to 9 P.M. Friday, 7 A.M. to 7 P.M. weekends. 100 N. Tustin Ave.; Anaheim; 714-974-0280.

Spectator Sports

BASEBALL

Los Angeles Angels of Anaheim (April–September): Angel Stadium of Anaheim; 2000 E. Gene Autry Way; Anaheim; call 714-634-2000 or visit *www.angelsbaseball.com*

Los Angeles Dodgers (April–September): Dodger Stadium; 1000 Elysian Park Ave.; Los Angeles; 323-224-1500; *www.dodgers.com*

BASKETBALL

Los Angeles Clippers (October–April): Staples Center; 1111 S. Figueroa St.; Los Angeles; 800-462-2849; *www.nba.com/clippers*

Los Angeles Lakers (October–April): Staples Center; 1111 S. Figueroa St.; Los Angeles; 800-462-2849; *www.nba.com/lakers*

Los Angeles Sparks (May–August): Staples Center; 1111 S. Figueroa St.; Los Angeles; 310-426-6033; *www.wnba.com/sparks*

HOCKEY

Los Angeles Kings (October–April): Staples Center; 1111 S. Figueroa St.; Los Angeles; 213-480-3232 (Ticketmaster); *www.lakings.com*

Anaheim Ducks (September–April): Honda Center; 2965 E. Katella Ave.; Anaheim; 213-480-3232 (Ticketmaster); *www.anaheimducks.com*

Surf & Sun

Beaches

Orange County's public beaches cover 42 miles of coastline—some dramatic, with high cliffs and crashing waves; others tranquil, with sheltered coves and tide pools. In summer, the water temperature averages 64 degrees but can get as high as 70; in winter, it's a nippy 57 to 60 degrees.

Beaches are open from around 6 A.M. to 10 P.M., with lifeguards on duty in the summer. Bicycles, in-line skates, and roller skates are available for rent. Public access is free, but parking in beach lots costs about $7. For more beach info, go to *www.surfline.com*.

BALBOA/NEWPORT BEACH: The Balboa Peninsula juts into the Pacific Ocean, creating beaches—Newport on the mainland, Balboa on the peninsula—that are long and horse-shoe-shaped, pleasant and sandy, and popular with families, surfers, and sightseers alike; *www.newportbeach.com*.

The largest small-craft harbor in the world, Newport Harbor shelters more than 9,000 boats. For the best view, drive south along the peninsula on Newport Blvd. to Balboa Blvd.; turn right on Palm St., and you'll find parking for the Balboa Pier and Fun Zone; *www.thebalboafunzone.com*.

> ### HOT TIP!
> For a scenic 45-minute walk, follow the harbor-hugging pathway around Balboa Island. For a mini-expedition, head to Little Balboa Island—it can be easily circumnavigated in about 20 minutes.

Throughout the fall and winter, the 1,000-acre Upper Newport Bay Nature Preserve and Ecological Reserve teems with great blue herons, ospreys, and other winged creatures. The park's partially subterranean Interpretive Center, at Irvine Ave. and University Dr., features exhibits on bird life, the watershed, and the history of Newport Bay.

During the migratory season (October through March), Newport Bay Naturalists and Friends leads free walking tours on the second Saturday of the month, pointing out birds, as well as fossils, marsh plants, and fish.

The reserve is generally open daily 7 A.M. to sunset. To get there from Anaheim, follow I-5 south to Highway 55 (which becomes Newport Blvd.) to Pacific Coast Highway south; turn left onto Jamboree Rd., take the first left onto Back Bay Drive.

To obtain updated driving directions and information about guided tours and various special events year-round, contact Newport Bay Naturalists and Friends (naturalists are on hand to give information on Tuesdays, Thursdays, and Saturdays); 949-640-6746; *www.newportbay.org*.

CORONA DEL MAR STATE BEACH: Secluded Corona del Mar State Beach is a favorite for swimming and snorkeling; and the lookout point above the beach is a great place to watch the sun set. There are picnic tables, grills, fire rings, a snack bar, and showers. For information, call 949-644-3151; *www.ocbeachinfo.com*.

HUNTINGTON BEACH: The self-proclaimed "Surf City, U.S.A." hosts competitions year-round (winter is best for wave height). Surfboards and wet suits may be rented or purchased; *www.surfcityusa.com*.

The long stretch of sand fronting the town is a popular place for jogging and beach volleyball. The pier provides an ideal spot for fishing and a good vantage point for observing the passing scene. For surf information, call 714-536-9303; *www.surfline.com*.

Bolsa Chica Ecological Reserve, 1,200 acres of Pacific Ocean marshland a mile north of Huntington Beach pier on Pacific Coast Highway, harbors fish, sea hares, and wetland birds. To get there, cross the bridge from the beach parking lot and follow a trail through the marsh; 714-846-1114; *www.bolsachica.org*.

LAGUNA BEACH: Thirty different beaches and coves line this seven-mile coastline, popular with surfers, kayakers, body boarders, and snorkelers. Laguna is one of the best spots in Orange County to scuba dive, though you need a wet suit year-round.

Laguna Sea Sports (925 N. Coast Hwy.; 949-494-6965; *www.lagunaseasports.com*) offers full rentals, guided beach dives, classes, general information, and more; there's a pool on the premises, and it's only about one block from the beach. Main Beach (the central strip of sand) offers basketball and volleyball courts as well as a playground.

A short walk from here, Heisler Park has picnic areas, beaches for swimming and sunning, cliff-top lookout points, lawn bowling, and shuffleboard; stairs lead to tide pools. Serious hikers like to head for Crystal Cove State Park, Aliso and Wood Canyons Wilderness Park, or Laguna Coast Wilderness Park. Watch the sun set from the gazebo near the art museum or from Laguna Village; *www.lagunabeach.com.*

Fishing

In Orange County, you can cast for bass, catfish, and trout in tranquil lakes; troll the Pacific for bonitos, barracuda, halibut, and more; and scoop grunions off the beach.

FRESHWATER ANGLING: At Irvine Lake, no fishing license is required, and there is no charge for catching fish, but there are restrictions on the type and amount of fish that can be caught. Gate fees are $20 for adults ($17 for guests 62 and older) and $9 for children 4 through 12; under 4 free; *www.irvinelake.net.*

Fishing poles, motorboats, rowboats, and pontoons may be rented, or you can launch your own craft for a $10 fee. A tackle shop and cafe are on-site. 4621 Santiago Canyon Rd.; Silverado; 714-649-9111.

GRUNION ALERT: One place to try your hand—literally—at catching grunion is at Bolsa Chica State Beach in March, June, July, and August, when the tiny fish come ashore to lay eggs in the sand and then head back out to sea on outgoing waves. They're slippery, and you have to catch them with your hands; fortunately, they also shimmer in the moonlight so they're fairly easy to spot. The best time to go: about an hour or two after high tide on the second through fifth nights after a new or full moon. For additional information, visit *www.dfg.ca.gov* or *www.parks.ca.gov* or call 714-846-3460.

Note: Grunion-catching is illegal in April and May. A fishing license is required for anyone 16 and older. The park closes at 10 P.M; gates close at 9 P.M.

SPORTFISHING: Boats set out from Davey's Locker, at the Balboa Pavilion in Newport Beach (949-673-1434; *www.daveyslocker.com*), and from Dana Wharf Sportfishing, at Dana Point Harbor (named for Richard Henry Dana, who wrote *Two Years Before the Mast*; 800-979-3370; *www.danawharfsportfishing.com*). Reservations are suggested. Licenses, necessary for deep-sea sportfishing, are available at either location and cost about $13.80 per day.

Parks

IRVINE REGIONAL PARK: Located in Santiago Canyon, near Irvine Lake, this peaceful place has hiking and equestrian trails that wind through 477 hilly acres and centuries-old sycamores and oaks. The oldest county park in California, it offers bike trails, the Orange County Zoo, playgrounds, and a small waterfall, lake, and picnic facilities. There is a $3 to $5 parking fee per vehicle year-round ($7–$10 on major holidays). 1 Irvine Park Rd.; Orange; 714-973-6835; *www.ocparks.com/irvinepark.*

MILE SQUARE REGIONAL PARK: It's one square mile in area—thus the name. Besides five miles of winding bike trails, the park has a walking course, a nature area detailing the park's plant and animal life, and picnic areas and shelters. Bicycles may be rented here on weekends and holidays. 16801 Euclid Ave.; Fountain Valley; 714-973-6600; *www.ocparks.com/milesquare.*

TUCKER WILDLIFE SANCTUARY: This 12-acre sanctuary in the Santa Ana Mountains' Modjeska Canyon is an oasis of flowers, plants, and wildlife. Naturalists answer questions, and there are hiking trails. A donation is suggested. 29322 Modjeska Canyon Rd.; Silverado; 714-649-2760; *http://nsm.fullerton.edu/tucker.*

YORBA REGIONAL PARK: These 175 acres in the Anaheim Hills cradle four lakes, picnic areas, playgrounds, and hiking trails, equestrian activities, horseshoe pits, model sailboating, volleyball courts, baseball fields, and biking (bike rentals on weekends). Visitors can walk or bike into the park without charge; parking is $3 to $5 ($7–$10 on holidays). 7600 E. La Palma Ave.; Anaheim; 714-973-6615; *www.ocparks.com/yorbapark.*

Orange County & Beyond

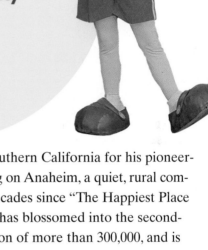

Walt Disney considered several spots in Southern California for his pioneering amusement park before finally settling on Anaheim, a quiet, rural community dominated by orange groves. In the decades since "The Happiest Place on Earth" welcomed its first guests, Anaheim has blossomed into the second-largest city in Orange County, with a population of more than 300,000, and is home to a Major League Baseball team, a National Hockey League team, and the largest convention center on the West Coast.

Like Anaheim, Buena Park is filled with family-oriented attractions; Santa Ana, the county's largest city, is developing an impressive museum mile; and Orange emanates small-town charm, with cafes, one-of-a-kind shops, and even an old-fashioned soda fountain. The beach communities of Newport and Laguna mix seaside culture with a vibrant arts scene, while nearby San Juan Capistrano bears witness to the area's mission heritage.

An hour's drive north from Anaheim, and a fun excursion, Los Angeles is a dynamic mix of culture, glamour, museums, shops, restaurants, and entertainment venues, interspersed with parks, palm trees, and traffic. Due west of L.A., legendary beaches attract beauty and brawn like a magnet. A 90-minute drive south from Anaheim, along coast-hugging I-5, leads to Legoland California, in Carlsbad, and to San Diego, with its world-famous zoo. There's no doubt about it: Southern California has something for everyone.

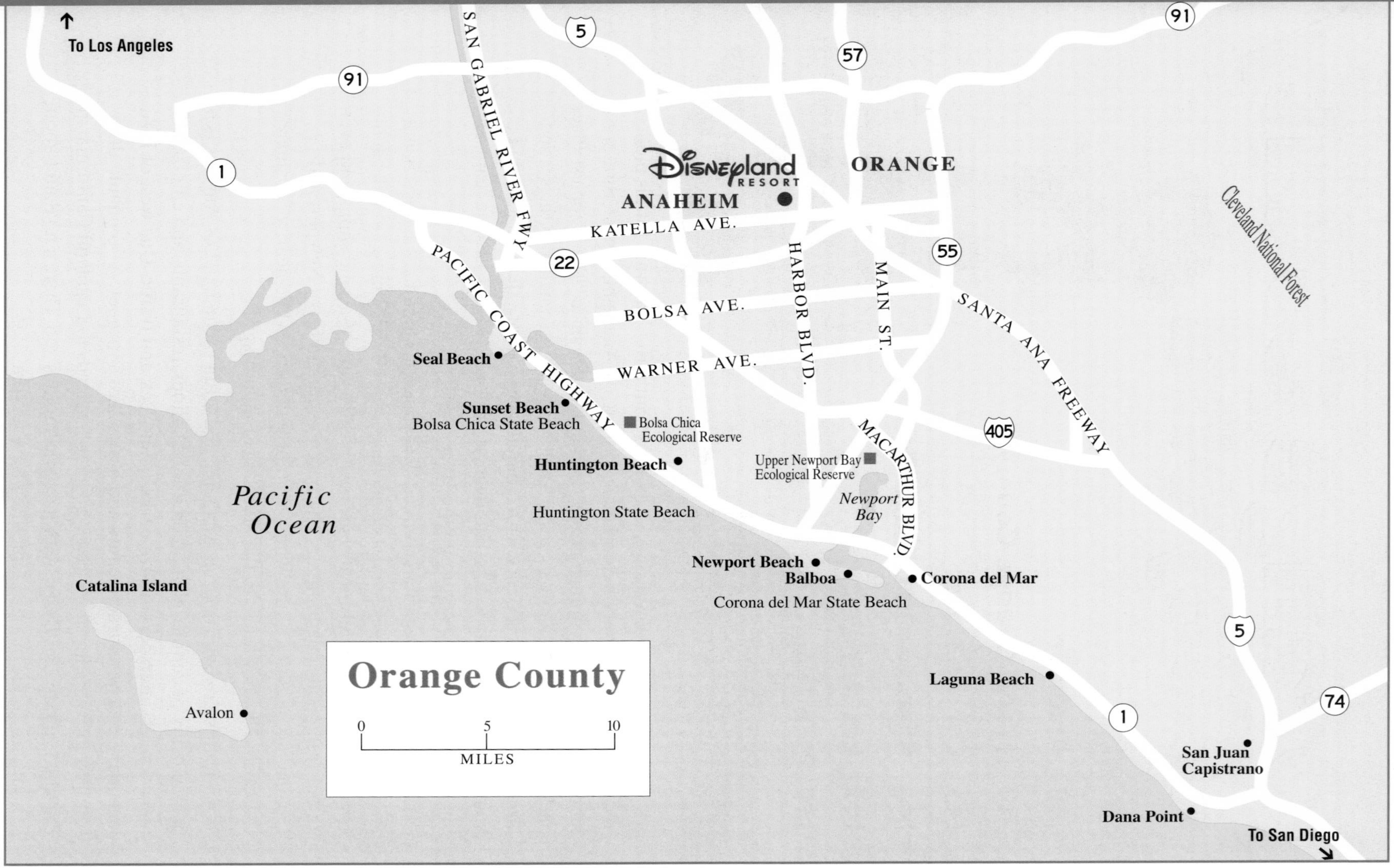

Orange County

To Los Angeles

Cleveland National Forest

Pacific Ocean

Catalina Island

Avalon

San Gabriel River Fwy

Disneyland RESORT

ANAHEIM

ORANGE

MAIN ST.

HARBOR BLVD.

KATELLA AVE.

BOLSA AVE.

WARNER AVE.

PACIFIC COAST HIGHWAY

SANTA ANA FREEWAY

MACARTHUR BLVD.

Seal Beach

Sunset Beach
Bolsa Chica State Beach

Huntington Beach
Huntington State Beach

Bolsa Chica
Ecological Reserve

Upper Newport Bay
Ecological Reserve

Newport Bay

Newport Beach

Balboa

Corona del Mar

Corona del Mar State Beach

Laguna Beach

San Juan
Capistrano

Dana Point

To San Diego

91

57

5

91

1

55

405

22

5

74

1

5

0   5   10
MILES

Orange County
Anaheim

MUZEO: This new complex encompasses the former Anaheim Museum's local history exhibit, located in the only remaining Carnegie library building in Orange County (there used to be five), as well as a new wing showcasing three traveling exhibitions every year. (Scheduled for 2009: "How to Make a Monster: The Art and Technology of Animatronics." The new urban cultural center prides itself on self-guided audio podcasts, available Wi-Fi access, interactive elements, and interchangeable displays. Open 10 A.M. till 5 P.M. daily. Admission fees vary by exhibition. Located about two miles from the Disneyland Resort. 241 S. Anaheim Blvd.; 714-956-8936; *www.muzeo.org.*

ANAHEIM ICE: Forget mild-weather outdoor pursuits for a moment to consider gliding over the ice in a building that resembles an escapee from Mickey's Toontown. Designed by noted architect and hockey fan Frank Gehry, Anaheim ICE houses an Olympic-size rink for public skating for all ages and skill levels, plus an adjacent NHL regulation rink where the Anaheim Ducks train. There's also pick-up hockey for men and women 18 and older, a pro shop, snack bar, and lockers. Day and evening skating sessions are available; birthday parties can be held here. Admission charge for skating. It's three miles from Disneyland Resort. 300 West Lincoln Ave.; 714-535-7465; *www.anaheimice.com.*

ANAHEIM GARDENWALK: This open-air mall across from the Disneyland Resort is anything but pedestrian. Garden Gate, the first of five themed garden areas, invites visitors into this alluring enclave of nationally recognized restaurants and stores such as the Cheesecake Factory, P.F. Chang's, and Hollister. Linger by the art and fountains of the Terrace Garden, enjoy the topiary and water features of the Wonder Garden, meditate by the peaceful rocks of the Zen Garden, or catch an impromptu performance at the Gala Garden.

Two hotels are scheduled to open here by the end of 2009, and a 400-unit time-share vacation property is slated for 2010. Located between Katella Ave. and Disney Way at Clementine; *www. anaheimgardenwalk.com.*

CAMELOT GOLFLAND: Five themed courses turn miniature golf into a faraway adventure. Try for a hole-in-one in a tropical jungle, a castle, a pagoda, or a Spanish fort with shooting water canons. Or hone your high-tech skills in the state-of-the-art Lazer Joust. This family entertainment center also features waterslides, an arcade, and a pizza restaurant. 3200 E. Carpenter Ave.; Anaheim. About seven miles from Disneyland Resort. Hours vary. Call 714-630-3340 for times and prices, or visit *www.golfland.com/anaheim.*

Inland Orange County

BOWERS MUSEUM: The original Mission-style Bowers building dates back to 1936, and with two major expansions since that time, the museum has become the largest in Orange County. It celebrates the fine arts of indigenous peoples—notably pre-Columbian, Native American, Oceanic, and African—and reflects the multicultural population of California. The museum hosts major traveling exhibits from Latin America, Europe, Africa, the Middle East, and Asia. The Bowers is also a repository for early California artifacts.

Tangata, far more sophisticated than most museum eateries, features California cuisine with French flourishes, while the museum shop sells artwork, jewelry, clothing, and other gifts from around the world.

Kidseum, part of the Bowers Museum but a short walk away (at 1802 N. Main St.), is a large, airy space where children get to learn in a hands-on way about the cultures of other places. Supervised activities here focus on art and music, and costumes are plentiful, colorful, and fun.

The Bowers Museum is open Tuesday through Sunday; Kidseum, Tuesday through Sunday (limited hours). There is a separate admission for each museum. They are closed on most major holidays. The museums are approximately five miles from the Disneyland Resort. 2002 N. Main St.; Santa Ana; 714-567-3600; 714-480-1520 (Kidseum information line); *www.bowers.org*.

CRYSTAL CATHEDRAL: More than 10,000 panes of glass cover a weblike steel skeleton and tower in this startling structure created by architects Philip Johnson and John Burgee. Established in 1980 by Dr. Robert H. Schuller and affiliated with the Reformed Church in America, Crystal Cathedral houses a 16,000-pipe organ, 52-bell carillon, Steuben glass cross, 33 marble columns, and 2,890 seats.

Schuller began his ministry in a drive-in theater, and worship here still has definite theatrical elements. A shop sells music, books, cards, and assorted gifts.

The visitors center is open from 9 A.M. to 3:30 P.M. Monday through Saturday. Free tours are available. Sunday services are in the main cathedral at 9:35 A.M., 11 A.M., and 6:30 P.M. (in English); 1:15 P.M and 6:30 P.M. (in Spanish). It's about 2.5 miles from Disneyland. 12141 Lewis St.; Garden Grove; 714-971-4000; 714-971-4013 (tour info); *www.crystalcathedral.org*.

DISCOVERY SCIENCE CENTER: This place gives new meaning to the term "hands-on." In several themed areas with more than 100 exhibits, guests get to experience an earthquake, lie on a bed of nails, climb a rock wall, create clouds, walk through a tornado, tread on a musical floor, fingerpaint electronically, pilot a plane, play virtual volleyball, make an impression in a pin wall, and interact with a two-story dinosaur. There is a shop, too.

Open daily, except Thanksgiving and Christmas. There is an admission charge (the 4-D laser theater costs extra). It's located about five miles from the Disneyland Resort. 2500 N. Main St.; Santa Ana; 714-542-2823; *www.discoverycube.org*.

KNOTT'S BERRY FARM: This is not a farm at all, but a themed amusement park depicting much of the history and culture of California. It began in 1920 as the Knott family's roadside berry stand. During the Great Depression, Walter Knott's wife, Cordelia, started a tearoom to help make ends meet, and her chicken dinners were such a success that Walter built a wander-through ghost town to keep hungry patrons from getting impatient. Things progressed from there.

Owned by the Knott family until 1997, the 160-acre park offers more than 165 rides (including eight roller coasters), shows, attractions, restaurants, and shops, in six themed areas.

Ghost Town (what remains of the original park) is home to GhostRider, a massive wooden roller coaster created from 2.5 million feet of yellow pine. Fiesta Village is a tribute to Spanish California and offers two coasters, one promising fun for guests of all ages. The Boardwalk combines California beach enclave with seaside amusement park. It features the Supreme Scream tower, one of the world's tallest descending thrill rides (with a 30-story, three-second drop), and Perilous Plunge, the world's tallest, steepest water drop ride (with a 115-foot drop at a 75-degree angle).

Recent additions to the thrill-ride family include Xcelerator, a high-octane launch roller coaster that sends riders from 0 to 82 mph in 2.3 seconds, and Silver Bullet, a coaster that climbs to 146 feet.

Wild Water Wilderness is a turn-of-the-20th-century river wilderness park with California flora and a whitewater raft ride. The Indian Trails area celebrates the arts, crafts, and rich traditions of Native Americans.

Camp Snoopy, a six-acre play area themed around the world's most beloved beagle, features Woodstock's Airmail (a mini-Supreme Scream), and the Red Baron biplane ride. Children get to meet Snoopy and his *Peanuts* pals here. It is also the site of the Sierra Sidewinder, a coaster with cars that rotate while taking dips, turns, and nose-dives.

Across Beach Boulevard from the park's main gate stands Independence Hall, Knott's replica of Independence Hall in Philadelphia. (Guests enter through a tunnel in the main parking area near the shops. There's never a charge to visit it.) Chandeliers, furniture, and the shape and size of the rooms are precisely reproduced, and there is a replica of the Liberty Bell, crack and all.

Also adjacent to the park is Knott's Soak City Orange County. This 13-acre water park boasts 22 rides, including tube and body slides, near-vertical chutes, a wave pool, a kids' wading pool, and a brand-new funnel ride all designed in the style of the 1950s California coast.

Knott's Marketplace is filled with shops and eateries. There is no admission charge for this area. Chicken dinners and boysenberry pies are still on the menu here, but try to dine early to avoid the crowds.

Knott's Berry Farm is open daily all year long (with Christmas Day as the lone exception); Soak City is open daily from late May through Labor Day and weekends through late September.

It costs extra to park a vehicle. However, if you come exclusively to shop, dine, or visit Independence Hall, you're entitled to three hours of free parking. Call for current park admission charges for adults and kids. Admission prices exclude Screamin' Swing, Pan for Gold, games, and arcades. Group rates (with a minimum of 15) are available. Children under age 3 get in free. Prices, operating hours, and attraction availability are subject to change without notice. 8039 Beach Blvd.; Buena Park; 714-220-5200; *www.knotts.com.*

OLD TOWNE ORANGE: For an idea of what Southern California was like before the advent of the freeway (or of Disneyland, for that matter), visit the historic area of

Orange. Highlights include a pharmacy (complete with an old-fashioned soda fountain) that's been in business since 1899, art galleries, antiques shops, two teahouses, a church that's now a restaurant (P.J.'s Abbey), a bridal museum where you can order a vintage-style gown, and Victorian and American Craftsman houses galore.

Old Towne Orange is approximately 20 minutes due east of Anaheim via Chapman Ave. The Visitor Bureau is located at 439 E. Chapman Ave.; 714-538-3581 or 800-938-0073; *www.oldtowneorange.com*.

RAGING WATERS: Raging Waters is a water park with acres of rides, slides, chutes, and lagoons. Highlights include Dragon's Den, the 10-story High Extreme, and Volcano Fantasea. Open weekends in May, early June, and September; daily from late June through Labor Day.

Guests 48 inches and taller pay full price. Kids under 48 inches pay less. Discounts are available after 4 P.M. Parking is extra. Raging Waters is about a half-hour drive from Disneyland (it's in a neighboring county). 111 Raging Waters Dr.; San Dimas; 909-802-2200; *www.ragingwaters.com*.

RIPLEY'S BELIEVE IT OR NOT! MUSEUM: Here you'll discover 10,000 square feet of curiosities amassed by cartoonist, world traveler, and collector of oddities Robert L. Ripley. The Riddler Room is an interactive area for kids. Open daily. Admission charge. It's about seven miles from the Disneyland Resort. 7850 Beach Blvd.; Buena Park; 714-522-7045; *www.ripleysbp.com*.

WILD RIVERS WATERPARK: More than 25 attractions include wave pools, a seven-story "mountain" with sheer-drop and high-speed slides, and small-scale rides and pools for young visitors. Open weekends from late May through mid-June and mid- to late September; daily from mid-June through early September. Admission charge. Parking is extra. It's about 20 minutes from Disneyland. 8770 Irvine Center Dr.; Irvine; 949-788-0808; *www.wildrivers.com*.

On the Coast

Corona del Mar

ROGER'S GARDENS: This public nursery fills 7 acres of landscaped grounds with splendid flowers, plants, shrubs, and trees; from mid-October through December 30, themed holiday trees draw enthusiastic crowds. Free lectures and demonstrations are given in the amphitheater on Saturdays and Sundays year-round (subjects and times vary; call for specifics). The gift shop sells items for the home, as well as holiday decorations year-round, including hand-painted glass ornaments designed by the world-famous Christopher Radko. The original Disneyland bandstand has found a home here, too.

Open daily, but opening and closing times change frequently. Closed Thanksgiving, Christmas, and New Year's Day. It is about 35 minutes from Disneyland. 2301 San Joaquin Hills Rd.; Corona del Mar; 800-647-2356; *www.rogersgardens.com*.

SHERMAN LIBRARY & GARDENS: The gardens are a veritable museum of plants and flowers ranging from desert flora to exotic tropical vegetation, displayed amid fountains and sculptures, brick walkways, and manicured lawns. They surround the library, which is a major research center devoted to the history of the Pacific Southwest, particularly the past century. A shop and café are on the premises.

The gardens are open daily from 10:30 A.M. to 4 P.M.; the library, from 9 A.M. to 4:30 P.M. Tuesday, Wednesday, and Thursday. Closed Thanksgiving, Christmas, and New Year's Day. Admission is $3 for adults, $1 for kids 12 through 16; free for kids under 12; free to all on Monday. It's a 35-minute drive southeast of the Disneyland Resort. 2647 E. Pacific Coast Hwy.; Corona del Mar; 949-673-2261; *www.slgardens.org*.

Dana Point Area

OCEAN INSTITUTE: There's a lab to visit at this institute, and a whale skeleton to admire; plus the tall ship *Pilgrim* may be toured, but only on Sunday, from 10 A.M. to 2:30 P.M. and excluding most of August. Educational cruises take place on weekends aboard the historic schooner *Spirit of Dana Point* and the *RV Sea*

Explorer. Prices, times, and themes vary. The institute is open to the public from 10 A.M. to 3 P.M. on weekends; the gift shop is open daily. Admission is $6.50 for adults, and $4.50 for kids 3 through 12. It's about a 45-minute drive from the Disneyland Resort. 24200 Dana Point Harbor Dr.; Dana Point; 949-496-2274; *www.ocean-institute.org*.

LOS RIOS HISTORIC DISTRICT: In this small enclave adjacent to the Capistrano train depot (1894), you'll find three adobe structures that housed original builders of the mission between the late 1700s and the early 1800s. There is also a collection of modest private homes and small stores built near the turn of the 20th century. Among them is the O'Neill Museum, which contains period furniture and the offices for the San Juan Capistrano Historical Society. It is open to the public; hours vary. Call 949-493-8444.

The district is within walking distance of Mission San Juan Capistrano. Take the train or I-5 south to the Ortega Highway to Los Rios; about 50 minutes from Anaheim. Contact the San Juan Capistrano Chamber of Commerce; 949-493-4700; *www.sjc.net*.

MISSION SAN JUAN CAPISTRANO: The famous mission near the southern tip of Orange County retains a wistful air of grandeur, even though these five buildings on 10 acres are all that remain of a one-time tract of 250,000 acres. Highlights of the self-guided walking tour include a 350-year-old gilt altar, a Moorish fountain, ancient pepper trees, a mission cemetery, the quarters of the early padres, and the Spanish soldiers' barracks. Once the most remarkable in the entire mission chain, the church was shattered by a powerful earthquake in 1812. The four bells of the tower and a small sanctuary called the Serra Chapel were miraculously spared; the chapel still holds services Monday through Saturday at 7 A.M.; call 949-234-1360.

The other local miracle is the return of the swallows to Capistrano every year around March 19 (Saint Joseph's Day). Some take this as a sign of the holiness of this place, while ornithologists explain it as no more than a predictable natural phenomenon. The Mission hosts a summer concert series, art and garden expositions, the Return of the Swallows Celebration, and other events.

Open from 8:30 A.M. to 5 P.M. daily (closed Thanksgiving and Christmas). Admission is $9 for adults, $8 for seniors 60 and older, and $5 for children 4 through 11. Take the train or I-5 south to the Ortega Highway to the mission; about 50 minutes from Anaheim. Corner of Ortega Hwy. and Camino Capistrano; San Juan Capistrano; *www.missionsjc.com*; 949-234-1300.

Huntington Beach

Life at Huntington Beach revolves around the surf—it's the perfect spot for catching a wave, or watching others do so. The Huntington Beach Conference and Visitors Bureau is at 301 Main St., Suite 208; 714-969-3492 or 800-729-6232; *www.surfcityusa.com*.

HUNTINGTON BEACH ART CENTER: Founded in 1995, this institution presents contemporary artists of national and international prominence working in all media. Exhibitions, musical performances, lectures, tours, and special events are presented all year. Open Wednesday through Saturday noon to 6 P.M.; Sundays noon to 4 P.M.; closed Mondays and Tuesdays. There is no charge for admission. It's about a 40-minute drive south of the Disneyland Resort. 538 Main St.; Huntington Beach; 714-374-1650; *www.hbarts.tripod.com*.

INTERNATIONAL SURFING MUSEUM: Expect to find all that's surfing-related here—artwork, jewelry, surfboards and paddleboards, even skateboards. Chances are you'll hear a bit of surfer music, too. Open noon to 5 P.M. Monday through Friday, 11 A.M. to 6 P.M. Saturday and Sunday. There is a suggested donation. 411 Olive Ave.; Huntington Beach; *www.surfingmuseum.org*; 714-960-3483.

PIER PLAZA: In the heart of town, this sweeping oceanfront plaza has a palm-tree grove with benches, bike and walking paths, and an amphitheater for weekend entertainment (visit *www.surfcityevents.com* or call 714-969-3492 or 800-729-6232 to get the schedule). It's about a 40-minute drive from Disneyland.

Laguna Beach

A professional artists' colony since 1917, Laguna Beach continues to thrive as Orange County's artistic hot spot, with more than 40 galleries, antique shops, and boutiques, displaying local artists' masterpieces. Painters find inspiration in the dramatic cliffs, carved-out coves, and pearl-white sand that define the beach's setting.

LAGUNA ART MUSEUM:

Founded in 1918, Orange County's oldest museum focuses its energies on and devotes its gallery space to work produced by the state's artists, past and present. Permanent exhibitions highlight early California Impressionism, while several changing exhibits feature contemporary artists. A visit here can easily be combined with browsing in some of the local art galleries, most within walking distance of the museum.

It is open daily from 11 A.M. until 5 P.M. and the first Thursday of every month from 11 A.M. to 5 P.M. Closed Thanksgiving, Christmas, and New Year's Day. There is an admission charge. It's about a 40-minute drive from the Disneyland Resort. 307 Cliff Dr.; Laguna Beach; 949-494-8971; *www.lagunaartmuseum.org.*

LAGUNA PLAYHOUSE: Now in its 88th season, this is the oldest continuously operating theater company on the West Coast. Since 1969, the Laguna Playhouse has called the 420-seat Moulton Theatre home. Screen star Harrison Ford was discovered in a Laguna Playhouse production in 1965. Actress Julie Harris has also appeared here, as did Bette Davis. The theater stages dramas, musicals, and comedies, often to rave reviews. It's about a 40-minute drive from Disneyland. 606 Laguna Canyon Rd.; Laguna Beach; 949-497-2787; *www.lagunaplayhouse.com.*

Long Beach

Settled along five and a half miles of sandy coastline, Long Beach is both a sophisticated urban center and a charming seaside community. Downtown's Rainbow Harbor offers shopping, dining, and amusement options at The Pike, while Shoreline Village also provides live entertainment, boat and bike rentals, and offshore water sports. The East Village Arts District is a gold mine of unique galleries; in addition, a variety of museums dot the downtown and neighboring landscapes. Performing arts enthusiasts can enjoy symphonies, operas, plays, and musicals performed by companies throughout the area. South of downtown, upscale Belmont Shore features dining, shopping, and entertainment at Second Street and Alamitos Bay. On Naples Island, an affluent community reminiscent of Venice, Italy, visitors can experience its canals on a gondola. And, of course, there are the beaches. Contact the Long Beach Convention & Visitors Bureau; One World Trade Center, 3rd floor; Long Beach; 562-436-3645 or 800-452-7829; *www.visitlongbeach.com.*

QUEEN MARY: If the Haunted Mansion leaves you "dying" for even more spooky encounters, take one of the tours that investigates the haunted history of this former transatlantic ocean liner. Follow a psychic through the paranormal "hot spots" not open to the general public; learn to use professional ghost hunting tools; or, watch wet footprints appear on the bottom of a swimming pool that is completely dry. For the less "spirited," there are traveling exhibits, concerts, special events and parties, lounges with live music, a dinner theater, an impromptu comedy troupe, and a Cold War–era Russian submarine to explore. Guests may even stay in one of the hotel's 307 original staterooms. There is also a spa and several dining options, including two award-winning restaurants and a champagne Sunday brunch in the ship's Grand Salon. The *Queen Mary* made its last voyage in 1967 and is now permanently docked at Long Beach Harbor. 1126 Queens Highway; Long Beach. Call 562-435-3511 for ticket information and hotel availability; *www.queenmary.com.*

AQUARIUM OF THE PACIFIC: Celebrating the largest and most diverse body of water on the planet, this aquarium is, itself, one of the largest in the United States. Its three main galleries and three major exhibits display the abundance of plant and animal life in the Northern, Southern, and Tropical Pacific. Among thousands of fish and other animals, guests can view puffins, otters, and sea dragons. Visitors may also feed nectar to lorikeets perched on their shoulders, stroll through a wetland sanctuary, visit sea lions, touch a shark, catch a 3-D movie, and observe sea life in a tank that is three stories high. Open every day from 9 A.M. to 6 P.M. except Christmas and the weekend of the Grand Prix of Long Beach. Admission charge. 100 Aquarium Way; Long Beach; 562-590-3100; *www.aquariumofpacific.org.*

Newport/Balboa

Pastimes here extend beyond beaches to celebrate the worlds of sports, history, and the arts.

BALBOA FUN ZONE: Established in 1936, this area looks like an old-fashioned boardwalk, complete with amusements, shops, and sweet treats. But most people come to admire the historic pavilion, enjoy a harbor cruise with views of ritzy shorefront houses, take the bridge, or board the car ferry to tiny Balboa Island to shop or dine. Ferry service is continuous. It's about a 45-minute drive from Disneyland. 600 E. Bay Ave.; Balboa Peninsula; for harbor tour information, call the Fun Zone Boat Company at 949-673-0240; *www.thebalboafunzone.com*.

BALBOA PAVILION: Built in 1906, this landmark building has been, among other things, a train station, a dance hall, an art museum, and a bowling alley. It is now the departure point in Orange County for Catalina Island, via Catalina Tours; 400 Main St.; 949-673-5245 or 800-620-3724; *www.balboapavilion.com*. It's about a 40-minute drive from Disneyland.

NEWPORT HARBOR NAUTICAL MUSEUM: Two new facilities invite guests to partake in exhibits, films, lectures, and classes that promote the nautical history of southern California and the eastern Pacific. The Model Pavilion presents a large collection of model ships, archival photos, and video programs. The East Wing Learning Center features a sportfishing simulator and a touch tank with living sea animals such as starfish, urchins, and limpets. Open Wednesday through Monday, 11 A.M. to 6 P.M.; closed Tuesdays. A small donation is suggested for anyone 12 and older. It's about 30 minutes from the Disneyland Resort. 600 East Bay Ave.; Newport Beach; 949-675-8915; *www.nhnm.org*.

NEWPORT SPORTS MUSEUM: View Muhammad Ali's gloves; jerseys worn by the likes of Michael Jordan, and Shaquille O'Neal, several Norris Trophy recipients, and all Cy Young Award winners; footballs signed by all Heisman Trophy winners; and seats from baseball stadiums built in the 20th century, including Ebbets Field, Fenway Park, and Yankee Stadium.

Open Tuesday through Sunday 10 A.M. to 5 P.M.; closed Mondays. Free admission; donations are welcome. About a half-hour drive from Disneyland. Located in Fashion Island; 100 Newport Center Dr.; Newport Beach; 949-721-9333; *www.newportsportsmuseum.org*.

ORANGE COUNTY MUSEUM OF ART: Taking its current name in 1996, this is the county's premier contemporary and modern-art museum. It focuses primarily on California art and sculpture from the early 20th century through the present day. The museum presents exhibitions and public programs that link historical and contemporary art, bridge local and global cultures, and aim to inspire creativity and imagination. There is a charge for those age 12 and older, but the third Thursday of every month is free. Closed Mondays, Tuesdays, and major holidays. It's about a 30-minute drive from Disneyland. 850 San Clemente Dr.; Newport Beach; 949-759-1122; *www.ocma.net*.

Catalina Island

A delightful day trip from Anaheim, this large island off the coast of Southern California resembles an unspoiled Mediterranean isle. Snorkeling, scuba diving, kayaking, whale-watching, sportfishing, golf, hiking, and horseback riding keep the more athletically inclined guests on their toes. Less active folks will enjoy a tour of the local "casino," an entertainment complex built in Avalon, the island's main town, by William Wrigley, Jr., in 1929 (dancing, not gambling, was the preferred form of entertainment here). Other island exploring possibilities include a marine tour in a glass-bottom boat, a voyage on a semi-submersible vessel for a fish's perspective of underwater life, and an island "safari" in a jeep for glimpses of buffalo (300 roam the island), bald eagles, wild goats, and deer (*www.visitscatalinaisland.com*).

From the Balboa Peninsula, Catalina Tours makes the 26-mile trip in about 75 minutes; 866-620-3724; *www.catalinatours.com*. The *Catalina Express* offers round-trip service to the island from Dana Point, Long Beach, and San Pedro; *www.catalinaexpress.com*; 800-481-3470. (The waters can be choppy, so plan ahead if you're prone to sea-sickness.)

For information, contact the Catalina Island Chamber of Commerce and Visitors Bureau; 310-510-1520; *www.visitcatalina.org*.

Shopping in Orange County

There is no question that the Disneyland Resort is full of fanciful shopping opportunities. But for those guests who crave even more retail fantasy, Southern California delivers. Specifics do change. Call for exact hours. At press time sales tax was 7.75 percent in Orange County.

FASHION ISLAND: This outdoor mall has nearly 200 stores and restaurants in a Mediterranean-themed setting of potted flowers, towering palms, and plazas with fountains, fish pools, sculptures, umbrella-topped tables, and a Venetian-themed carousel. The three major department stores here are Bloomingdale's, Neiman Marcus, and Macy's; the enclosed Atrium Court houses a variety of stores, including Barnes & Noble. The mall also features seven cinemas, Daily Grill, California Pizza Kitchen, and The Cheesecake Factory, in addition to other dining spots.

The mall is on Newport Center Dr., in Newport Beach, about a half-hour drive south from the Disneyland Resort; 949-721-2000; *www.shopfashionisland.com.*

IRVINE SPECTRUM CENTER: The hundreds of palm trees and lovely tiled courtyards and fountain in this gigantic shopping and entertainment zone makes you think you're in the south of Spain. Aside from Target, Macy's and Nordstrom, there are more than 120 retailers and a 21-screen movie theater complex (with a total of 6,400 seats!), including an IMAX theater. And for the little ones, there's even an antique-design carousel with horses and menagerie animals, as well as a 108-foot-tall Giant Wheel, hand-crafted in Italy. The center is located at 71 Fortune Dr.; 949-753-5180; *www.shopirvinespectrumcenter.com.*

WESTFIELD MAINPLACE: Formerly known as Mainplace Mall, this place is home to a Disney Store, with its character-conscious toys, videos, books, gift items, collectibles, and clothing for adults and children. You'll also find Macy's, Nordstrom, Abercrombie & Fitch, and JCPenney, along with many other shops and restaurants, a cinema complex, concierge desk, and a bank. 2800 N. Main St. (at the intersection of I-5 and Highway 22), Santa Ana; located about four miles from Disneyland Resort; 714-547-7800; *www. westfield.com/mainplace.*

SOUTH COAST PLAZA: Festive, airy, upscale, and downright enormous, it's home to more than 300 restaurants and shops, including a Disney Store, Macy's, Nordstrom, Saks Fifth Avenue, Coach, Chanel, Christian Dior, the Rainforest Cafe, and Wolfgang Puck Cafe. A bridge connects the two sides of South Coast Plaza. Shuttles operate to and from Anaheim hotels. At the intersection of the San Diego Freeway and Bristol St. in Costa Mesa, approximately 13 miles from the Disneyland Resort; 714-435-2000 or 800-782-8888; *www.southcoastplaza.com.*

"MALL-TERNATIVES": If you've had your fill of the local shopping mall scene, check out The LAB, a self-proclaimed "anti-mall" with indoor/outdoor shops, cafés, and free entertainment for teens and families; 2930 Bristol St.; Costa Mesa (714-966-6660. *www.thelab.com*). Or try the fine Gallery Store at The Bowers Museum; 2002 N. Main St.; Santa Ana (714-567-3600; *www.bowers.org*); and all the shops at the Disneyland Resort, with special emphasis on those at Downtown Disney. (Refer to page 128 for additional information on Downtown Disney.)

Los Angeles

From the rugged ridges of the Santa Monica Mountains to the vast San Fernando Valley to downtown L.A. itself, Los Angeles County spreads over 4,084 square miles (including 81 miles of shoreline), knit together by 650 miles of freeways. To get to L.A. from Anaheim, take I-5 north and Route 101 or 10 west. For information, contact the Visitor Information Center; 685 S. Figueroa St., Los Angeles, CA 90017; 213-689-8822; *www.discoverlosangeles.com.*

Attractions
Downtown

EXPOSITION PARK MUSEUMS: There are three museums here, all served by one parking lot. At the California Science Center, hands-on exhibits probe everything from a single-celled amoeba to a 100-trillion-celled human being. Take a ride on the High Wire Bicycle, the Motion-Based Simulator, or scale the Ecology Cliff Climb. There is also an IMAX Theater; 323-724-3623; *www.californiasciencecenter.org.* (Museum open daily except major holidays; IMAX open every day. Permanent exhibits free; charge for attractions and IMAX.)

The California African American Museum highlights the art and achievements of African Americans; 213-744-7432; *www.caamuseum.org* (free; open Tuesday through Sunday). The Natural History Museum of Los Angeles County features dueling dinosaurs and an insect zoo; 213-763-3466; *www.nhm.org* (admission fee except on the first Tuesday of each month; open daily except major holidays). Parking costs between $6 and $10. Exposition Park is at the corner of Figueroa St. and Exposition Blvd., west of the 110 freeway.

FARMERS MARKET: An L.A. fixture since 1934 and popular with locals for Sunday brunch (among other meals), it's filled with stands piled high with fresh produce, plus prepared foods. The French Crepe Company's sweet and savory crepes are not to be missed. Tables allow for casual outdoor dining. Shops offer souvenirs and cooking items. For information, visit *www.farmersmarketla.com.*

Farmers Market is open Monday through Friday 9 A.M. to 9 P.M.; Saturdays 9 A.M. to 8 P.M.; and Sundays from 10 A.M. to 7 P.M.; 6333 W.

Third St. and Fairfax Ave., Los Angeles; 323-933-9211. (Its next-door neighbor is a big draw, too. The Grove is a shopping, dining, and entertainment mall, complete with a 14-screen movie theater and dancing water fountains; *www.thegrovela.com.*)

LA BREA TAR PITS: If you have ever wondered what Los Angeles looked like before the studios and skyscrapers, visit the 40,000-year-old pools of *brea* (Spanish for "tar") in Hancock Park, where a replica depicts one unlucky mastodon perpetually trapped in the mire. Next to the tar pits is the Page Museum, displaying bones excavated from the area and (living) paleontologists doing research in a lab. Open daily. There is an admission charge for the museum, but you can gaze at the pits for free. It's free on the first Tuesday of each month; closed on major holidays. 5801 Wilshire Blvd.; Los Angeles; 323-934-7243; *www.tarpits.org.*

LOS ANGELES COUNTY MUSEUM OF ART (LACMA): Expect to be dazzled by the permanent collection of Islamic and African art, costumes and textiles, and a distinguished collection of 19th- and 20th-century art and photography. Free after 5 P.M. and on the second Tuesday of each month. Closed Wednesdays and major holidays. 5905 Wilshire Blvd., Los Angeles; 323-857-6000; *www.lacma.org.*

OLVERA STREET: The street is the site of a pueblo built in 1781 by original settlers of Los Angeles. Now it's home to strolling mariachis, Mexican shops, and food stalls. Free walking tours are offered Wednesday through Saturday from 10 A.M. to noon. El Pueblo de Los Angeles Historic Park; 845 N. Alameda St.; Los Angeles; 213-680-2525; *www.olvera-street.com.*

WALT DISNEY CONCERT HALL: When Lillian Disney made the initial donation for this project, she envisioned it as a tribute to Walt Disney's devotion to the arts. The end result, designed by noted architect Frank Gehry, would make her proud. In addition to the L.A. Philharmonic, this world-class venue presents an eclectic array of musical entertainment—including jazz, opera, and world music. Tours are available for a fee. 111 South Grand Ave., Los Angeles; 323-850-2000; *www.laphil.com.*

Hollywood

DISNEY'S EL CAPITAN THEATRE: Built in 1926 to present live stage shows, this lavish Hollywood landmark became the Paramount movie house after premiering Orson Welles's film *Citizen Kane* in 1941. It was restored to its former grandeur by Buena Vista Pictures Distribution and Pacific Theatres and reopened, once again, as the El Capitan in 1991. A movie here includes Disney tunes played live on an organ and, often, a chance to see sets from the film. Disney's Soda Fountain and Studio Store are right next door. 6838 Hollywood Blvd., Los Angeles; 800-347-6396; *www.disney.go.com*.

GRIFFITH PARK ATTRACTIONS: The largest park in the U.S. that is surrounded by a city, 4,210-acre Griffith Park is home to the Los Angeles Zoo and its more than 1,200 inhabitants; the Autry Museum of Western Heritage, which salutes the American West; an equestrian center; and many walking trails.

Having just completed a $93-million renovation, the famous Griffith Observatory is open again to the public, at 1,134 feet above sea level. Peer at the stars and planets through the Zeiss telescope, catch a show in the completely overhauled Oschin Planetarium, or explore other new exhibits that focus on celestial observation. Shuttles take visitors to the site on weekends, from 10 A.M. to 10 P.M., for a fee. Shuttle reservations do not guarantee the ability to purchase tickets for the planetarium. Closed Mondays. Call 888-695-0888 for information or visit *www.Griffithobservatory.com*. Ranger Station; 4730 Crystal Springs Dr., Los Angeles; 323-913-4688; *www.laparks.org*.

HOLLYWOOD MUSEUM: Ensconced in the restored Art Deco Max Factor building, this nostalgic spot salutes Tinseltown, from the silent era to the present, with costumes, props, posters, and more. Admission charge. Open Thursday through Sunday 10 A.M. to 5 P.M. 1660 N. Highland, Los Angeles; 323-464-7776; *www.thehollywoodmuseum.com*.

MANN'S CHINESE THEATRE: Better known to movie fans around the world as Grauman's Chinese Theatre, this is one of the most visited sites in Old Hollywood. (Ted Mann took it over in 1973.) The theater's forecourt contains the world-famous celebrity handprints and footprints, immortalized in cement. Inside is one of the world's most impressive and elaborate movie palaces. Tours of the stars' homes depart from here. 6925 Hollywood Blvd., Los Angeles (for theatre tours, call 323-463-9576; for movies, 323-464-8111; *www.manntheatres.com/chinese*).

UNIVERSAL STUDIOS HOLLYWOOD: First-timers to this theme park might start with the 45-minute Studio Tour, which has passed sets from such films as *Jurassic Park*, *Jaws*, and *War of the Worlds*. Other attractions include Jurassic Park—The Ride, complete with dinosaurs. Tamer, by comparison, are Nickelodeon Blast Zone, where kids can let loose with flying foam balls and water spritzers, and Universal Animal Actors, a live show featuring athletic dogs, affectionate apes, and other animals.

There is an admission charge. Open daily, except Thanksgiving and Christmas; hours vary.

Outside the park, you'll find Universal CityWalk—an outdoor promenade lined with shops, restaurants, a 19-screen cinema complex with IMAX, 3-D facades, and neon galore; there is no admission charge here, but parking is $10. CityWalk is open daily; 818-622-4455.

Universal Studios is located off the Hollywood Freeway (aka Route 101) at Lankershim Blvd. It is served by Metro Rails's Red Line (Universal City Station); 100 Universal City Plaza; Universal City; 800-864-8377; *www.universalstudioshollywood.com*.

Tours & Tapings

See the posh homes of movie stars in L.A. and Beverly Hills with **Starline Tours**; 800-959-3131; *www.starlinetours.com*.

The **Warner Bros.** studio tour costs $45 per person. It's located at 3400 Riverside Dr., Burbank. It's closed weekends. Kids under age 8 will not be admitted. Prices are subject to change. For reservations, call 800-972-8687; *http://www2.warnerbros.com/vipstudiotour/*.

The **Sony Pictures** tour costs $28 per person (guests must be at least 12). It runs Monday through Friday, 9:30 A.M. to 2:30 P.M.; 10202 W. Washington Blvd., Culver City. For information or to make a reservation, call 310-244-8687; *www.sonypicturesstudios.com*.

NBC Studios tours cost $8.50 for adults, $5 for kids (under 12). 3000 W. Alameda Ave., Burbank. For information, call 818-840-3537.

Tapings: Nab a free ticket to *The Tonight Show* by calling NBC; 818-840-3537 (long before your visit). For free tickets to other programs, call Audiences Unlimited; 818-753-3470, ext. 812; *www.tvtickets.com*.

San Diego

The country's seventh-largest city, and California's second largest, San Diego lies about 100 miles south of Anaheim, a 90-minute drive away on I-5 (or I-15 if I-5 is congested). The city is known for its perennial springlike weather, its sporty lifestyle, and its cultural scene. It's home to ballet, modern dance, opera, theater companies, and a symphony, along with myriad art galleries and museums.

San Diego is also the site of the world's largest military complex. The nation's first warm-weather, year-round, multisport Olympic training complex, the ARCO Training Center, is in nearby Chula Vista. The largest urban park in California, 5,800-acre Mission Trails Regional Park, is eight miles away. Tijuana, Mexico, is 17 miles due south, easily and inexpensively reachable via trolley.

La Jolla (pronounced *La HOY-a*), 12 miles north of downtown San Diego, is actually part of the city. One of the most picturesque communities in Southern California, it is known for its upscale shops, romantic restaurants, ocean views, and theater. La Jolla Playhouse was founded in 1947.

For additional information, contact the San Diego International Visitor Information Center; 1040 1/3 West Broadway at Harbor Dr.; San Diego, CA 92101; 619-236-1212; *www.sandiego.org*. Also contact the San Diego North Convention & Visitors Bureau, 360 N. Escondido Blvd.; Escondido, CA 92025; 760-745-4741 or 800-848-3336; *www.sandiegonorth.com*; the Carlsbad Convention & Visitors Bureau; 760-434-6093 or 800-227-5722; *www.visitcarlsbad.com*; the Coronado Visitors Center; 619-437-8788; *www.coronadovisitor center.com*; and La Jolla Visitor Center; 619-236-1212; *www.lajollatc.org*.

BALBOA PARK: This

1,200-acre oasis just north of the downtown area is home to 15 extraordinary museums, which appeal to such diverse

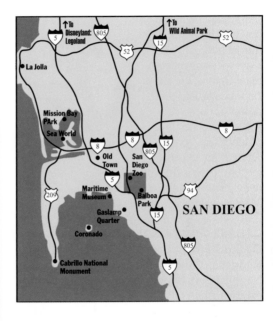

areas of interest as art, photography, sports, science, astronomy, aerospace, model railroads, automobiles, Russian icons, and Japanese gardens.

The nationally acclaimed Globe Theatres are here, along with the Mingei International Museum and the Museum of Photographic Arts. On Sundays at 2 P.M., the park hosts a free concert on the world's largest outdoor pipe organ.

Park entry and tram service are free, but admission is charged at most of the museums; on Tuesdays a few museums waive their admission charge. You can save money by purchasing a one-week coupon book for all of the museums. Open daily; museum hours vary. Follow signs from I-5. 1549 El Prado, Suite 1; 619-239-0512; *www.balboapark.org*.

Don't miss the opportunity to have a meal at The Prado restaurant, a full-service restaurant featuring creative cuisine (619-557-9441).

BIRCH AQUARIUM AT SCRIPPS:

Part of the world-famous Scripps Institution of Oceanography, this popular attraction is actually an aquarium and a museum. The two are connected by a plaza with its own man-made tide pool overlooking the Pacific Ocean and Scripps Pier. The aquarium contains 60 marine-life tanks and a 13,000-gallon shark tank; the museum itself has a selection of interactive displays focusing on climate change, the art of camouflage, and the power of ocean currents. There are three outdoor tide pools, too. There is an admission fee, but there is free 3-hour parking. Open daily. 2300 Expedition Way; La Jolla; 858-534-3474; *www.birchaquarium.org*.

CABRILLO NATIONAL MONUMENT:

Dedicated to the arrival here in 1542 of Juan Rodriguez Cabrillo, and supervised by the National Park Service, this monument offers exhibits, films, talks by rangers, and tide pools to investigate. A statue of the explorer and a lighthouse dating to 1855 are on the grounds. Views are great; you might spot migrating whales from mid-December to mid-March. Open daily. 1800 Cabrillo Memorial Dr.; San Diego; 619-557-5450; *www.nps.gov/cabr*.

CORONADO: A separate municipality from San Diego but connected to it by the striking, two-mile-long San Diego/Coronado Bridge — and accessible by car, bus, or ferry —

Land-Ho!

The decommissioned USS *Midway* has docked at the Embarcadero and assumed a new role: the interactive *USS Midway* Museum, a tribute to those who serve in the U.S. Navy and Air Force. Take the self-guided audio tour of 60 locations on and around the ship (it's narrated by Midway sailors). You can also see 25 aircraft on site. For more information, call 619-544-9600 or visit *www.midway.org*.

Coronado is the quintessential beach town. The highlight of a visit is the Hotel Del Coronado. Built in 1888, it's one of the largest and most beautiful wooden structures on the West Coast. You can take a self-guided tour through the hotel (parts of the classic film *Some Like It Hot* were shot here), then a walk on the beach, which is especially lovely at sunset.

Other town attractions include the Coronado Historical Museum, 15 miles of bike paths (it's possible to rent a bicycle), lots of public tennis courts, an 18-hole bayside public golf course, professional and community theaters, and walking tours. Coronado Visitors Center; 1100 Orange Ave.; 619-437-8788; *www.coronadohistory.org*.

GASLAMP QUARTER: This 16½-block collection of 93 restored Victorian-style commer-

cial buildings in the heart of San Diego is the center for dining, shopping, and nightlife downtown, with traffic jams and many valet parking options to prove it (Croce's has long been a favorite for contemporary American cuisine spiced with live jazz and R & B). Most of the buildings in this part of town date from 1870 to 1910. The quarter is bounded by Fourth Avenue, Broadway, Sixth Avenue, and Harbor Drive. Horton Plaza shopping complex is adjacent. For information, contact the Gaslamp Quarter Association; 619-233-5227; *www.gaslamp.org*.

LEGOLAND CALIFORNIA: The first American outpost of the famous Danish park opened in March 1999 on a hill overlooking the Pacific. Eight themed areas created from 35 million Lego bricks surround a man-made lake. For the uninitiated, this park has 50 rides, shows, and attractions, outdoor and indoor theaters, live entertainment, restaurants, food stands, and even a driving school for kids.

The park's target audience is ages 2 through 12, but grown-ups are captivated, too—especially by Miniland, USA, with its scaled-down Lego versions of New York City, San Francisco, Washington, D.C., New Orleans, a New England harbor and town, and the California coast. Even the people on the streets and in the vehicles of Miniland are made of Lego bricks.

There is an admission charge to Legoland, which is open daily (closed Tuesdays and Wednesdays in the off-season). It's on the coast, 30 miles north of San Diego, in Carlsbad. To get there, take the Cannon Road exit off I-5; 760-918-5346; *www.legolandca.com*.

MARITIME MUSEUM OF SAN DIEGO: This floating museum is triply blessed, with the full-rigged merchant ship *Star of India* (1863), the steam-powered ferry *Berkeley* (1898), and the steam yacht *Medea* (1904). Each vessel's colorful history begs onboard exploration. From here, you can easily stroll along the Embarcadero to Seaport Village for shopping, or take the ferry to Coronado Island.

There is an admission charge. Open daily. At the foot of Ash St. on N. Harbor Dr.; 619-234-9153; *www.sdmaritime.com*.

MISSION BAY PARK: This 4,235-acre aquatic park has playgrounds, picnic areas, 27 miles of bayfront, 17 miles of oceanfront beach with six designated swimming areas, and paths for biking, jogging, and skating. The bay is popular for windsurfing, sailing, Jet-Skiing, water-skiing, scuba diving, and sportfishing and whale-watching excursions. Mission Beach draws surfers year-round. Nearby Belmont Park, with its giant wooden roller coaster, is pure California. To get there from downtown San Diego, follow I-5 north to the Clairemont Drive exit; 619-276-8200.

OLD TOWN: The flavor of Mexican California pervades the place where San Diego was born, especially in Old Town San Diego State Historic Park, with seven original and thirteen reconstructed buildings from the 1800s, two museums, and Bazaar del Mundo, a south-of-the-border-style shopping and dining complex. Free walking tours leave from the

Lodging

In addition to its resort hotels, luxe spas like the Golden Door and La Costa, and moderately priced hostelries, San Diego offers elegant bed-and-breakfast inns in areas such as Old Town, Balboa Park, La Jolla, and Hillcrest. For more information, contact the San Diego International Information Visitors Center; 619-236-1212; www.sandiego.org; or the San Diego Bed & Breakfast Directory; 619-297-3130; www.sandiegobandb.com.

Visitors Center daily at 11 A.M., 12 P.M., 2 P.M., and 3 P.M. You can stroll to other historic attractions from here; Mission San Diego de Alcalá is nearby. Open daily. Old Town San Diego State Historic Park; 619-220-5422; and Old Town San Diego Chamber of Commerce; 619-291-4903; *oldtownsandiegoguide.org*.

SAN DIEGO ZOO: A fabulous home to 4,000 birds and beasts, the 100-acre zoo claims the largest breeding colony of koalas outside Australia (about 30 of them). Giant pandas Bai Yun (a female), Gao Gao (a male), and their female cubs, Su Lin and Zhen Zhen are on loan from the People's Republic of China

HOT TIP!

The Southern California CityPass offers substantial savings on admission to Disneyland, Disney's California Adventure, Universal Studios Hollywood, SeaWorld Adventure Park, and the San Diego Zoo or the San Diego Zoo's Wild Animal Park. CityPass booklets are sold as a package and are valid for 14 days from the first day of use. Call 866-557-1173 or visit *www.citypass.com*.

and reside in a lush compound that includes a large viewing area. The zoo is also home to Polar Bear Plunge, Ituri Forest, Gorilla Tropics, Sun Bear Forest, and Tiger River, along with a petting zoo and an animal nursery. Admission charge. Open daily. Follow I-5 to Park Boulevard. 2920 Zoo Dr.; Balboa Park; 619-234-3153 or 619-231-1515; *www.sandiegozoo.org*.

SEA WORLD: Four-ton killer whales glide through the air, astounding fans in 7,000-seat Shamu Stadium. Dolphins, sea lions, otters, walruses, and birds steal a few shows. In Wild Arctic, guests spy polar bears, beluga whales, walruses, and harbor seals; in Manatee Rescue, they view the endangered species from an underwater gallery; and in Shipwreck Rapids, they brave churning seas, waterfalls, and a ship's propeller. For $160, visitors can splash with dolphins. Admission charge. Open daily. Exit I-5 onto Sea World Drive and turn right. 500 Sea World Dr.; Mission Bay; 619-226-3815 or 800-257-4268; *www.seaworld.com*.

WILD ANIMAL PARK: Here, some 3,200 wild creatures roam free over most of the 1,800-acre facility. In the 32-acre Heart of Africa, you can go on a walking safari and actually feed the giraffes. Take a 60-minute railway ride through remote landscapes of Africa and Asia; or trek through the Hidden Jungle, a replica of a tropical rain forest, or Nairobi Village, a collection of engaging animal presentations. Or join a Photo Caravan tour or a Roar and Snore sleepover (additional charge, reservations required).

Admission charge. Open daily. It's 30 miles north of San Diego; follow I-5 to Highway 78 east to I-15; go south to the Via Rancho Parkway exit and follow the signs. 15500 San Pasqual Valley Rd.; Escondido; 760-747-8702; *www.wildanimalpark.org*.

Index